TO BONEGILLA FROM SOMEWHERE

By the same author

Roadside Contemplatives (2007)
Long Road to Rezekne (2008)

TO BONEGILLA FROM SOMEWHERE

Wanda Skowronska

Connor Court Publishing

Published in 2013 by Connor Court Publishing Pty Ltd

Connor Court Publishing Pty Ltd.
PO Box 224W
Ballarat VIC 3350
sales@connorcourt.com
www.connorcourt.com

ISBN: 978-1-922168-733 (pbk.)

Cover design by Janusz Tydda

Printed in Australia

Note: The photos used in this book are largely the author's own. Some are reproduced with kind permission from the National Archives of Australia and Albury Library Museum while others are available in the public domain. The Albury Library Museum is referred to in the text as the Albury Library Museum. The exhibition/museum known as the Bonegilla Migrant Experience is referred to as the Bonegilla Migrant Experience Museum.

CONTENTS

Dedicated to those who came to Bonegilla and all the other Australian 'camps'. And particularly to those who did not make it and whose stories are unknown.

Acknowledgements

I would like to thank those who have assisted me in this telling of Bonegilla's story: Karlie Hawking and the staff at the Albury City Library, the volunteers at the Bonegilla Migrant Experience Museum and Father Paul Stenhouse, editor of *Annals*, who encouraged the first short article on this subject. I would also like to thank Grazyna Tydda, Associate University Librarian at Macquarie University Library, for her invaluable advice; Janusz Tydda and Gerard Haffner for their patient help with some technicalities of cyberspace; Gail Instance and Jane Instance for their friendly ongoing interest in the place they'd once 'never heard of before'; and the people from Bonegilla and other refugees, and descendants of refugees, who shared their stories on the following pages.

Introduction

Bonegilla might seem a strange name to some people. But it is not strange to the indigenous inhabitants who had long sought rest and water there from the intense heat of the day. Nor is it strange for very different kinds of nomads who came to Australia many years later from distant, even unheard of lands. Bonegilla was the first home for many of the refugees called Displaced Persons of the immediate post-World War II years – known as the DPs. They were the 'first wave' to come to Bonegilla and it is about them that this book has been written.

The DPs were dispossessed and homeless survivors who found themselves without a country to go back to after the political victors had redrawn the borders of Europe after World War II. Among them were Hungarians, Latvians, Lithuanians, Poles, Estonians, Ukrainians, Slovenians and Czechs. In 1947, two years after the war had ended, there were still 1.6 million DPs in 920 refugee camps mainly in Germany who fell under the purview of the IRO – the International Refugee Organisation set up by the United Nations in 1946 to deal with this pressing problem. What do you do with so many people with nowhere to go? The DPs had already been blown about like leaves in the uncertain fortunes, journeys and destinations of war. In the end there was nowhere left to run and, as officially designated 'Displaced Persons' living their camp life under the care of international welfare agencies, they waited to be accepted as Placed Persons by anyone who would take them. Once accepted – usually by America, Canada or Australia – they were taken one last time to their more permanent destination. In the case of those destined for Australia, many ended up in Bonegilla which operated between 1947-1971, a place which was to become indelibly imprinted in the minds of the new nomads who had come from what one might call another 'dreaming'. For that first wave of post-war immigrants, the DPs who came between 1947-1952, Bonegilla was a hope-filled bridge between the horror of war and a new life in a country they had never imagined they would set foot in. And that bridge town Bonegilla took on a vivid life of its own, gradually weaving itself into the memory of its inhabitants in a way that combined sorrow and hope, compelling needs with ineffable dreams, strangeness with that familiar territory of the heart that seeks enduring answers and solace in the deserts which wars create.

The first DPs from Eastern Europe disembarking in 1947 at Port Melbourne with their worn coats, old suitcases, gaunt frames and European manners no doubt looked around at their new country with puzzled, attentive eyes. No doubt some burly wharfies stared back at them with equal curiosity as the DPs made their way in lines to the train that would take them through Melbourne and on through the bush heading north. Their long train journey would take them to the border of NSW and Victoria, to this unpronounceable 'Bonegilla', a place with symmetrically laid out long barracks, with corrugated iron roofs in the bush about 10 kilometres from Wodonga. After the horrors of war and displacement, here was their new temporary home in the faded greens and browns of the Australian countryside under endless blue skies – this respite, this end, this beginning.

What made Bonegilla so memorable, were the stories of the 'ordinary' people who came there. The original DPs, however, had come from experiences that were far from 'ordinary' for one cannot call ordinary an era of bombings, gas chambers, the Third Reich and the Soviet Union. Among these DPs at Bonegilla were two survivors of World War II who arrived on separate transport ships in 1950 – my father, Bogdan Skowronski, from Lublin in Poland and my mother, Valerie Klucnieka, from the environs of Rezekne in Latvia. Already citing the names of the towns they came from is to intone some strange litany and hints of that mysterious 'other' world they carried to Bonegilla. It was this strange world which inevitably permeated the residents' lives, including mine as a 'Bonegilla kid' during my first five years in the camp and beyond. The stories of Bogdan and Valerie were only two among so many others, part of that post-war 'first wave', but in many ways their footprints echoed the dreams of so many who came to this inland ex-army camp. This book recounts something of why Bonegilla came to be. It recounts some outlines of the 'somewhere' these two DPs came from and what brought them – along with so many like them – to come and tread a dry, grassy path from a bush railway siding to the long huts of Bonegilla in the first place.

I

Bonegilla: a place for the displaced

Little known is the fact that the place called 'Bonegilla' was the largest migrant camp in Australia's history. Over 320,000 people passed through it between 1947-1971 and it is as close an equivalent to New York's Ellis Island as Australia has ever had. This place in the Australian bush witnessed of 'one of the largest peace-time movements of people in the history of the world'.[1] In present Australia, when one considers families and descendants, it is estimated that about 1.5 million people can claim a connection to the place and if one includes workers and others who stayed there, this number would surely be higher.[2] Australia's post-war society was increasingly threaded with ex-Bonegillians whose memories of this unique post-war migrant town have given its transient nature an enduring significance in Australian migration history.

It is perhaps strange that the memories of Bonegilla have a grip on many its former residents – like a dream, a haunting melody that never goes away. Isn't this too great a claim to make about a place one just passes through? The Displaced Persons (known as DPs) who passed through the migrant camp known as 'Bonegilla' from 1947 onwards came to know only too well, however, that it was not just any 'transit point'. It was their first contact after their individual quasi Homeric odysseys, and it would take years for them to find words to describe what had happened to them. This first wave of post-war immigrants, the DPs who were soon to be called 'New Australians' were survivors of the murderous regimes of the Nazis and Soviets. And suddenly here they were standing still looking at eucalyptus trees, blue skies, far horizons and the innumerable details of this land yet to reveal its mysteries to them.

Bonegilla was a world on its own – perhaps because of its relative isolation in the bush and because of its unique post-war, European-Australian ambience. It was as if a spaceship had landed in the Australian countryside. Yes, this was Prague, Warsaw, Budapest, Vienna, Riga or Vilnius in the bush. Australia had never seen anything like it. In its first phase, after the devastation of World War II which displaced over 12 million people in its immediate aftermath, it was precisely these longer term 'displaced' who came there. Bonegilla was filled with Hungarians, Czechs, Poles, Latvians, Ukrainians, Estonians, Germans, Romanians and Lithuanians who, with little or nothing, had waited in post-war Displaced Persons' camps. Those chosen to be 'placed' in Australia walked Bonegilla's streets filling the air with multilingual communication. They had all come from 'somewhere' and were all on the way to 'somewhere.' They talked, observed, reflected, laughed, wept, hoped and wondered what their future life in Australia would be. They walked from one block to another, from the 'mess' to their rooms, to the bush, to the camp shop, to English classes, to the post office and to the employment office. The streets of Bonegilla were alive with colour and sound, with the hopes of former nurses, cooks, soldiers, doctors, professors, foresters, cleaners and young people ready to 'have a go' in Australia.

As a child of Displaced Persons or DPs who themselves spent seven years in Bonegilla (an unusually long stay) and as one who spent my first five years there, I have some vivid memories of this migrant town. This place was the first I can ever recall on the earth. It was a kind of Eden for me, a mélange of European manners, possums, open land, stories of intense and remembered worlds from far away. In a strange way, I felt I was Bonegillian before I knew I was Australian for like most children who lived there, the stories of our families seeped into our very being – as transmitted memories from a kind of European dreamtime, a dreamtime which had turned into an abyss of loss on the one hand and of compelling curiosity on the other. Their stories were our stories too and the very fragmentation of their lives were pierced into our consciousness as children and all throughout the years to come. They became our Australian stories. In recounting what led to Bonegilla's existence and what brought my parents here – mingling historic details and hindsight with personal reflection – perhaps some fragments of that once alive town will emerge on these pages from its increasingly silent shadows.

Stamped for Australia

In Germany, around 1949-50, some Australian immigration officials whose names I will never know, deemed my parents, 23-year-old Bogdan Skowronski and 25-year-old Valerie Klucnieka suitable for migration to Australia. Bogdan was one of the 60,000 Poles accepted by Australia at this time, the largest single group comprising more than a third of the total 170,000 Displaced Persons received in Australia during 1947-1953.[3]

The Poles outside Poland were in an acute situation after the war. The Poles in Poland were now under the tyranny of Soviet rule and the Poles outside Poland had few if any options. Many of the latter had survived German concentrations camps, labour camps, Soviet gulags and the partial or total loss of immediate families. There were some who were sole survivors of families. Some were airmen, who as Polish allies fought in the Battle of Britain, soldiers who had fought in Tobruk, Normandy, the Battle of Monte Cassino, the Warsaw Uprising and other battle fields. Some of them had been released from Soviet detention in the one and only release of its kind in the course of the war in 1941-2 – from Arkhangelsk, Vorkuta, Kazakhstan and Kolyma (in the Arctic circle) – to find their way to the west to fight under General Władysław Anders who formed the second Polish Corps in exile, fighting alongside the Western Allies, the first consisting of those who had escaped to England after the Germans invaded in 1939. In fact the Poles comprised the fourth largest group within the Allied forces. After the war, however, unlike other allied soldiers who could return home, these soldiers had no 'home' to go to. The displaced Poles were 'non persons' in Soviet occupied Poland in the geopolitically rearranged post-war world and were a 'problem' to many of the Allies. At the Yalta conference of 4-11 February 1945, Churchill, Stalin and Roosevelt handed over much of Eastern Europe to Soviet control. The soldiers of the Polish Home army (Armija Krajowa), my father Bogdan among them, who had fought for an independent Poland desperately hemmed in between Nazi and Soviet forces, and those Poles who had fought for the Allies, were not part of the new Soviet agenda. There were stories of survivors of concentration camps or the Warsaw Uprising being arrested or shot on re-entry into Poland by the newly installed Soviet officials. This gave Poles outside Poland an idea of what their fate would be if they returned. They faced imprisonment or death as they were deemed 'enemies' of the Soviet Union though they had fought the Nazis with heavy losses. They were totally caught between new geopolitical narratives about what had happened and were not only 'displaced' but also did not 'exist'.

My mother Valerie, was one of the smaller group of Latvians accepted by Australia at this time. Approximately 19,700 Latvians,

10,000 Lithuanians and over 6,000 Estonians came to Australia as Displaced Persons during the first phase of post-war migration.[4] These were Calwell's 'beautiful Balts' or alternately 'bloody Balts' as they were sometimes described. These refugees from the Baltic countries had fled – as had Valerie – often just a few steps in advance of the Soviet take-over of their countries in 1944 and were also 'non-existent' as far as the new Soviet regime was concerned. It was not only that returning to their original countries meant certain imprisonment or death – because of the 'crime' of having set foot in the west – but in the current Soviet hyper-control of its citizens, even writing a letter home would have had dire consequences for their families still living there, as those who lived through this era will readily attest. Lithuanian scholar Linus Saldukas made the following observation of Lithuanians making it to post-war camps, but it could well have been said of all DPs fleeing the Soviet takeover of East European countries:

> These people (refugees) met with more favourable fates than the Lithuanians who had remained in their country, and far better ones than those who were forcibly exiled to Siberia and other distant territories of the USSR. At the time these refugees were fleeing Lithuania, they certainly could not guess their ultimate destinies. All they knew was that they were facing the unknown, heading into a sort of total vacuum.[5]

Finding themselves disconnected from their families and from their past history, the DPs hoped to build a new life on the fragments of whatever was left them. So it was for Valerie. A few Latvians had fled to Sweden (and Swedes handed back some Latvians to the Soviets) but the majority – among the 200,000 Balts in all who left their countries – had waited in the post war chaos of Germany, for a chance to live somewhere. Many of them went to the United States and Canada. Some had been accepted in Germany. And some found themselves sailing to Port Melbourne in far away Australia. In Victoria, there had only been 108 Latvian born people in the entire state prior to World War II. This was about to change dramatically. The post-war 'invasion' by the Balts and other East Europeans meant a rapid increase of over 5,000 Latvian permanent settlers in this state alone.[6]

Bogdan and Valerie had in fact been offered other destinations as well by the Australian Immigration officials. In the case of my mother it was Canada, in the case of my father it was Britain – but they each opted for Australia – as a better choice. Like other DPs they gazed at atlases and maps to see where this land was and there must have been a sense of going to the farthest reaches of the universe. On arrival by transport ship in 1950, they could have been sent to Greta, Bathurst or any other of the many smaller migration holding centres all around Australia. But again some Australian immigration officer had picked Bonegilla for them, and thus decided the course of their lives and mine. Had Bogdan and Valerie not come to Bonegilla it is unlikely they would have met, nor would I have been born. Similarly had they not survived innumerable brushes with death prior to this, these pages would not have been written. But before looking in detail at their stories, at the 'somewhere' from which they came, it is interesting to consider now some of the reasons for Bonegilla's existence, for this in itself is an interesting aspect of Australia's migration history.

What and where exactly was Bonegilla?

The full formal name for this camp was Bonegilla Migrant Reception and Training Centre. It began operating as a migrant camp in December 1947 and closed in 1971 and took in people of more than

30 nations. Of this largest and longest operating migrant reception centre, the Australian Heritage Commission site says the following:

> It forms an important part of Australia's recent collective memory and symbolises the central role of Bonegilla in the peopling of Australia with immigrants in the post-war years. It is estimated that there are over 1.5 million descendants of migrants who spent time at Bonegilla. It represents the role of Australia as the 'host' nation.[7]

There were distinct phases in its operation. It first accepted Displaced Persons from Eastern Europe between 1947-1952. Then in its second phase, it accepted 'assisted migrants' mainly from southern and western Europe until it closed in 1971, although during the second phase, there were also intakes of refugees from Hungary after the 1956 uprising, 'White Russians' from China in the early 1960s and Christian Armenians from Egypt in the later 1960s.

Bonegilla is inland from the coast, located on the shores of Lake Hume not far from Wodonga and Albury – both border towns. Wodonga is just inside Victoria and Albury is just inside New South Wales. About 320 kms north of Melbourne and 600 kms from Sydney, Bonegilla is located around 10 kms from both Albury and Wodonga. It is surrounded by hills and lakes and is as scenic a location as one can find in Australia. Bonegilla's post office opened in 1878 and much of the development of the place was due to the development of the Cudgewa railway line. This was the railway track which in the future was to transport the DPs from Station Pier in Melbourne to this hastily organised refugee – and later immigrant – town in the bush. In its early days Bonegilla's inhabitants in fact outnumbered those of Wodonga.

Bonegilla – faithfully pronounced as 'Bon-a-gilla' by most of its residents in a quasi Italiate way whatever one's nationality – was in reality a border town to the state border towns of Albury and Wodonga, its very 'border' quality already lending a symbolic significance to its location. It was a border between one life and another, one way of knowing and another – a geographical, social and spiritual transition to a new realm.

When the first transport ship, the *General Stuart Heintzelman*, arrived in Melbourne in December 1947 with its 839 DPs, the newcomers were to experience a very iconic Australian journey by train into the mysterious interior of their as yet unknown land. Once out of the port, the DPs would have seen the outskirts of Melbourne, the ever smaller towns with ever smaller weatherboard houses. They would have glimpsed the increasingly open horizons, where the pale green-grey eucalyptus trees and telegraph poles were the only things to see against a stark blue sky. They would have seen the sun shimmer on faded green foliage and brown earth, with the innumerable shades of intermingled pale yellow, brown and grey. They would have wondered at the new colours they were seeing. In time the outlines of the bush would have become dark and spidery in the quiet shadows of the night. And so, one might say, as these newcomers crossed from one life to the next, an ancient dreaming touched a newer one. The new displaced and dispossessed from Europe entered a place of profound meaning to the original inhabitants in turn bringing their personal histories and burdens of memory which would soon interweave with the emotional and spiritual accommodations they would make with their new country.

In more pragmatic terms, the beginning of Bonegilla Migrant Reception and Training Centre was a response to the times – specifically to the events of the post-World War II assessment of Australia's defence and economic situation. In common terms this was the realisation of the need of Australia to 'populate or perish.' Bonegilla housed refugees who were part of the post-World War II migrations of peoples, and who became the second largest wave of migration in Australia's history. The previous largest group was that of the Chinese arrivals during the gold rushes of 1850-51 which in itself had transformed Australian society. Given that previous immigrants had mainly come in steadier, smaller streams from Britain, Scotland, Ireland and New Zealand, this post-war shift of focus was a dramatic change, some viewing it as 'the most important change in government immigration policy' up to that point in Australia's history.[8] As part of this change in immigration policy, which was underpinned by economic and political aims to build Australia as rapidly as possible, Bonegilla played a central role in Australia in the post-war years and was most significant demographic change in Australia during the 20th century up to that point. However to understand how it came to be, a little must be said of its pre-Bongeilla history.

A step back into origins and wartime history

Prior to its use as a migrant holding centre, Bonegilla was well known to the indigenous people – the Dhudhuroa, Minubuddong and Wiradjuri and their many associated clans.[9] The word 'Bonegilla' derives from an indigenous word meaning 'where the waters meet', in this case the waters of the Mitta Mitta, the Murray and the Kiewa rivers. It has also been called 'deep water hole' and there was certainly no lack of water in the area in the form of rivers and lakes. Ann Tundern-Smith, in her account of the early settlers in Bonegilla, entitled *Bonegilla's Beginnings,* lists details of the early indigenous inhabitants and of the early farmers and other settlers in the area – the Raspeys, the Pollards and the Cummins – and includes several photographs and maps of historic interest in her account of the early DP arrivals.[10] From the

1830s onwards, pastoralists cleared and worked the area, establishing their runs along the rivers. The Australian Heritage Database website states that in 1835 Charles Ebden established 'Bonegilla' as 'one of several large pastoral runs close to the principal Murray River Crossing Place on the route between Sydney and Port Phillip. That run was subsequently subdivided into smaller farms. By the time of the Second World War the area was a cleared grazing landscape.'[11]

After the start of World War II, the location of Bonegilla came to the attention of the Australian army which used the area for artillery practice before commencing construction of a more formal base in 1940. As Bruce Pennay describes in his well-referenced account of this era, *The Army at Bonegilla 1940-1971*, four core teams of civilian contractors employing over 800 men built the new 'city' in the bush.[12] It was considered strategic good sense to move army installations to country districts away from vulnerable cities and coastal centres. The construction of over 800 buildings for a 'hutted military camp' on 240ha (620 acres) of resumed land at Bonegilla proceeded rapidly through late 1940. Soon there were 23 self-contained blocks, a hospital block, organised into rows containing 20 huts each with kitchens and messes built for allocated sections of the camp. They were unlined timber framed huts. The 2/24th Battalion from Wangaratta as well as a Battalion from Seymour were stationed at the camp. In fact, twenty training units were stationed there at various times during the war, also among them 2/23rd Infantry Battalion from nearby Albury, known as 'Albury's own' which had been formed in 1940. The soldiers from this Infantry Battalion had marched into the camp with great fanfare from Albury showground.[13]

The Australian Women's Army Service started to arrive in 1942, by which time the camp was a hive of activity. During the war years, there were approximately 1,000 women at Bonegilla who were nurses, medical attendants, store managers, clerks and signallers. Signallers for the Australian Army's Australian Special Wireless Group were trained to interpret Japanese coded radio traffic on receiving sets at Bonegilla Signals Training Camp. Other groups located there during this time were an Infantry Officers Training School, an Army Gas School, a Small Arms School and a Bomb Disposal Unit. At one stage the camp had a hospital with 1,200 beds, in particular treating soldiers suffering from tuberculosis. Italian prisoners-of-war were accommodated at Bonegilla from May 1944 to March 1946 and worked on nearby farms. Block 19 which still exists, was initially used as an Officer Training School.[14]

Post-war perceptions

After the wartime soldiers and signallers had dispersed, the Bonegilla camp site was considered for other purposes. At this time, Ben Chifley, Prime Minister of Australia from 1945 to 1949, had commissioned a report on Australia's population needs, and concluded at the end of the war that Australia was indeed in a most vulnerable demographic situation. Given this urgent need of a larger population and failing all other avenues of expansion, displaced persons were to be considered. So it came about that in 1947 the Australian government of the time saw Bonegilla as a place to house the homeless from Europe and as a revolutionary geographical launching pad for the expansion of Australia. The principal reason for the large intake of refugee immigrants at this time – over and above the need to fill the labour shortage – was defence. Viesturs P. Karnups says that 'as early as 1943, Prime Minister Curtin had said that a population of twenty-five million was essential for Australian security and this could be achieved by the end of the century if immigration was sustained.'[15] The pressure to 'populate or perish' was well and truly on. Of the more than 170,000 Displaced Persons scattered in German camps who were accepted by Australia under an agreement signed in 1947 with the IRO (the International Refugee Organisation), about half of ended up in Bonegilla.

The Department of Immigration took over control of the large tract of land in and around Bonegilla to prepare a place for the imminent wave of new arrivals. Eventually seven government departments in addition to teaching and health personnel were to be stationed there. However the operation of the camp was, initially at least, to be based on a military model for no other models were readily at hand.

Arthur Calwell had been appointed as Australia's first Minister of Immigration in 1945 by Chifley and had earlier decided on an ambitious program of 'mass immigration' to address Australia's population needs principally by attracting British immigrants via 'The U.K. Free and Assisted Passage Agreement' signed in 1946. Calwell's reassuring statement that 'for every foreign immigrant there would be ten people from the United Kingdom' reflected the attitudes and wishes of the majority of Australians at that time. The White Australia Policy was still in force. Where other foreign immigrants were concerned, the principal problems lay in their 'suitability' and the means of transporting them to Australia. 'Suitable immigrants' at this period were generally considered to be anyone from the British Isles, and those of French, Belgian, Dutch, Danish and Norwegian background. The East European DPs did not originally figure high on the list. However, as time went on, it seemed unlikely that enough of the 'suitable' group would come. This was due largely to the fact that there were protracted delays with shipping. There were simply not enough ships in post-war Europe to bring British immigrants quickly enough and in sufficient numbers. It was after this realisation that attention shifted to other possibilities and some comments were made in the Australian parliament in 1946 about the 'unfortunate' men women and children languishing in the German displaced persons' camps. Despite this, Calwell wavered in his response in considering them 'suitable'. Could these 'unfortunates' ever be considered suitable? No doubt for mixed motives, as Glenda Sluga outlines in her study of the period, the spotlight eventually did turn to the DP camps in Germany.[16] It was thought that although the DPs would be seen as Aliens (initially, at least, this was their designation), they could be housed en masse at reception and training centres, away from urban centres and then go on to fill acute labour shortages and thus help build Australia's economy and ultimately her defence capabilities. Thus from a variety of motives, Calwell altered the focus of the immigration 'conversation' from that of attracting 'desirable' Britons, to one which included homeless refugees in German DP camps, it being both altruistic and expedient to give a chance to these young, potentially new Australians.

In July 1947, Calwell headed to Europe and visited a DP camp in Bremen. While there, he inspected a ship leased to the IRO by the US Army with a US Navy crew which had been used to transport displaced persons to various countries. When he met with IRO officials, they made the attractive offer of paying the future shipping costs of any DPs to the accepting host country. The offer seemed too good to refuse. Whether this was the tipping point or not, after consultation with German, British and American officials, in July 1947 Calwell signed the fateful agreement to accept, initially, 12,000 post-war displaced persons with the IRO (the number rapidly increased) which led to the first 'processed' DPs coming to Bonegilla on the ship called *General Stuart Heintzelman* in the same year. One observer of the times writes:

While Calwell was in London he heard about the existence of the DPs languishing in camps in Europe. Calwell visited the camps and soon thereafter signed an agreement with the International Refugee Organisation (IRO) to allow the refugees to emigrate to Australia. This wave of refugee immigration was the first large influx of non-British immigrants since the Chinese migrations of the last century. It broke the long tradition that only British immigrants would be assisted to come to Australia.[17]

This large group of post-war DPs were to help stem a labour shortage, and prevent Australia from perishing. They were to come in massed groups to migrant camps all over Australia – but mostly to Bonegilla. The official Bonegilla website says the following of this period of burgeoning growth of post war immigration:

> Bonegilla was big. At one time it could accommodate 7,700 people, with an additional 1,000 in tents, if need be. Through 1950 about 1,000 migrants arrived each week. The Reception Centre became intent on processing large numbers rather than trying to meet individual or family needs. It was not possible to accommodate family units together, and women and children were sent to Holding Centres in places like Uranquinty, Cowra and Benalla.[18]

After 1951, as well as accepting displaced persons, Bonegilla also accepted other non-British assisted migrants, many from Greece and Italy. Throughout the 1950s Australia negotiated migration agreements with several other European nations such as the Netherlands, Germany, Malta, Austria, Spain, Belgium, Finland and the Scandinavian countries. These agreements led to further agreements with other countries in subsequent decades. The 'tin hut town in the bush' type of migration town did not persist, however, as the favoured method of accommodating and assimilating migrants. The assisted migrants of the second phase were not as quiet in their acceptance of the barrack style of accommodation as had been the first phase of post-war displaced persons. The times were changing and the new waves of immigrants had come to Australia because they had chosen to even though they had the choice of remaining in their own land. They had not been dispossessed and some did return to their countries of origin. DPs like Bogdan and Valerie had no choice of return and this in itself constitutes a major difference between the first and subsequent waves of immigrants, even though the memories of Bonegilla would be similar in some respects for all who passed through its gates.

When Bonegilla closed in 1971, this unique manner of 'processing' migrants to Australia had already begun to lodge itself in the communal and cultural memory though the form these memories would take was as yet unknown. In time ex-Bonegilla residents would live in every part of the country and have an indelible effect on Australian life.[19]

Tin cups and plates: labourers and domestics

The DPs came on the basis of agreeing to do two years labour for the Australian government. Whether one was a farmer, student, professor or scientist, one was designated as 'labourer' or 'domestic'– even if vague reassurances about the future were given. Most were happy to sign the agreement as they had little choice. James Jupp observes:

> The decision to select economically assimilable Displaced Persons in 1947 is often hailed as 'the greatest humanitarian act that Australia has ever undertaken'. In fact it was a coolly calculated drive in competition with the United States to draft workers into Australia without upsetting the domestic labour or housing situation. It was humanitarian in that families were allowed to accompany male workers, provided they were healthy. It was less than human is splitting those families on arrival in Australia, sometimes for as much as two years.[20]

This labour could be done anywhere in Australia, from Dalby to Hobart, from Cooma to Perth, and hence, as soon as requests for some specific labour came through to Bonegilla, the new arrivals would be allocated a job and would leave to fill the new positions. The separations of wives and husbands was the cause of considerable distress and only increased the determination of the separated couples to reunite, whatever it took. Some of the work offered was in the camps themselves, as was the case with Bogdan and Valerie, but usually people had to move elsewhere.

An advertisement of the time gave an enticing impression:

> In the middle of sunny fields and on the banks of Australia's greatest river, the Murray, lies Bonegilla, the reception camp established by the Australian Government for European citizens. The new arrivals spend their first weeks in their new homeland here in order to become acquainted with its customs and mores and thereby ease their passage into the Australian way of life. (Advertisement to encourage Displaced Persons to come to Australia).[21]

One can almost hear the birds twittering in the background to this optimistic advertisement. Bonegilla was indeed located on a site of natural beauty. However its actual construction was the simplest and most pragmatic available at the time. Bonegilla's accommodation consisted of the recently used barrack type rows of huts, one after the other, made mainly of fibro and corrugated iron, set out in neat rows among the gum trees of northern Victoria. One description of the barrack type building goes thus:

> The walls of the huts were made of corrugated iron without linings. There were no ceilings under the roofs. A gap between the roof and the top of the walls provided

for ventilation. The huts offered shelter but not insulation from extremes of heat or cold.[22]

The first 839 newcomers at Bonegilla entered a camp with very simple amenities. They were initially in dormitories and, like a swagman, had a tin cup and plate. They must have looked around and wondered at what they saw. The Army initially provided transport, security and catering services and thus military routines and disciplined queues were the order of the day where the issue of stores such as eating utensils, linen and blankets were concerned. Each newcomer was issued with grey woollen blankets and crockery, cutlery and other items to be returned on leaving Bonegilla. Army clothing was supplied when needed and organisation was geared to group provisions and group management. By 1948, there were a hall, kitchens and messes, a Department of Labour and National Service office, quartermaster, ration store, linen store, post office, regimental aid post, lecture room and accommodation for administrative staff as well as migrants. Apart from providing accommodation, the main function of the centre was to provide Alien Registration, accommodation, transport and to allocate employment. Thus the whole focus of camp activity was to place the DPs and migrants in work as quickly as possible and to expedite all the matters that accompanied this.[23]

The army barrack buildings, though primitive and spartan, were practical for accommodating large numbers of people as they had done in the war years. Certainly, the surrounding scenery could not have been more typically Australian or picturesque, for those whose recent memories included being caught in crossfire and bombings (as were my mother and father) barely escaping with their lives. After the horror of war, coming to Bonegilla must have seemed like travelling on the Spaceship Enterprise to the moon and landing on the Sea of Tranquillity. For some it would have been disorienting to come to such an isolated place, having been urban dwellers, but the gum trees, lakes, ubiquitous possums and the languid calm of the Australian bush soon exerted their influence and Bonegilla became for many as good a respite as any that might be found in the world. Most expressed gratitude such as Hilja Opik from Estonia who said, 'We never regretted it even for a second. We got away from the displaced persons camp. We were pleased that the Australian Government brought us here and gave us a chance for life.'[24]

Before the transport ships to Bonegilla

But when did the DPs' journey begin? Or when does any journey really begin? Is it in the stamp of a document, or is it an idea, a word, the passport photo, or is it in the boarding of a train or ship? Is it in the loss of a former life, the thoughts that hold the mind in the strangeness of being caught between two destinations? Perhaps it is not possible to untangle all the threads of any journey, as one leads to another, then to another and another. One part ends, another unfolds and so on forever. For those who came to Bonegilla, while it is hard to find the exact moment when it all really started, one can find some initial footing if one considers the places and times in which they lived not so long beforehand.

Prior to Bogdan and Valerie stepping off onto Bonegilla railway siding in 1950, their stories, as for other DPs, begin before World War II in places very far from Australia. So this account will go like a storyteller's boomerang and return to another time with different outlines, shadows, realities and fateful portents. It cannot bring back all of the pieces of the journey, for some are inevitably lost forever but it tries of capture that 'somewhere' from which Bogdan and Valerie and many DPs came, and to reveal something of 'who' in fact the DPs were.

2

Bogdan before Bonegilla:
a place called Lublin and another called Vilno

For my father Bogdan the journey to Bonegilla begins in Lublin, a large town in south-eastern Poland where the blues, greens and blacks have a deeper intensity than those colours in Australia. The crowded streets of pre-World War Two Lublin are framed with the contours of solid ochre and brown buildings of past centuries, black lace ornamental balconies, church spires, old town walls, narrow cobbled alleyways and synagogues. Birch and oak trees line the roads on which men, women and children head to their daily destinations and some horse pulled carriages can still be seen along with cars and trams. Along the various paths of purpose and activity walk merchants, bankers, artists, scholars, paper sellers, children, rabbis, priests and all the inhabitants of a pre-war Eastern European town. The trees in Spring 1939 would have blossomed just the same as in any other year, as deep-voiced conversations, shouts and laughter mingled and echoed around them and as children ran past in their carefree attitude (oh, could it really be joy?). The children ran along the streets as if the world was theirs, calling out to friends and family with their myriad sounds in the especially mellow summer light of that year, a light full of unimaginable portents.

In that time called the inter-war years – as if the content of that time can be grasped as an interval between two monuments of time

– ordinary Poles enjoyed music, theatre, going to church, discussing politics, telling stories – in fact all that a developed European city had to offer. It was for many an idyllic time, like a dream, yet with a nightmare looming, dark beyond imagining. It was a time where many did not see what was coming, a time when those who did see something, hoped it was not coming. The roads leading away from busy Lublin went to the fields beyond, dotted with horses, carriages, storks' nests, and birds circling above the country houses. The roads led to the east and to the west, to places planning Poland's extermination.

It was in this south-eastern Polish town of Lublin that Bogdan Skowronski was born on 1 February 1928 in the old town centre. Lublin lies about 160 km southeast of Warsaw, the capital of Poland and it takes only a few hours to reach the capital from there by train. Bogdan's name was really Bohdan, an older form of the name. Bohdan when pronounced correctly sounded like 'b-och (och as in 'Loch) dan. Scots would have no difficulty saying it. But people actually said 'Bogdan' in everyday conversation – Bogdan with a 'g' and for ease of understanding this form Bogdan will be used in this story. In both forms the name means 'gift of God', as does Theodore in Greek.

Lublin was often referred to as the place where 'east meets west', though perhaps the city of Lwów (now in the Ukraine and called Lviv) merited that title more appropriately and also that area to the east of Poland generally known as the Kresy, the Borderlands. These were border areas over which there was fierce fighting in 1920 when the newly formed Soviet Bolsheviks wanted to take over Poland (and the rest of Europe) and did not succeed. In any case, Lublin was always thought of as 'eastern Poland' and although not on the border itself, it was still not far from the areas bordering the Soviet Union in

1939 and hence of stragetic importance where Soviet intentions were concerned. Towns near borders are very conscious of their identity, of signs of friendliness and signs of threat, it is part of the heightened if not hypervigilant sense of geographic reality their inhabitants are born with.

Bogdan's father, my grandfather Stanisław Skowronski, a tall imposing man with a long diagonal nose, was a notary who had married my grandmother Wanda Maria Bogdanowicz when she was only 17. Wanda Maria, a lively, kind and devoutly religious brunette, who all her life liked to tell witty stories, was the youngest daughter of a patriotic Polish family of five children and was born in Ciechanowiec, north east of Warsaw in an area of Poland called Podlasie. Her father – my great-grandfather – was Leon Antoni Bogdanowicz and her mother – that is my great-grandmother – was Helena von Brakiel, of aristocratic, part Prussian background. Leon Bogdanowicz was a member of the minor landed gentry who had had his own country manor and land in the 19th century. He lived in a Poland which was under Russian occupation. However, Leon lost all his land and property because of the family's participation in the Uprising in 1863, in which Poles tried to regain their freedom from Russia, one of the powers which had partitioned their country and wiped Poland off the map of Europe. People may have varying views of nationalism, but to delete a country and race entirely is another thing and it is natural that people try to avoid it happening, a forlorn hope for many in the past century. Leon's brother, 26-year-old Kazimierz Bogdanowicz, fought with a group of insurgents in this 1863 uprising. He was arrested and was shot dead by the Russians for his participation, as were many other Poles. He is buried in a tree-filled cemetery in central Lublin, along with other resistance fighters.

After the loss of his property (a punishment for being involved in the Uprising) my great-grandfather Leon had to find a job. Being an educated man, he was able to live and work as a legal notary in other people's manors (that is, in those areas where people had managed to retain them after the uprising of 1863) to support his large family. The owners of the manor in which Leon lived would have watched the children grow up. Leon must have heaved a sigh of relief when his daughters got married and went off to a better life. And especially he would have been happy when his youngest daughter Wanda Maria got married to Stanisław, the tall, imposing man of letters, who fought in the army under Pilsudki's command and who came from the Lublin area. They were my grandparents and faced a future full of hope.

Wanda and Stanisław initially lived in Lublin after my father was born there in 1928. Then they moved to Vilnius with their young son, Bogdan, as Stanisław obtained a secure position there. He went to work for the mayor of Vilnius, or Vilno as it was known to Poles, in a relatively well paid role as secretary to the mayor who had social democrat leanings. And there, Bogdan's sister Alicia was born. Brother and sister recalled a relatively happy early childhood in beautiful inter-war Vilno, city of lively streets, artists, poets, musicians, the 'Paris' of the east, a 'Jerusalem' for the Jewish population. Bogdan's and Alicia's early years there were very different from what was to happen to them during the remainder of their childhood – Vilno was a kind of past 'Eden', which they referred to poignantly in later years.

What follows in these paragraphs is not a comprehensive history of pre-war Poland for such is not the purpose of this story. Histories of the inter-war and war years can be found in more detailed accounts elsewhere. This is more like a snapshot of some aspects of the life Bogdan once knew and the thoughts that would have been in his mind and those of his contemporaries – the world of a DP. Of course this

*Bogdan (left) with his sister Alicia. This is one of very few photographs
to survive World War II*

Bogdan's father Stanisław Skowronski in uniform – he fought in Piłsudski's army in 1919-20 against the Bolsheviks

Another photo to survive the war. Taken in 1938, Alicia is on the right, Bogdan is second from the left. They stand in Kiwerce in eastern Poland (now part of the Ukraine) with their Grandmother Helena, second from right and a little friend

The grave of Kazimierz Bogdanowicz – author's great-great uncle – and his fellow compatriots who participated in the 1863 Uprising against the Russian occupiers. Kazimierz was 26 when arrested by the Russians and shot. All family property was confiscated henceforth

involves giving some historical details and description of the events which formed his early years but these are just strokes of the brush and not any 'final' interpretation of those times. It gives the broad outlines of Bogdan's life before Bonegilla – the geographical, political and psychological worldview he would have known and thought about as he sailed to Australia.

What Bogdan knew – a brief historical detour

In his childhood Bogdan would have learned about the origins of the area in which he was born. For Polish children, history is a most important subject and for most Poles inevitably remains so all their lives. How could it be otherwise? It is not an option to be unaware of it when you live between great empires. It is different for countries surrounded by mountains and the sea. But this is not the case with Poland. History and context are of utmost importance where so many immediate lines of influence touch everyday life. Thus a sense of identity and historic outline comes naturally through daily contact with others and continual hearing of historic tales.

Where Lublin's historical origins are concerned, there are several theories. One general view is that the earliest significant settlements began in the area in the sixth century, on a hill located in the area of Czwartek – which in the Polish language means 'Thursday'. Perhaps the town's name was a reference to the fact that much of the trade around this strategically located town occurred on its market day, Thursday. Certainly Bogdan would have known, as standard general knowledge for any Polish child, that Polish King Mieszko I married the Czech Princess Dabrowka in 965 AD. He converted to Catholicism in 966 AD in western Poland with most of the country converting after him, Poland truly became an eastern bastion of Catholic Europe beyond which the world of Russian Orthodoxy began. The following expresses a standard view of this event as Bogdan would have understood it:

> … it is Mieszko I who is recognised as the founder of the Polish state. It was during his time that conquests were completed and the tribes whose languages and cultures showed great affinity were united. The prince reorganised the new territories and united them into a uniform state system. In 966, Mieszko was baptised, thus placing the Polish state in the political system of Central Europe and determining the European and Christian road of development of the Polish state and society.[25]

The decision of Prince Mieszko I to convert to Catholicism inevitably shaped Poland's relations with the Holy Roman Empire and determined her future development and participation in the states of Europe. So all Polish children learned and still learn that the son of and successor to Mieszko was Boleslaus the Brave (992-1025 AD) whose statue stands in Gniezno in central Poland, in fact the ancient capital of Poland.(To this day, whoever is the Bishop of Gniezno is the Catholic Primate of the whole of Poland). Boleslaus went along the same path as his father, increasing Poland's independence at the early stages of his rule. In 997 he organised a mission by the Czech Benedictine monk-Bishop Adalbert (many Polish children are named Wojciech or Wojtek, the Polish version of this name) to the lands of the Baltic Prussian tribes. After Bishop Adalbert perished as a martyr, Boleslaus the Brave paid for his body and brought it back to place in Gniezno Cathedral. The canonisation of this martyr raised the status of Poland in the eyes of the surrounding nations and became engraved as part of the nation's history. There are constant tours to Gniezno cathedral and Polish children just 'know' about Saint 'Wojtek' as part of their communal history.

During the general political, spiritual and economic development of Poland after the conversion of Mieszko I, Lublin developed into an important trade centre in the 10th and 11th centuries, and continued to grow around its 12th century castle. Being on the eastern border of Poland, the city was a target of attacks by Tartars, Ruthenes, Yotvingians and Lithuanians. It was destroyed a number of times. Lublin, however, achieved some importance as a town when it received a 'city charter' in 1317 from King Ladislaus the Short (Władysław I Łokietek, also known as Władysław the Elbow-high), a sign of upward mobility for a town of its size. After devastating Tartar invasions from the East in 1341, King Casimir the Great, appreciated the strategic importance of the site and fortified the city. He funded further work on the castle in 1341 and encircled the city with defensive walls and battlements.

Later in the same century there occurred an event of great importance in the form of a marriage which altered the course of Polish history. It concerns a Lithuanian prince from adjacent Lithuania whose name also falls easily from the mouth of every Polish school child – even if it may seem unpronounceable to English speakers. The name is Władysław Jagiełło (1351?-1434) whose strange looking surname is pronounced Yagewo, the letter 'ł' in Polish being pronounced as 'w'). He was grand duke of the small neighbouring country, Lithuania, and his life, role and actions had profound consequences for the region. As duke, Jagiełło had considered conversion to Russian Orthodoxy for a while but he opted for the Catholic faith of Poland and was baptised on 15 February 1386 in Wawel Castle in Kraków (or Cracow) which was then the capital of Poland.

It was considered to be beneficial for both Poland and Lithuania if he could marry a Polish queen and so attention turned to the young Jadwiga of Poland (1373-1399) who was originally a member of the Capetian House of Anjou, the daughter of King Louis I of Hungary and Poland and Elizabeth of Bosnia. Jadwiga could claim lineage from the earlier Piast dynasty of Poland. When Louis I died, his eldest daughter Mary inherited the Hungarian throne but, the Poles wishing for a ruler independent of Hungary, chose his younger daughter Jadwiga as their ruler. Interestingly, Jadwiga came to Kraków on 16 October 1384 and was crowned *King* of Poland – she was named *Hedvig Rex Poloniæ* even though she is commonly called Queen Jadwiga. While Polish law had no provision for a female ruler it did not specify that the King had to be a male. Thus Jadwiga was a monarch in her own right not a queen consort. Jadwiga had previously been the subject of earlier attempts to marry her off, at an even younger age, to Wilhelm of Austria. However the latter suitor was put aside for the good of the country now that attention shifted to the neighbouring suitor in the form of the Lithuanian grand duke. No doubt the young Polish Jadwiga who was only 12 or 13 at the time, felt some trepidation when she married the older Jagiełło on 4 March 1386, soon after the latter's conversion.

With this marriage, while Jagiełło became King of Poland, Jadwiga retained her monarchical rights. This marriage forged a link between the two neighbouring countries of Poland and Lithuania that would be highly significant for the future culturally and politically, especially in terms of their proximity to the adjacent lands of Russia. Jagiełło, and his queen ruled together as co-monarchs and Jadwiga took an active role in governing her country and achieved the unique feat of gaining the affection of her people. She did in fact die young, at age 25, along with her child, three weeks after giving birth in 1399. In her short life she had built a reputation for helping the poor for protecting her people and established a University in Kraków at which the future Pope John Paul II was to study (known now as the

Jagiellonian University). Jadwiga was even the subject of canonisation by Pope John Paul II who could openly refer to her in his public addresses to Poles, knowing that every Pole knew who she was, for she has a permanent place in the nation's memory.

Bogdan's youth would have been replete with stories of the 'great marriage' of the great Jadwiga and Władysław Jagiełło. He would also have learned that after his conversion, Jagiełło, as winter fell in 1386, had set out for pagan Lithuania to begin the Christianisation of his country. Lithuania, along with Latvia and Estonia was a country filled with pagan tribes who regularly indulged in fire ceremonies, and who were fiercely resistant to the initial approaches of Christian missionaries, as were all the Baltic tribes. Once in Lithuania, Jagiełło worked hard to persuade his people to abandon their pagan ways and removed the outward symbols of the pagan religion. He took the dramatic steps of dousing the pagan flames at Vilno, felling the sacred groves and disposed of the serpents that traditionally lived in the temples under house doorsteps. Apparently, he also personally instructed the people in Christianity – as much as he knew of it at the time – primarily via the Lord's Prayer and the Apostle's Creed. His preparation for Baptism had taken no more than a few days although he would have known enough to distinguish Catholic Poland from her orthodox neighbours. Massed baptisms were done all throughout Lithuania and the whole country was made Catholic more or less in one fell swoop. In that act, its entire historic trajectory was changed. For here were two Catholic countries allied in the face of their Russian Orthodox neighbour. In fact, Jagiełło went on to have a long and relatively peaceful reign during which accords between Poland and Lithuania grew ever stronger. Lublin was at the hub of this process, being not far from Lithuania and became an important trade centre, carrying a large portion of commerce between the two countries.

Lublin was already a prosperous commercial centre when another historic event of great importance occurred which Bogdan would have known as a fundamental fact of its history. While the Jagiellonian dynasty did not last, the historic link between Lithuania and Poland did. In 1568 the historic treaty between the Kingdom of Poland and the Grand Duchy of Lithuania was signed in Lublin Castle, with long lasting consequences for the two countries. As an official Polish government history site relates:

> The Jagiellonian dynasty became extinct through lack of a male heir (1572). In 1569 King Sigismundus Augustus effected the statutory union of Poland and Lithuania, up till then joined by a personal union. Henceforth the Kingdom of Poland and Grand Duchy of Lithuania would be an elective monarchy, with the entire noble (equestrian) estate enjoying the right to elect their king.[26]

Poland's elective monarchy and how it operated is the subject of ongoing fascination for historians. It was, and is, common knowledge to Polish children that the Union between the two countries existed and the two countries were united in a spiritual and cultural bond. There was continual movement between Warsaw, Lublin and Vilno and vice versa. It was nothing unusual for communities of Jews to live within all towns of the Union – for Hassidism to flourish in Lublin and various groups of orthodox Jews to flourish in Vilno and Trakai. One of these groups were the Karaim people, Jews of Turkic origin who impressed the Lithuanian King Vytautas who first encountered them on the Black Sea and who invited several hundred of them to return with him and live in Trakai. The Lithuanian-Polish union, with its centuries of co-operation, its cultural and economic ties, persisted much longer than one might have expected of such an alliance and provided an 'unparalleled degree of constitutional, intellectual and religious liberty'.[27] The Union of the Two Kingdoms, became a powerful Commonwealth, a bulwark against numerous enemies, a major European power stretching from the Baltic to the Black Sea. The role of Poland in European history was largely seen as that of the defence of Europe, its freedom and Christianity from the invaders coming from the East: the Tartars, the Turks, and ultimately the Russians. This culminated in the famous battle of Vienna (1683), where a devastating charge of Polish cavalry wiped out a grand Turkish army laying siege to Vienna, the gateway to Europe.

In memory of this union there is a monument located in central Lublin in a place called Litewski Square – that is, Lithuanian Square. It is a reminder of the Lithuanian gentry who came to Lublin to attend parliamentary debates and were stationed here. The original monument from the 16th century was destroyed on the Tsar's authority. In 1826, however, a new monument, created on the initiative of Stanisław Staszic in honour of the Lublin Union was unveiled in the form of a cast iron obelisk. The monument was in the form of two women and the national emblems of Poland and Lithuania commemorating the historic union of the two countries. While the current era is termed post-colonial, post-empire, post-post-modern and post many things, the Polish-Lithuanian Commonwealth has its place in the historic annals of Eastern Europe as a significant multi-ethnic union which was a basis for the further development of the area in terms of culture, commerce and relative political stability. That is how Bogdan, his family and peers saw the Commonwealth of Poland-Lithuania – as a union of hope against formidable enemies.

Invasions and take-overs

The Commonwealth did not last forever but it did last until its collapse in 1795 due to increasing invasions and partitions of Poland by surrounding powers. Again these dates of partition are well known to Polish schoolchildren and thus would have been well known to Bogdan. The country was partitioned (i.e., divided up and given to other countries) three times, again events of communal remembrance of loss to every Pole. Poland was partitioned for the first time on 22 September 1772 between Prussia Russia and Austria. Poland was partitioned for the second time on 23 January 1793, between Prussia and Russia. The third partition on 24 October 1795, after which the country of Poland ceased to exist altogether on the map of Europe, brought with it the end of the commonwealth. 'Partition' here is a euphemism for the total loss of the nation's existence on the map of Europe. This annexation of Poland's territory during this and subsequent partitions did not dampen Poland's memory of its own history, as many literary and historic works of the time attest – an historical example of memory surviving such destruction. Not without reason, the national anthem begins with the words 'Poland has not perished yet' – a rousing song composed by Joseph Wybicki in 1797, shortly after the first partition of Poland, and made the official national anthem in 1926. A flowering of literature, in the early and mid Romantic period often written by émigré Polish writers who fled to Paris took up the themes of a loss and gain in a national context. Each educated Polish child knew of the towering figures of writers Jan Kochanowski, Adam Mickiewicz, Juliusz Słowacki, Zygmunt Krasiński and Cyprian Norwid (the latter being one of the favourite poets of the late Pope John Paul II).

So close had been the alliance of Poland and Lithuania prior to these partitions, that it was and is not in any sense unnatural for generations of Polish children to say, along with their Lithuanian peers, the opening lines of Poland's and Lithuania's best known poem, the 1834 epic *Pan Tadeusz*, written by the great poet Adam Mickiewicz (1798-1855). The poem begins thus – 'Oh Lithuania my fatherland, you are like good health: I never knew till now how precious till I lost you'. Mickiewicz was born in Lithuania and was educated at the University of Vilno and wrote these lines about Lithuania in Polish. In the same poem, Mickiewicz goes on to describe the well known Marian shrines of the Virgin of Częstochowa in Poland and the Virgin of Ostra Brama in Vilno (also known as 'Our Lady of Mercy') seeing the common faith of the two nations in terms of heavenly providence, as a union affecting the fates of the two countries. Mickiewicz felt no less a Pole using the terms 'my fatherland' about Lithuania, and Lithuanians proudly claim him as their own. Plaques on buildings in Lithuania mark the places where he stayed. To this day Polish and Lithuanian children learn to recite these lines and in Vilno in the mid-1930s so did young Bogdan and Alicia.

In addition to the awareness of the union between Poland and Lithuania there was also awareness of the intersection of the Byzantine and Catholic worlds. This was especially evident in the integration between the Byzantine and Western art, the world of Russian Orthodoxy and Western Latin Rite Catholicism. In Lublin Castle there was, and still is, an ancient 'Trinity chapel' built in the time of the first King Jagieło. It stands as a great example of artistic union of east and west – in having both Western Gothic arches and Byzantine frescoes. Actually these frescoes, which have often sent art historians into various states of frenzy for their sheer beauty, have only recently been restored. Only now, in the post-Soviet era, the painstaking cleaning of the chapel by art restorers has fully revealed the paintings on all the walls and the ceiling in this extraordinary Gothic and Byzantine artistic union. One of the frescoes in Byzantine style depicts king Jagieło kneeling with head bowed before a bishop.

Although Bogdan loved his years in Vilno, he also loved Lublin and deeply imbibed the history of the place where he was born. He would have walked past the various churches, synagogues and historic building and monuments. For example he would have known about the church of St. Brigid in the street called Narutowicza in Lublin – a church whose building was funded by King Jagiełło after the victory over the Teutonic Knights in Battle of Grunwald (1410). The battle of Grunwald is an expression as familiar in Polish memory as would be the name of Gallipoli to Australians. The battle of Grunwald involved King Jagiełło I along with the Grand Duke Vytautas (Witold) in an early battle involving the Polish-Lithuanian alliance. These rulers fought and decisively defeated the invading Teutonic Knights led by Grand Master Ulrich von Jungingen. Throughout Poland there are reminders of this historic battle. In Lublin, near the church commemorating the Grunwald victory stands the monument to Jan Kochanowski the most eminent poet of the Polish Renaissance, much beloved by the future pope, Karol Wojtyła. Kochanowski was an ardent supporter of the Polish-Lithuanian Union of 1569 and lauded it and the developments of the day in his poems. He actually witnessed the oath of allegiance paid to the Polish King Sigismund Augustus on 19 July 1569 in Lublin by Prince Albrecht II Frederic von Hohenzollern, a fact noted for posterity in the extraordinarily detailed painting of the Lublin Union by Jan Matejko.

Bogdan would have pondered the paintings of Matejko and the span of historic events included in his art. As part of his education in Polish history, Bogdan would also have been aware of the events of the Reformation which affected the development of Poland. In the second half of the 16th century, Reformation movements arose in Lublin and of note, a large group called the Polish Brethren established themselves there. The Polish Brethren were a non-trinitarian group who were variously labelled Arians and Socinians but eventually became known as Unitarians. Also at around this time, one of Poland's most significant Jewish communities in Lublin rose to prominence and was one of the most renowned and flourishing in all of Europe. This community of scholars were referred to as the Jewish 'Oxford' and students came from everywhere to study the Talmud and the Kabbalah at the great Rosh Yeshiva of Lublin, a centre of learning which had rights equal to other Polish universities after 1567.

Like every Pole, Bogdan would also have known of the history of the Polish cavalry, especially the Hussars with their spectacular metre high wing formation and the various battles in and beyond Poland in which they were victorious – among them the battles of Orsza (1514), Obertyn (1531), Byczyna (1588), Kluszyn (1610) and Kircholm (1605). In particular he would have heard of the Siege of Vienna in 1683, when the Ottoman Turks threatened to overrun Europe. He would have heard of and read about Jan Sobieski going to the aid of besieged Vienna with his 30,000 troops, after praying at the shrine of Our Lady of Częstochowa. Sobieski spearheaded the charge of hussars who descended in mighty formation looking like avenging angels with their high winged plumage, sending the Ottoman Turks into terrified flight. Sobieski's hussars were a force to be reckoned with and had considerable influence on the course of the battle, to the gratitude of the other participants in the battle and the rest of Europe.

Bogdan learned that Lublin, like the rest of Poland, had fought for its survival against the Swedish invasions of the 17th century. Then, not long after being partitioned for the third time in its history, Lublin was under Austrian rule from 1795 onwards, as mentioned above. It then passed to Russian rule in 1815. It regained its freedom again after the First World War, in the Polish republic of 1918 which was a source of immense joy and relief after the long years of occupation. Literature, the arts, political life all began to flourish with renewed vigour. The Catholic University of Lublin was established in 1918 and was to play an important role in preserving the eastern and indeed the western European cultural and spiritual legacy in the times to come.

The battle of 1920 and beyond

Another sombre fact in this historical legacy absorbed by Bogdan was the aftermath of World War I. While the war had ended for most of western Europe in 1917, it did not end for the Poles who now had Lenin's plans for world expansion of the Communist idea to contend with. While celebrating their newly found independence the Poles saw that the Soviet powerbrokers to the east, in their revolutionary fervour, had plans for eastern and western Europe. As historian Adam Zamoyski put it:

> Karl Marx had only ever envisaged communism working in an advanced industrial society. Its triumph in the backward agrarian economy of Russia had been something of a freak, and to Lenin and his comrades the best way of ensuring its survival appeared to be to export the revolution to Germany. Humiliated by defeat in the Great War, awash with unemployed and disaffected soldiers, German seemed fertile ground. Between Russia and Germany lay Poland...[28]

The plans for Soviet expansionism led to an invasion of Poland by the Soviet army in 1920 just after Poland had regained its freedom. The Soviet invasion was intended to overrun Poland rapidly as an 'example' to other western European countries of the kind of revolutions awaiting them. However things did not go according to plan. The easy victory did not occur, to the great surprise of Lenin and Stalin, because the Poles fought back expressing an overwhelming desire not to become Communist.

The invading Bolshevik/Soviet army had to contend with a

person greatly revered by Poles in general. This was the indefatigable Marshall Józef Klemens Piłsudski, a name evoking awe and respect the length and breadth of the country. It had a special resonance in Bogdan's family for his father Stanisław fought the Bolsheviks in Piłsudski's armies. Piłsudski was a larger than life figure, a brilliant strategist who had no illusions about the Bolsheviks, who viewed their grand claims with a sober and skeptical eye and knew their means of operation. He had had ample earlier contact with the Russians as he had dealt with them in Tsarist times and knew the complex, internecine conflicts and conspiracies of the era. Piłsudski possessed military and political cunning in battles which even the young Charles de Gaulle appreciated. De Gaulle came to Poland and participated in this anti-Bolshevik war thus giving him training in resistance against the occupying Nazis in the future. Even less known is the fact that an American pilot Merian Cooper, greatly inspired by Tadeusz Kościuszko's aid to George Washington in the American Civil War, went to Warsaw to offer his services to Piłsudski as he 'wanted to act in Poland as Kościuszko had acted in my own country'.[29] He convinced seventeen other American pilots to join in, thus forming the Kościuszko Squadron and aiding the Poles, inflicting considerable damage on the Soviet army. Cooper was shot down and imprisoned by the Bolsheviks but managed to escape. He was awarded Poland's highest military honour Virtuti Militari by Józef Piłsudski himself. Interestingly this extraordinary pilot on returning to America, went on to become a Hollywood director and produce the very first film of *King Kong* in 1933. He never lost his passion for flying and served as chief of staff for the US Fifth Air Force's Bomber Command in World War II.

The Poles never forgot that Piłsudski saved Poland from the Bolshevik threat. The two decades of freedom from communism after 1920, called the 'inter war years', in fact 'provided much of that part of the Continent with its first taste of some kind of democracy'.[30] Piłsudski's name would have been hailed at many hall meetings, churches and dinner tables of Lublin and throughout the whole of Poland. Having been born in Lithuania, he had defended Poland against great odds at a point where Western Europe ended and the Soviet empire began. Even some of his Russian opponents grudgingly showed him respect, though the Soviets nursed their grievance and sought to avenge it.

Meantime, Piłsudski's name was revered by Poles as hero, saviour and symbol of persistence against the more numerous Bolshevik Russians, the new Soviet regime. Thus while, at the end of World War I, Byelorussia and Ukraine were mercilessly suppressed by Bolsheviks, Poland had resisted the westward surge of the Soviet expansionists, much to the Soviets' chagrin (Lenin reportedly raged in anger at the Bolshevik defeat). In fact some viewed Poland's defeat of the Communists in 1920 as a victory of great significance for the West in general. A British diplomat, who reflected on the significance of this 1920 Russo-Polish battle remarked:

> If Charles Martel had not checked the Saracen conquest at the Battle of Tours … the interpretation of the Koran would be taught at the schools of Oxford … (And) had Piłsudski … failed to arrest the triumphant advance of the Soviet Army at the Battle of Warsaw, not only would Christianity have experienced a dangerous reverse, the very existence of Western civilization would have been imperilled.[31]

The heroism of Piłsudski against the invading Soviet army constituted a large part of the world view of my father, grandfather and many other Poles of his generation. Bogdan breathed an air resonating with stories of near destruction and heroic survival. In fact he had a very patriotic pedigree in having a great uncle who died in 1863 fighting the Russians, a father who fought under Piłsudski as a cavalryman. Then he himself was to become a resistance fighter. However, for the time being in the inter-war years, it was in this interlude of freedom in Poland and eastern Europe, this post-Piłsudski era with its rich tapestry of historic memory, its literature, music, poetry, journals, its foxtrot dancers, its accordion players on the streets, its varied society during which my father and Alicia acquired their memories, their 'dreaming' – everyone's hopes were for the continuance of civilisation and the retreat of totalitarianism.

One of the few family photos not destroyed in the Second World War shows Bogdan standing in a square, not in Lublin as it turns out, but in Kiwerce, where the family was holidaying at the time. Kiwerce was formerly part of Poland not far from Rivno and in this surviving photo taken in 1938 Bogdan stands lightly smiling with his sister, his grandmother Helena Bogdanowicz and another young friend. It is one of those carefree, mellow moments of childhood where Bogdan and Alicia stand in a square looking on shy but content. In the photo, my father holds a newspaper with inter-war comic strips visible on the opened page, the page he was reading. His proclivity for humour and what became a fine sense of irony is evident in its early phase of growth. The querying spirit is already evident in his intense eyes and the stories he had heard of the past, such as have been recounted in the previous pages, were already part of who he was. He stands with both hands down in front of him, wearing shorts and sandals in a relaxed pose. Little did he know what awaited him.

My father's grandmother Helena died not long after the photo was taken and she is buried in Vilno. During Bogdan's and Alicia's time in Vilno, the Nazi build-up in Germany would not have been unnoticed by the family and all those around him, as well as an increasing sense of apprehension about Hitler's intentions as regards

Poland. Looking east there would have been the simultaneous realisation that the intentions of the Soviet dictators were far from benign and Piłsudski's victory in 1920 had not been forgiven or forgotten. Kenneth Koskodan writes that 'by the spring of 1939, Polish intelligence had located and identified 36 German divisions moving to within striking distance of Poland's western frontier' and while Poland tried in earnest to build defences, she was hampered by pressure from France and Great Britain not to activate her military lest she 'provoke' Hitler.[32] The treaty of mutual defence signed in the spring of 1939 between Britain, France and Poland had as its central point that if any one of the signing parties was attacked, the other two were immediately to give aid in its defence. Koskodan states with some irony the widely held view that this 'was considered a great achievement in diplomacy and was thought to be a major deterrent to Hitler's aggression'.[33] But despite Germany's evident aggressive intent Poland was asked not to prepare for war as if this in itself might deter Hitler from his plans.

Bogdan's childhood in Lublin and Vilno came to an abrupt halt when Hitler invaded Poland from the west on 1 September 1939, and darkness fell over Europe. Then soon afterwards the Soviet Army invaded Poland from the east on 17 September 1939. There was a scramble by many to return to Lublin ahead of the Soviet army which was racing to take over large areas of wherever it could. Then there were chaotic attempts to escape from west to east too. But where could people really run between two criminal regimes hemming them in on either side? My father was 11 years old and already in Lublin when Hitler invaded Poland. The momentary idylls of Lublin and Vilno were shattered never to return. The beautiful summer of 1939, the hopes, the artistic growth, the respite, the ever disappearing peace, all gave way to the inescapable contours of a war which now began to forever define all their lives.

The church and monastery of the Bernadines in Vilno with a side view of the statue of Adam Mickiewicz, the most revered poet of Poland and Lithuania

A street in old Vilno (Vilnius) in the 1930s

A corner of Lublin's Old Town

Lublin Castle, used as a Gestapo jail during World War II, where Bogdan's mother, Wanda Maria, was imprisoned after being tortured. From here she and fellow Lubliners were taken to Ravensbrück concentration camp

3

Wartime and resistance

The invasion of Poland at 4.45 am on 1 September 1939 by Nazi Germany came with unimaginable violence and fury, marking the beginning of war for Poland and the beginning of a global geopolitical shift whose movements few could foresee. When the German cruiser *Schleswig-Holstein*, moored in the port of Danzig (Gdansk), started to fire at point blank range at the Polish fort of Westerplatte, two million German troops crossed the Polish border in immense waves at various points in the west, north and south accompanied by hundreds of planes and tanks. Many Poles, Bogdan and Alicia included, sat at tables and listened to radio transmissions which informed them that their country had been invaded at several points and that their armed forces were fighting back. With time they would have realised that the Polish counter-attacks were not adequate to repel the massive German forces and that their lives were radically changing around them. It would have been hard to find some still point in the chaos that had been unleashed in ever intensifying forms around them. They heard with some hope that the United Kingdom, Australia and New Zealand had declared war on Germany on 3 September 1939, soon followed by France, South Africa and Canada, among others, and waited for help. They pondered immutable facts which increasingly restricted their lives and demanded some immediate plan though little action seemed possible. How does one plan when one cannot see one step forward in the midst of chaos?

One cannot understand why Bonegilla ever came to exist, nor the people who came there immediately after the war, without understanding how some of the major events of those times impacted on those living through them. What follows are some aspects of the dark realities that entered the lives of my father Bogdan and so many of his generation, who had as yet little knowledge of the evil now facing them in the Nazi occupation, the General Government, the determination to kill the Jews and Poles and the subjugation of a country which had so recently regained its nationhood. Whatever one's internationalist sympathies, it is understandable that the people in Poland, freed from over a century's domination by other powers, would feel keenly the tragedy of this new assault on their national freedom. What follows in this chapter is no definitive history but is rather an account of some of some salient features of those times which of course are open to differing interpretations and I claim no final word on any of these. It is a brief account of the way many who lived through the events saw them then, or came to see them later – of course filtered through their communications to me and through what I have read and seen. These were experiences which formed Bogdan's teenage years and the memories he carried to Bonegilla as young man.

As the German battleship *Schleswig-Holstein* opened fire in Gdansk, and as the Wermacht poured into Poland, dive bombers attacked from the air. Simultaneously panzer divisions invaded the country at several points, attacking relentlessly to secure the Baltic port and move inland. The Poles put up fierce resistance and the mayor of Warsaw Stefan Starzyński (later shot in Dachau in 1943) rallied the spirit of his people. Kenneth Koskodan points out that the Poles inflicted more damage on the invading German forces than is generally acknowledged, writing that 'for more than a month Polish forces had fought, retreated, regrouped, then fought and retreated again as planned' while waiting for a hoped-for invasion of Germany by France, which would have slowed the German invasion but which never materialised.[34] The cost of the Polish campaign for the Germans he adds was 16,000 killed and 32, 000 wounded with much equipment destroyed including '674 German tanks, 319 armoured cars, 195 heavy guns, 285 aircraft and over 11,000 truck and motorcycles.'[35] While the British, French and other nations were 'gravely shocked' and 'appalled', in reality Hitler's attack was at a comfortable distance and no immediate help was forthcoming. In reality the Poles' defence of their country bought precious time for France though in the end this was to no avail.

The invasion of Poland occurred one week after the signing of what has become known as the Nazi-Soviet pact, the Hitler-Stalin pact or the Molotov-Ribbentrop Pact, named after the Soviet foreign minister Vyacheslav Molotov and the German foreign minister Joachim Von Ribbentrop. It was signed in Moscow by both parties in the early hours of the morning of 24 August 1939 and was a treaty of non-aggression between Germany and the USSR. It was a deadly document in which the fate of Poland was sealed as the Russian and German foreign ministers felt free to divide up Poland between them – literally to the last square metre. It was a pact agreeing on simultaneous invasion of Poland from the west by Germany and from the east by the Red Army. It was as if China and Indonesia carved up Australia for themselves without telling anybody and then proceeded to enact their plans. At that time no-one in Poland knew their lives and land had been signed away by this pact. With the simultaneous invasions the Soviets and Germans raced in for their land grab, at a pace faster than the Western Allies reacted to the events. After the German invasion from the west, Lublin found itself the victim of a swift invasion by the Soviet army from the east over the Bug River in the same month. For Lubliners, suddenly there was nowhere to run, only inescapable realities to adapt to.

The Soviet army was simply co-operating with Germany in overrunning eastern Poland after its invasion on 17 September. By 1 October, less than a fortnight later, both Germany and the Soviet Union had completely overtaken the country, although the Polish government never formally surrendered but tried to escape southwards as quickly as possible. In this way the government and many of Poland's remaining land and air forces were evacuated to neighbouring Romania and Hungary. Over 100,000 Polish soldiers escaped making their way, despite encountering extremely dangerous situations, to France and many on to England. The aim of those escaping was to preserve some remnant of the existing Polish government and to re-form an army which would fight alongside the Western forces with the aim of helping them and freeing Poland.

Disappearing millions

While the Germans established their anti-Semitic and anti-Polish regime, the omnipresent Soviet regime in the east began a new chapter of what was its hallmark activity – spreading terror based on 'class'. The Soviet terror had already killed over 3.5 million Ukrainians in the forced famine of 1932-3 when the Soviet regime insisted that Ukrainian peasants hand over all their grain, even their growing seeds to the Soviet collectors and collaborators who simply killed those who did not comply. The crime here was to own land and to be able to fend for oneself – this was odious to the Soviet view of the world where all were forced to be 'team players' in unworkable co-operatives. The terror had continued in 1937-8 when many hundreds of thousands more Ukrainians were suspected as enemies of the Soviet state. They weren't but they were killed anyway.

When the Soviet Army entered eastern Poland, they had prepared lists of names of those who worked in any position, in the government, whether railways, postal or police services. Then began the knocks on the door by day and night and arrests of large sections of Polish society in eastern towns. This constituted a Russian blitzkrieg that rivalled the Nazi one. Many Poles were killed by a bullet at point blank range in a deliberate policy to decapitate Polish society of its leaders, its intelligentsia or any citizens involved in any of its functioning organisation. One example from the many millions is that of Lucjan Lucjanowicz Jankowski, a policeman from Lwów, then in southern Poland. Lucjan was last seen by his cousin at the end of September 1939 among the mayhem of people rushing to the east, away from the Nazi invasion in the west. He was spotted by his cousin at an eastern station for Lucjan wore his policeman's uniform and his cousin urged him to take it off as the Soviets were after anyone in a uniform. Lucjan told his cousin that he took an oath to serve his people and would not take off his uniform. He was arrested and killed around April/May 1940. The story is known because of the release of some 'death lists' from Russian archives in the post-Soviet era and because of an unusual detail. Lucjan was able to send a small postcard to his family en route to his imprisonment and death with a Russian postage stamp stating, 'I have been arrested by the Russians. I don't know what will happen to me'. Virtually none of these types of notes got through – some were thrown from railway carriages in the hope a stranger might find them and send them on. The archival material released in recent years reveals a list of deportees to be shot. Some surviving descendants of Lucjan – Jolanta and Stanislaw Kotowicz – who live in Sydney got hold of a photocopy of the original list with Lucjan's name on it and showed it to me. Lucjan was taken to a forest and shot by the Soviet militia but the whereabouts of his grave is unknown. This is one of millions of stories of deportees who are buried in unmarked graves and whose 'crime' was simply to exist.

Another deportee was Jan Pacewicz, grandfather of Anna Pacewicz from Sydney. Jan was arrested by the Soviets when they invaded Poland, also for the 'crime' of being a policeman. Initially he was held in Rowne prison where the family sought him out and were able to visit him taking him food by passing it through the bars. On the last such visit Jan said to his son 'it's not safe here, tell Mama to go quickly, run'. On 28 March 1940 Jan was transported to Kiev, in USSR controlled Ukraine, and sentenced to death by the Soviet secret police, the NKVD, without trial. He was accused of article 54-13 of the Ukrainian Criminal Code ('committing crimes against the working class or revolution movement') and was executed by the NKVD (shot in the head), most probably in the NKVD Kiev headquarters. Jan Pacewicz was on the 'Katyń, Ukraine List', included in the order by Stalin of 5 March 1940 which clearly commanded the execution of 22,000 officers, police, border guards and anyone considered to be intelligentsia. He lies at the mass burial site of Bykownia in the Ukraine. His body has not been exhumed but Anna his granddaughter has been on pilgrimage there to pay her respects to the grandfather she never knew.[36]

Another deportee was Lucjan Wisniowski – the paternal grandfather of Stefan Wisniowski (also from Sydney). Lucjan was a civic leader and district magistrate in Brody in eastern Poland before 1939. Stefan's father was only nine at the time he was deported with his father Lucjan (and the entire family) to Soviet captivity in sub-Arctic Archangel on 10 February 1940. The family was released in late 1941 under a temporary Soviet-Polish agreement (about which more will be said later) but Lucjan died soon after from frozen exposure on the harrowing winter's trek to freedom and it is not known where he was buried. Zbigniew his son, who is Stefan's father, was evacuated with General Anders' army to Iran but there were many more who perished in the gulags than survived in this way. The descendants of those who 'disappeared' – such as Lucjan's grandson Stefan – have spent much of their lives trying to piece together information about their family's fate during this era. In fact Stefan has gathered many of their stories on a site of historic significance, Kresy Siberia Virtual Museum.[37] 'Kresy' here refers to the 'borderlands' – that is, the borderlands of the eastern European countries from which millions disappeared during the early years of World War II and after it and whose fate tended to be forgotten in subsequent histories with the spotlight focused on events in Western Europe at the time.

In addition to the shooting of Polish officials, officers and anyone deemed suspicious, deportations of ordinary citizens from Poland to distant Siberian prison camps and to Kazakhstan began in earnest. It is difficult to say how many were taken, for it all happened so quickly but the figure is anywhere between 1 and 1.5 million people.[38] Many certainly perished en route or in the camps. One of the deportees, Jan Onoszko, was a child at the time and recalls the day of arrest and the disappearance of his father whose crime was to own a butcher's shop. One of the few to survive this period, he recounts his mother giving her daughter – whom she was never to see again – to relations just before leaving. Onoszko describes the harrowing journey, during which his baby brother died of hunger and his mother almost died (she was to die later) and of their constant battle against cold and starvation in Siberia.[39]

Enter Władysław Anders

Another of the deportees was Władysław Anders who had been in charge of a Polish cavalry regiment in western Poland when the Nazi invasion occurred. He had a reputation for heroism dating back to World War I and was to become an even greater hero to Bogdan's generation who knew and forever extolled his courage and daring in the chaotic terror which had seized Poland. Born in 1892 in Krośniewice–Błonie he had distinguished himself in battle and was known as a good strategist. As a member of the Protestant Evangelical Augsburg Church, he made a prayerful promise while in a Soviet prison that if he survived and regained strength in his legs (he was seriously injured) he would convert to Roman Catholicism. He did survive, and did indeed convert and continued his military career in a most extraordinary way. Like many in the Polish cavalry, Anders moved from western Poland to the east with his forces, after the 1939 German invasion, away from where he had been stationed at Lidzbark, trying to counter the German attack. While about 140,000 Poles were taken prisoner of war by the Germans (at this stage random killing was intermingled with some 'prisoner of war' status) some, like Anders, tried to escape east hoping things were better there. As he rode east, Anders noted in his account of the war – *An Army in Exile* (1949) – that the streets were filled with the swelling crowds of refugees running in fear. He also records hearing about the heavy bombardment of Lublin which my father, his sister and their parents and the rest of the family were experiencing at close quarters at the time after having fled from Vilno at the outbreak of the war.[40]

Given the Molotov-Ribbentrop pact, Anders, along with many other Poles in the east, had simply fled one enemy and fallen into the hands of another. He was subsequently arrested yet again and imprisoned by the Soviet army. He was tortured in Moscow's Lubianka jail. However the Russians, including Stalin, knew of his extraordinary military abilities and a number of the NKVD, including the brutal torturer Beria himself, tried to induce Anders to join them. Getting him to come over to the Russian side would aid Soviet plans. Stalin himself interviewed Anders several times asking him to 'come over' to the Soviet side knowing that many Poles would follow him. Anders refused and was repeatedly imprisoned in order to wear him down and win over the Poles.

Anders is one who lived to tell the tale of these mass deportations of Polish soldiers and civilians to the Soviet concentration camps about which little is well known except for the word 'gulag' which is the Russian word for such a camp.[41] The Soviet plan to exterminate any persons with education or position in Poland was a premeditated one. As previously stated it aimed to destroy any future leadership of the country, just as the Nazis were doing with efficiency in their daily activities. One of the methods of eliminating Polish officers was to round them up in large numbers and kill them without any trials or warning. This is what the Soviets did in what is known as the Katyń Massacre (which involved several massacres in several places) where the mass graves of 4,000 Polish officers were found in one place alone in 1943. The total number of murdered officers is between 15,000 and 22,000 and involved many areas, not only Katyń. The officers simply 'disappeared' at various sites within Russia – among them Kalinin, Kozielsk, Starobielsk and Katyń, not far from Smolensk.[42]

As far as these 'Katyń Massacres' were concerned they were carried out with such relentless efficiency that they even gave the Germans pause for thought which is saying something. When the Germans uncovered the graves during their 1941 invasion of the Soviet Union, they broadcast their findings to the West. The Germans were taken aback by the extent and volume of the killings, or perhaps pretended to be, but in any case some measure of human outrage was demonstrated. When they heard of the German discovery of the mass graves, the Russians blamed the massacres on the Germans who then in turn explained that this type of point blank shooting was not their style of execution – at least not in these particular circumstances. It is not that they did not shoot prisoners in the head, it was that they did not do it precisely this way, or so the story went. While the Nazis showed little angst at their own unspeakable mass executions, on this occasion, strangely, they happened to be telling the truth – the Soviet Army was guilty of this particular massacre. The officers killed were not just military men being engineers, botanists, professors, doctors as many educated men were officers and it was not uncommon for academics to take on military service as commissioned officers.

The Soviet plan targeted them precisely because of their education. Their families had no idea what had happened to them until the mass graves were unearthed in the course of the war and the horrifying possibilities began to sink in about what had happened. The events of Katyń became a deeply embedded part of the national identity not only because of the murder of the Polish elite, but because of the reluctance of the Allies to accept than an 'Ally' had done this. In fact, it took decades for these facts to be accepted as part of the events of the war as they involved the Soviet Union – then a Western 'Ally'. The recognition of the events demanded thought and analysis which many in the West did not wish to apply to the Soviet Union at that time but the facts came to light in the post-Soviet era with the release of some documents and Mikhail Gorbachev's admission that Soviet Russians were responsible for Katyń, though this was not followed with any further elaboration or explanation.[43]

The Polish Government in Exile and the deportees

My father Bogdan, like his compatriots caught in this pervasive web of terror and killing, would have had a hard time in trying to deduce what it all meant and what was going to happen next. His daily life was one of living amidst two totalitarian regimes, destroying everything he had ever known. Then there was the problem of trying to follow the bizarre twists of the war. For while the Soviet Union was the 'friend' of Nazi Germany at first, it then did a volte-face and became an 'ally' of the West. This major change in the progress of the war occurred when 4.5 million German troops invaded Russia along a 1,800 kilometre front on 22 June 1941 in Operation Barbarossa – that is how they came across 'Katyń' and other sites of mass murder, as mentioned above, while engaging in a murderous invasion themselves.

Suddenly the geopolitical winds of the war – and one could say the entire century – shifted direction. In shock at the German invasion, Russia's becoming one of the Allies resulted in an interesting turn of events which affected the fate of the Poles. To understand how it happened one has to appreciate what happened to the Polish government which had escaped southwards after the Nazi and Soviet invasions of 1939. They in fact passed over the power of the government to key figures with the purpose of forming a Polish government outside Poland. Thus the Polish government in exile came into existence on 17 September 1939, when the then president of Poland, Ignacy Mościcki, who was in the southern Polish town of Kosow, signed an official declaration appointing Władysław Raczkiewicz as President of the Republic in accordance with Article 24 of the Polish constitution. The Polish government did not resign and in this way it continued outside Poland. Raczkiewicz took on the role of President and based the government-in-exile first in Paris in 1939 and then moved it to London. He appointed Władysław

Sikorski, Prime Minister and Commander-in-Chief of the Polish Armed Forces, (Sikorksi died in 1943 in a mysterious plane crash) and who was succeeded later by Stanisław Mikołajczyk. At first the Polish government-in-exile established diplomatic relations with the Soviet government but this was broken off by the Soviets in 1943 when the Soviets took offence at being accused of the Katyń massacre. The Polish government-in-exile continued to operate in London for the remainder of the war and beyond, even after the Allied governments ceased diplomatic relations with them in the new post-war realities, recognising the Soviet-backed Communist puppet regime in Warsaw.

The Polish government-in-exile was already established in Britain when Germany attacked the Soviet Union in 1941. When the Soviets suddenly changed sides, the Poles saw a window of opportunity to seek information on the missing million-and-a-half citizens. They asked Churchill to put in a plea for the missing Poles (those still alive) spread out over gulags across Russia. Such pleas would normally have led to no result, as they were meaningless with the Soviet regime, except that in this case, Russia was particularly vulnerable after the German invasion and were courting British help. Knowing this, Churchill intervened and offered to 'feed and arm' the scattered Poles, and told Stalin with some tongue-in-cheek that he would help him get rid of these 'nuisances', if they could be found and disgorged from the gulags throughout Russia. In a one-off decision Stalin, who was desperate for Western support, agreed and his order was sent out across the wide Soviet terrain. Though many did not get to hear of this order, others did, and thus a considerable number of Poles were freed in this way. Over 100,000 Poles, though emaciated, made their way from Siberia, Kazakhstan and all parts of Russia to an agreed meeting point to join up with Anders, once the news filtered through about this once in a lifetime amnesty.

After the call went out that Poles could be released, Anders worked at feverish pace, for he had met Stalin personally on a number of occasions, had witnessed his criminal pathology at close quarters, and thus knew this unique event could easily be overturned at any moment. Anders established a Polish recruiting centre in Buzuluk in Russia and as soon as these Poles arrived, telling their horror stories of imprisonment and torture, he enlisted the released men into an army which he was forming. The remarkable rarity of this 'amnesty' in 1941, needs to be appreciated in the light of the fact that it was only after repeated Allied requests that Anders and his confreres from the gulags were released. For those who made it, there began one of the most extraordinary journeys of all time, something like the biblical Exodus. Anders left Russia and the 'Anders Exodus' with groups of emaciated Jewish and Polish deportees, who had been in concentration camps in Siberia, used every available means of transport to get away, realising this opportunity was unlikely to ever arise again.

Anders' Escape

This extraordinary escape march of Anders and his deportees, by train, lorry, horse and on foot is one of the lesser known stories of World War II. The journey took Anders and his enormous group down from Russia to the Persian Corridor into Iran, Iraq and Palestine. The Polish Jews in Anders' group had a historic encounter with the Jews of Iran.[44] In Anders' group was none other than Menachim Begin who was to have a great influence on the future history of Israel. Once they reached Palestine, the half-starved men of Anders' Exodus group recuperated, the orphans were cared for and a whole new organisation was set into being. From this group of survivors, Anders formed and would lead an army which was to be of immense service to the Allied cause – the Polish Army in Exile – the 2nd Polish Corps.

Moreover, Anders never ceased to agitate for the release of Polish nationals still in the Soviet Union who had not made it out (that is, the majority of the Poles arrested in 1939). Anders, who had met Stalin and Molotov, was later to meet Churchill and the British commanders and to link his army with the British forces in the Mediterranean.

Many in the West know of the Polish pilots who fought in the Battle of Britain and of the Polish troops in England, Scotland and France but few know of this army in exile, whose epic exploits came to be widely known during and after the war by young soldiers such as Bogdan. Anders reflected the hopes of those left behind and Bogdan and his peers would have seen Anders as a hero and future saviour of their country. They listened avidly to any news of Anders through illegal radio broadcasts and his extraordinary courage helped fuel the resistance movements in Poland.

Anders had been given official charge of his army in 1941 by the Polish government-in-exile and led the 2nd Polish Corps in numerous battles gaining the respect of all the Allied commanders he met. Of particular note was the assault that finally captured the Nazi held stronghold of Monte Cassino, site of the Benedictine Monastery established by St Benedict in the sixth century, which the Nazis had taken over as a headquarters. Two allied assaults had previously failed to capture it. The heavily populated nearby cemeteries give witness to the extraordinary battle which took place in early 1944, which involved soldiers scaling Monte Cassino as Germans fired on them from above, the ascending soldiers hoping enough would get through the barrages of fire. Bogdan followed the events and cheered Anders on, inspired by his feats. And the oppressed Poles waited for him to return to Poland and help liberate their country.

After the war, Anders wrote his account of these extraordinary events in the work referred to above, *An Army in Exile*, which Harold Macmillan described in its introduction as 'an epic … like the march of the Greeks under Xenophon. It will long remain a classic of military prowess and courage.'[45] Anders, never ceased trying to learn of the fate of his deported confreres who had been arrested in the Soviet blitzkrieg of 1939 and not made it out of the Soviet Union with him in 1941, about whom most Poles, like Bogdan and his generation knew and grieved. While many in the West knew of the German atrocities in Poland, few knew of the Russian atrocities, deportations, assassinations and death camps. In his assessment of the 1939-41 period, Anders describes the difficulties of giving an account of the events:

> I tried to assess the real figure of Polish citizens deported in 1939-41, but it was extremely difficult. After many months of research and enquiries among our people who were pouring from thousands of prisons and concentrations camps spread all over Russia, we were able to put the numbers at 1,500,000-1,600,000 people. Statistics obtained afterward from Poland confirmed these figures. But unfortunately, it was clear that most of these poor people were no longer alive. God only knows how many of them were murdered, and how many died under the terrible conditions of the prisons and forced labor camps.[46]

The Poles who escaped subsequently joined up with the Allied forces in France, French-mandated Syria, the United Kingdom and Anders' 2nd Polish Corps. In subsequent perceptions and evaluations of the war it was not so well known that that in their combined presence in the Allied army, air force and navy, the Poles became the fourth largest Allied military formation.

Darkness everywhere

After its initial invasion of eastern Poland the Soviet army subsequently withdrew from Lublin according to the conditions of the Nazi-Soviet pact, restraining further ambitions for the time being. After the Soviets left the Lublin area, the German army moved in and occupied south-eastern Poland. Here on 26 October 1939 they set up what was known to the Germans and to the horrified inhabitants as the General Government – the German administration of Poland. On 9 November, Odilo Globocnik (who was responsible for erecting the death camps of Majdanek, Belzec, Sobibor, and Treblinka) became head of the district police and the SS. The 'Governor General' was the German lawyer Hans Frank – known as the 'butcher of Poland' who was later tried at Nuremberg and executed.[47]

Lublin was made the specific German headquarters for Operation Reinhardt, the main German effort to exterminate the Jews in occupied Poland. The Jews in Lublin, who numbered approximately 40,000, about a third of the town's population, were forced into the Lublin ghetto established around the area of Podzamce. The majority of the ghetto's inhabitants were deported to the Bełżec death camp in 1942, others were killed in Belzec and Majdanek, the latter concentration camp built by the Germans in the same year on the outskirts of Lublin as part of their occupation and control of that city. The floor to ceiling piles of shoes and glasses of those murdered there are evident to this day. The General Government area also contained three other extermination camps which were set up for killing alone – the Nazi death camps of Treblinka, Sobibor, and Belzec/Zamost to which Jews were brought from the Warsaw ghetto and other parts of Europe. Treblinka was the largest of these and Jews literally walked from the train carriages into the gas chambers. Chil Rajchman only survived as he had to carry the dead bodies and sort clothes as he recounts in his work entitled *Treblinka: A Survivor's Memory* (2012, 2009).[48] Rajchman describes a revolt by the starved inmates in Treblinka on 2 August 1943 (those left alive to carry bodies, sort clothes and remove gold-filled teeth would also soon be killed) which destroyed much of the camp, and it was closed in November 1943. However the pace of killing had been such that between six to eight thousand were gassed each day (as in the other death camps). In fact Hitler seemed impatient for the task of extermination of Jews and as many of Poland's citizens as possible. In an entry to his diary on 23 August 1939, Admiral Canaris notes Hitler as saying:

Genghis Khan had millions of women and men killed by his own will and with a gay heart. History sees him only as a great state-builder ... I have sent my Death's Head units to the East with the order to kill without mercy men, women and children of the Polish race or language. Only in such a way will we win the Lebensraum that we need. Who, after all speaks today of the annihilation of the Armenians.[49]

Hitler took the genocide of the Armenians at the hands of the Ottoman Turks (70% of the Armenian population perished in the years 1915-1918) as the example he wished to follow in his planned extermination of the Jews and Poles and then the other 'untermenschen' of eastern Europe.

While walking through the former Jewish area of Lublin, I came across a Jewish home for disabled children whose inhabitants down to the last person were killed by the occupying Germans and a plaque on the building recounts the events. There are many plaques throughout Poland indicating where groups of people, whether men, women or children were killed by the Germans. They are particularly frequent in Warsaw where each day Poles faced random shootings, arrests and every variety of terrorism.

Disbelief beyond Poland's borders

Jan Karski, a Home Army courier who faced death several times by moving in and out of Poland on behalf of the resistance, brought news of the mass murders occurring in Poland to the outside world. In particular he gave eyewitness accounts of the systematic extermination of the Jews to Allied leaders in 1943 but many would not believe him. Karski had managed to get smuggled *into* the Jewish ghetto and witnessed first hand the starvation and brutality within it. In his powerful work *The Story of a Secret State: My Report to the World* (2011, 1944), Karski describes the underground 'state' within Poland and its relations with the Allies, in particular how he tried to alert the West to the 'final solution' already in progress.[50] Dr Shmul Zygielboym, the delegate of the Jewish Socialist Bund of Poland to the Polish government in exile, tried to communicate, along with Karski, the evil beyond imagining occurring in Poland. Feeling that he faced a world that was not listening, Zygielboym committed suicide saying in a suicide note of 1943, that while the responsibility for the crime of the murder of the entire Jewish nation rested with the perpetrators, indirect blame must be borne by humanity itself, stating:

> My comrades in the Warsaw Ghetto fell with arms in their hands in their last heroic battle. It was not given to me to die together with them, but I belong to them and to their mass graves. By my death I wish to express my strongest protest against the passivity with which the world observes and permits the extermination of the Jewish people.[51]

While Hitler scorned Judeo-Christian moral norms, and despised Judaism and Christianity, he expressed admiration for pagan myths and

Islam as stronger more 'manly' types of belief. The Jewish population of Lublin were initially forced into a ghetto, then were systematically exterminated in concentration camps in mass killing sprees such as that which occurred on 22 April 1942, when approximately 2,000-2,500 Jews, mostly women with children, were taken to the Krepiec Forest and shot.[52]

The extent of Nazi genocidal activity was difficult to assimilate at the outset of the war but finally Poles, Bogdan among them, realised they were dealing with horror beyond measure. Entire villages of people were killed, random shootings were frequent events, the final solution was taking shape. My grandmother Wanda Maria was told by a friend that an arrested Jewish woman threw her baby out to a stranger on the street begging the woman to take care of her child, which the stranger immediately did. The Jewish mother did not survive, but the baby was saved and the suddenly appointed guardian lived to tell the tale.

Some in Warsaw, hearing from rare escapees of what was happening in the death camps, found it difficult to believe, as did Western reporters. Meanwhile the Soviet Union had been conducting its own reign of genocidal terror in the Ukraine and Byelorussia which had been subjected to purges and constant terror throughout the 1930s. The comment of Norman Davies here expresses views which had been common knowledge among Poles, before being recorded as part of his history of the war:

> Stalin's purges defy comprehension by people who demand rational explanations. They were not undertaken simply to weed out opponents or unreliable elements. They were often directed against his most loyal servants, against Communists, who had welcomed the earlier

purges of Troskyists and old Bolsheviks ... who had never uttered a word of dissent. Yet they proceeded on a scale and with a ferocity unparalleled in European history. In the 1930s Stalin ordered the deaths of more human beings than Hitler had killed in the whole of his career. And he didn't stop in 1939. He did it from motives of pure terror, to render the very idea of independent thought unthinkable.[53]

Stalin had defied rationality in his killing sprees and extended the purges among his own citizens within every level of society, a fact which not even the Census officials could keep up with. Again as Davies notes:

The Soviet Union involved in a series of purges and mass murders whose scale at the time was unimagined. In 1939 the Census officials lived long enough to do their jobs, saying 17 million had disappeared during the previous decade, before they themselves were purged.[54]

Caught between twin vortexes of destruction surrounding them in Lublin and given the historic imprint within the Polish character to fight for freedom, many Poles set about trying to sabotage the Nazi efforts wherever they could. Resistance organisations sprang up all over the country. Bogdan's mother, Wanda Maria, and her sister Janina, while at first just putting their efforts into survival then turned their thoughts to how they could help as did many Poles around them. There were a number of resistance groups which were not as yet united into one larger group as eventually happened when they coalesced in 1942 and became the Armija Krajowa – or the AK. Wanda Maria and Janina enlisted in a resistance group in Lublin (as far as I know it was the White Eagle group) to do undercover work in a restaurant often patronised by German soldiers. Not that they had any training whatsoever in espionage. They pretended to be waitresses, smiled and listened to German and Polish conversations as they served food, in an attempt to garner information from Nazis frequenting the Lublin restaurant. The ploy did not last long and many involved in this espionage effort, including the two sisters Wanda and Janina and Janina's daughter, Jadwiga, were arrested by the Germans. There was no chance of a farewell to any members of the family. By this stage Bogdan's father Stanislaw was in hiding in a remote part of the country, a candidate for instant death by the Germans because of his work as Secretary to the Mayor of Vilno who had had socialist leanings. He no doubt assumed that that his children were in good care but Wanda and her sister were now arrested, as Bogdan and Alicia watched helplessly. Hiding where they could, they now had to fend for themselves and knew the reality of hunger.

Wanda Maria and Janina and Janina's daughter Jadwiga were first imprisoned in the Gestapo prison in Lublin – familiarly known as the place 'under the clock' on 14 February 1941 where they were questioned and tortured. Wanda remembered a Nazi guard entering the cell and throwing a chair against her face which threw her to the ground and caused lifelong damage to one eye. Then they were transferred to Lublin Castle, now a prison, and remained incarcerated until they were transported to Ravensbrück Concentration camp, located in northern Germany about 90 kms north of Berlin.

My grandmother Wanda Maria told me, years later in Australia, that the arrested group sat terrified in Lublin Castle prison prior to transportation to the concentration camp. Wanda thought of her children and hoped someone would take care of them. As with many in her cramped cell, she began to pray and at one point the Polish prisoners, mainly Catholics, began to sing the 'Litany of the Saints' pleading for divine intervention. One prisoner called out the names of the saints in rhythmical chant. The cantor, however, could not remember the whole litany from memory, as there are many saints on the list, but he managed to stumble through it as best he could. At one point, after having called out a number of saints' names, he then sang in perfect rhythm 'Saint – I can't remember his name.' Instead of the usual chanted reply – 'please pray for us', someone in the arrested crowd, replied, again in the strict Gregorian chant and rhythm of the litany, 'Well you should have left him out' – which struck all the hapless prisoners as funny. They managed some laughter in their desperate state, which enraged the German guards nearby who shouted at them to cease, even striking some of the prisoners in their anger.

The arrested group among them Wanda Maria, Janina and Jadwiga were put into cattle trucks and transported on the Sondertransport from Lublin in September 1941 to Ravensbrück concentration camp, a camp for women only. There my grandmother and her sister Janina and Janina's daughter Jadwiga were incarcerated for nearly four years, until the war's end, enduring all manner of horrors in a place where death by starvation, beating, torture, hanging, and shooting happened daily. At one stage Jadwiga was operated on in the camp by Nazi doctors who conducted bizarre experiments on the muscles of her leg. This is described in the following way in an account of what happened to the victims of Ravensbrück, giving individual details:

> During her time in Ravensbrück, on 23/11/1942 she (Jadwiga) became the subject of pseudo-medical experiments In her case the experiments involved infections caused by series of injections with gas gangrene bacteria into her right lower leg muscles. The experiment aimed to check the effectiveness of sulphonamides (abacil) in the treatment of such infections. The experiments

conducted on her resulted in pus abscesses on her thigh
and in her groin which required surgical treatment.[55]

The surgical treatment involved taking out the muscles in one
of her legs. She walked with great difficulty for the rest of her life,
with one leg lacking much muscle tissue.[56] My grandmother Wanda
escaped such an experiment – she was also was to be operated on in
a similar way one day, but an air raid by the Allies on Ravensbrück
saved her from the macabre procedure as all had to run for cover.
But along with the inmates she had to work for 12 to 14 hours a day
during her years of imprisonment. The three women, though starving
and near death on many occasions during their ordeal, survived their
years in Ravensbrück in which the majority of the 132,000 prisoners
died. Jadwiga the young girl who was operated on returned to Poland
(with her mother and aunt) and became a chemist, was married to
Wlodimierz Mojejko and had two daughters. Of course in 1941
Bogdan did not as yet know all this. He wondered if he would ever
see either of his parents again.

Into the Armija Krajowa

With his mother in a concentration camp and his father, who had a
price on his head from many quarters and fleeing from village to village
to survive, my father Bogdan at 12, along with his sister Alicia who was
only nine at the time, ended up in a Warsaw orphanage run by religious
sisters. In fact their father Stanislaw re-emerged from hiding and had
placed them there thinking they were probably safer with nuns than
with him. Bogdan, hearing of the Polish efforts of resistance, ended
up leaving the orphanage, joining the growing Armija Krajowa in
Warsaw – that is, the Polish underground army – which had gathered
together all the resistance groups formed throughout Poland soon
after the Nazi invasion. The previously disparate resistance groups

were uniting into one larger underground army and those who could joined it – boy scouts, men, girls, women, young and old. Alicia, very young and suffering from malnutrition and tuberculosis remained in the orphanage until the end of the war, although Bogdan saw his sister saw as often as possible, risking death in these attempts, for moving around Warsaw was dangerous. Many Poles recall thinking daily that one did not know in the morning if one would be alive in the evening. Not that Alicia was any safer in the orphanage for neither religious sisters, paramedics nor orphans were spared in the relentless bombings. Alicia with the sisters and other orphans were to run from building to building looking for shelter throughout the bombardment of Warsaw during the Uprising in 1944.

In that underground resistance movement, known as the Armija Krajowa, or AK in Warsaw, Bogdan at age 12 started out, as many young people did, as a child messenger – called a 'goniec', doing errands in situations of great danger, crossing several battle zones in the city on any given day. This was an effective means of communication between the Poles. As far as education was concerned, Hitler wanted no education for the Poles, for like the Jews, he considered them to be 'subhuman'. He not only targeted all people of education or artistic or professional achievement, he also closed all high schools. Though all high school education was banned for Poles under pain of death, the Underground immediately organised a network of schools and Bogdan attended regular classes in one of these and was able to study several subjects this way. He was gifted with a natural intelligence, good memory and skill in languages, although the circumstances in which he advanced in knowledge were less than ideal in occupied Warsaw. Thus, in accordance with the law of unintended consequences, in refusing to allow formal education to Poles, the Germans only caused the intelligence, ingenuity and talents of the occupied Poles to be used against them. My father recalled that one boon to this dangerous life in the underground resistance inside Nazi occupied Warsaw was getting a meal a day – which was more than could be guaranteed otherwise. It was also a boon to be able to acquire perfectly printed 'papers' in the Polish underground, whose printing presses the Nazis never could locate and destroy. At the same time, like many of his compatriots, Bogdan suffered malnutrition, tuberculosis (from which he recovered) and scurvy as food scarcities increased and illnesses became more common.

At one stage, when Bogdan was about 14 or 15, he was unlucky to find himself arrested by the Germans in Warsaw after a street round-up. He was thrown into Warsaw's infamous Pawiak prison from which few emerged alive. After being tortured and revealing nothing, he was placed on a list for execution and recalled being given a cigarette by a fellow inmate as a friendly farewell gesture as he counted the remainder of his life in hours and minutes. How the rest happened is not entirely clear to me for Bogdan did not speak about it much when he was alive and I did not think to ask for the details, respecting his silences. Bogdan's father, Stanisław, who was still alive and hiding from the Nazis and the Soviets was contacted somehow in his remote village hideaway as soon as Bogdan was arrested. By what elaborate means he managed to slip into Warsaw in disguise, I do not know. Perhaps he pretended to be an illiterate country yokel as this is the 'disguise' he used for a while when in hiding in the country. In any case, he paid a considerable bribe to a German official for his son Bogdan's release. Of course this was not to be a true release. Virtually no-one was released from Pawiak, as Kulski, the 15-year-old AK soldier notes in his first hand account of this period.[57] Kulski himself was imprisoned there and released through the intervention of numerous people, knowing that the release was in the hope of the person leading the Germans to other Polish resistance hideouts and thus exterminating them.

Bogdan was released onto the street on the day he was supposed to die in Pawiak prison. The Germans truly thought that this young resistance fighter would lead them to other resistance cells. So a German soldier was assigned to follow Bogdan who was sick, feverish and hardly able to walk. This planned 'release' had been done with other rare 'releases' who were promptly re-arrested and shot after leading the Germans to their prey. In response to these events, the underground army had drilled its young soldiers telling them if they were ever caught they were to go to a particular part of Warsaw and enact certain gestures. This would be a signal of the released prisoner's situation to any AK partisan in the vicinity. Each AK soldier was told very little that he could reveal under torture in any case. So, on release, the AK soldiers who could were instructed to go to a certain spot in Warsaw, and wander around aimlessly in that place, making the specific gestures, known only to the AK.

My father could hardly see out of his eyes when he walked out of Pawiak, as he had scurvy and his cheeks were puffed with purulent abscesses, the swellings covering his eyelids and restricting his vision. He recalled in later years being unable to see much of what was before him and making his way step by step holding on to the walls of the buildings he passed. In his hungry, dizzy, ill state, he walked alone, shaking, onto the street and noticed out of the corner of his better eye which was not totally covered by abscesses that a German soldier was following him. Bogdan recalled also looking into the glass of such window panes as were still there in buildings he walked past and seeing the German pursuer ever at his back. Still, he walked on and went to the place assigned by the AK for those released from prison, and hardly conscious, wandered aimlessly in the area as he had been instructed to do. It must have been for a long time, and perhaps the pursuer thought he had lost his mind or was deliberately diverted from his task by other members of the AK who spotted him. Suddenly Bogdan found he had been grabbed from behind by two people, a blanket put over his head. He was thrown into the boot of a car and the boot was quickly slammed shut. He had no idea how long he was there in the boot, nor whether Nazis or Poles had captured him but he was taken on a journey of several hours, not knowing where he was going. When the car stopped, he found that it was the Polish resistance group, the AK, who had caught him in this way and bundled him into the boot blindfolded. This was so he could never come to know the area to which he had been taken, so its secrecy as a resistance hideout could be protected. Bogdan could barely stand, as on top of his scurvy and malnutrition, he also had tuberculosis which had greatly weakened him. One of the small resistance group of men in this forest hideaway who was billed as the 'doctor' but probably had no more than a little first aid knowledge, began to lance the large boils on his face, and to wash the resultant pussy mess from it. Then Bogdan was given the 'cure' for tuberculosis which was the only one available at the time. He was wrapped tightly in a sheepskin rug and put outside onto the snowy ground under some pine trees to breathe fresh air each day, all day. He was given some food and he particularly remembered the fact that he had an orange a day – to build up his strength, a rare luxury at the time. As primitive a cure as this was, it apparently worked and my father, who had been so near death, recovered and grew stronger. After some months, Bogdan was strong enough to return to Warsaw to join the underground army. Tragically however, after this fateful rescue, he was never to see his father again.

Bogdan's sister Alicia became very ill with tuberculosis herself in the orphanage run by nuns on the outskirts of Warsaw. On his return to Warsaw, after his 'cure' my father went to visit Alicia in the orphanage which was increasingly dangerous to do. These visits entailed crossing several Nazi occupied zones and Bogdan risked being shot dead each time he visited her. However, the brother and sister had deep affection for each other and they were all they had of their immediate family so each looked forward to the visits. Bogdan sometimes got hold of a few sweets to give her, a fact Alicia remembered all her life, even saying the names of the sweets with the greatest affection – 'chrowki' – little caramel type sweets wrapped in paper. How my father got hold of these I don't know, but he had learnt quickly to be resourceful as Poles under occupation had to be.

A boy's response to evil

Bogdan, like many of the young soldiers in his situation, was confronted with an abyss of evil when not long out of childhood. He was living, to adapt Timothy Snyder's term, in a pervasive 'bloodlands', where the mutually competing murderous Nazi and Soviet regimes sought to reshape reality, seeing the deaths of millions as necessary to the realisation of their crazed utopian ideas.[58] He could not separate himself from the daily realities as could others who were at a distance. He was caught in it and had to live it. He reflected seriously at a young age on matters which do not confront most people till much later in their lives, if ever. While forced into pragmatism and realism, he nonetheless had a capacity for reflection. He would have weighed up the realities of the situation, weighed up options for himself and pondered the events around him as they changed – always with the long threads of history acquired in childhood informing them. In spirit, the Home Army was the heir to Piłsudski's Legions of the previous generation and my father would have been no different, though his views always moved beyond any conventional appraisal of things. When I asked him later in Australia of his thoughts as a child during the war, he simply replied that he realised 'that there were things worth fighting for and dying for.' Freedom, nationalism, honour, courage – all meant something to him even at his young age. At age twelve and thirteen, in the midst of brutality and immorality beyond measure, he made moral decisions. From what he did say to me later in life, he not only was faced with daily issues of survival, but seemed to have a profound sense of what mattered – and knew that some things only come with sacrifice. He had come to some wisdom, beyond his years, with no intervening time to enjoy the lighter pursuits of youth. He would have awoken each day, aware that people would try to kill him and that this day might be his last. As did so many confronted with isolation and terror at the time, he carried this knowledge across the sea to Bonegilla, knowledge which was an ineradicable part of the journey. From my earliest childhood years in the camp, I sensed this inner seriousness in him which echoed from this past, a wordless bond, an inaudible communication from some other realm which I did not as yet understand but which I sensed then I would understand one day, for it inevitably transmitted his 'story' to me and became part of my story too. An imprint was transmitted and, without understanding how, I stored it away for a future time when I would understand and engage in journeys in reverse that revealed what the imprint meant.

Being so young, there would have been no compulsion for Bogdan to join the underground army and of course not all children did as those with parents nearby would have been discouraged or prevented from doing so. However, Bogdan, like many children, had made the decision on his own. Thus the meal a day was not the primary motivation, nor could it always be guaranteed in any case. From what he told me it was a sense of the value of civilisation, of human life, of the value of true freedom and an all too early insight into the murderous forces which strive to take away that freedom. He did not often speak of these times later in Australia but when he did some raw emotion rose to the surface, not for himself but for his friends who perished in the Gulags, the concentration camps and in the Warsaw Uprising, whom he never wanted to forget. The silences in his accounts and his piercing eyes spoke as much as his words and so it is for many who inherit the legacy of war. It was his way of mourning and honouring his young soldier friends – an unforgettable, perpetual remembrance. As young boys they dreamt of freedom, of speaking together without fear, of being with families, listening to songs, music, of being together – simple things. As boys in the underground resistance, increasingly gaining expertise in warfare, they ceaselessly planned for their longed-for dream to come true.

4

The 1944 Warsaw Uprising

After being a 'goniec', a messenger in the underground army in Warsaw, Bogdan became accustomed to the training in fighting, the use of arms and the unpredictable events life presented to him. The actions of this underground group of which he was a member came to a head in the battle called the Warsaw Uprising in 1944. In this chapter the terms 'Home Army', 'Armija Krajowa' and 'AK' will all be used to refer to the same group who instigated the uprising, which was in reality an affiliation of many underground groups in Poland. This was the setting of Bogdan's life for several years as a young teenager.

In the living hell of occupied Poland, where killing was random, where helping Jews was punishable by death, where street roundups were common, Bogdan, like other members of the Armija Krajowa or AK, prepared for one final stand that Poland would make against the German army. This final stand for independence informed the experience and thoughts of many of his generation to such an extent that one can say it was of central importance as regards their journey to Bonegilla. In fact, Bonegilla's largest group in the first phase was comprised of Poles, and this cannot be fully understood without considering what happened in this extraordinary battle as many who came in this group were survivors of it and even if they were not immediately involved, it loomed large in their understanding of their personal fates. In a sense their lives were determined by it. After many of Poland's leaders had been murdered by the Russians and Germans early in the war, the Poles in the AK fought on as armies tried to annihilate them too, as superpowers bargained coolly about them and as horror surrounded them at every turn. Bogdan, and many other DPs, could not but carry the memory of this nightmare with them to Bonegilla. It shaped what many saw as the 'fine young DPs' who alighted from their ships in Australia after the war.

What follows in this chapter is not a comprehensive history of this partisan uprising, for there are several accounts available which fulfil this purpose, but an account in broad outline of some events of Bogdan's life accompanied by some individual stories of battle and survival. It also includes some reference to well documented accounts of the Warsaw Uprising which provide details and perspectives of this battle about which little was known in the West in the post-war years and about which little is known even now.[59] This was due to political agendas in the east and west – in the Soviet Union, any knowledge of the very existence of the Home Army was suppressed in the post-war years – one risked one's safety, even one's life by even referring to the independent non-Soviet army in post-war Poland – and in the West, it jarred with the view of the Soviet army as an ally.

Before proceeding further, the battle termed the Warsaw Uprising of 1944 needs to be distinguished from the Jewish Ghetto Uprising of 1943 in Warsaw. The latter occurred after the Nazis crammed much of Warsaw's Jewish population into a small area in central Warsaw, without basic food or water. They then abandoned the 380,000 Jews to die from starvation in the ghetto and then implemented the 'Final Solution' of the death camps such as Sobibor and Treblinka. The Jews were rounded up in the ghetto, literally walking from there onto the train and then from the train into the gas chambers. Anyone who tried to escape was shot, like the young Jewish girl of about twenty who ran with her hands raised crying piercingly 'No, no no!' Czesław Miłosz saw this young girl fleeing and writes in his account of it that 'the necessity to die was beyond her comprehension' but 'the bullets of the SS guards automatic pistols reached her in her cry'. As she cried out 'no, no, no', she fell to the ground crumpled in a heap and then was 'kicked aside by an SS boot'.[60]

Having visited Sobibor in eastern Poland, I found it does not take long to walk from the railway siding to the place where the gas chamber was, the final destination of many Jews locked up in the ghetto and transported from western Poland. A memorial now stands there and I stood in silence with Jewish visitors to the site, 'hearing' the silence of the surrounding trees and grey skies, a silence to which no human words can respond, a silence which is inconsolable. Some Poles sought to help their Jewish compatriots encircled by Nazi guards in the ghetto, trying to scale the walls and being killed in the attempt. Among those who gained access to the ghetto was the heroic Irene Sendler, a Polish Catholic social worker, who by an complex series of ruses gained rare entry. She worked quickly in her limited time allowed in the ghetto and saved 2,500 Jewish children from certain death by issuing them with false papers and finding them safe houses with Polish families on the outside. Another person who got inside the ghetto was Jan Karski who then was sent by the underground army on a mission to London to give his eyewitness report.[61] Within the ghetto a group fought the Nazis to the death in 1943 in a final act of extraordinary courage in which most of those remaining were killed. After killing the remaining Jews, another camp – called Concentration Camp Warsaw – was erected on the site of the ghetto and became another macabre site of almost daily killings of Jews and non-Jews, where those prisoners ordered to burn the bodies of those who had been shot, were then themselves shot until the next group to be killed arrived.[62]

As reports came through of Nazi reverses, especially after the failure of Hitler's Operation Barbarossa, his attempt to invade and take over Russia in June 1941, his failure in the largest tank battle of World War II, the Battle of Kursk in July-August 1943, the attempt on Hitler's life in 1944 and resistance in France, hopes grew that the tide might be turning towards an Allied victory. The Poles hoped to seize some initiative in the midst of these reverses. They were also aware of the Soviet march into Lublin in July 1944 in order to begin a wholesale Soviet takeover of Poland. The Soviets began to publicise 'the Committee of National Liberation' in Lublin, a group of little known Polish fanatics, Communists and left wing sympathisers who shared the Soviet view of the world. The Poles in the AK knew that the Soviets, who were playing a deadly, deceptive game with the Allies' hesitation, aimed to present this group as representative of Poland and as a fait accompli. Delay was not an option in these circumstances. As historian Timothy Snyder notes:

> Although the British and Americans could afford to have illusions about Stalin, Polish officers and politicians could not. They had not forgotten that the Soviet Union had been an ally of Nazi German in 1939-41, and that the occupation of eastern Poland had been ruthless and oppressive. Poles knew about the deportations to Siberia and Kazakhstan and about the shootings at Katyń.[63]

The Poles' understanding of Soviet intentions were based on the realities of the former actions of Soviet armies whose members, often at gunpoint, had forced ex-gulag internees into their army which was planned to take over Poland, as a supposedly 'Polish-Soviet' force. Many AK units in eastern Poland had tried to attack German communication targets in early 1944 but were then uncovered and dissolved by the Soviet Army who still killed Polish officers they found and forcibly conscripted remaining young Poles into a 'Polish-Soviet' army on pain of death for themselves and their families. Bogdan's contemporaries in the AK, the only surviving 'free' army in Poland, were forced to take an ultimate stand hoping for Allied intervention – for they and the Allies knew they could not do it alone.

In 1944, preparations were made for this final uprising involving men, women, children – all who could fight joined in. Each AK soldier was given assigned roles such as that of soldier, scout, messenger, printer or medical helper. The level of organisation was highly detailed and there was a wordless mutual sense of alertness on the streets as members passed each other. Religious priests and sisters helped in whatever way they could. The AK had few resources, but held great hope that the country might be finally released from the Nazi exterminators under whom all had lived for so long.

Norman Davies writes that the Warsaw Uprising was 'the biggest military action undertaken by any of the wartime resistance movements.'[64] In his landmark history of the second world war entitled *No Simple Victory: World War II in Europe, 1939-1945* (2008), Davies states that this was a most unevenly matched battle in terms of weapons and other matériel, the Poles having little or no access to arms and being pitted against a well armed, larger army. Everything had to be planned on the basis of how to make fewer resources more effective. J. Zawodny similarly states that 'nowhere during the Second World War was there a battle of such magnitude in which the enemies were so unevenly matched.'[65] Only about ten percent of the combatants were armed and the arms were hardly a match for German tanks, planes, self-propelled artillery, railway mortars, tanks and armoured trains. The determination to make a stand, however, had now reached a critical mass. Bogdan, along with all in the AK, knew there would be a moment when the fight for liberation would begin and eagerly awaited this hour. They did not as yet understand the increasingly cool detachment of the Western powers as to their fate.

Rising from darkness to hope

Jadwiga Nowak, a young girl at the time who had the 'code-name' 'Greta' in the AK (all members had a code name) describes the atmosphere in Warsaw, just hours before the Uprising:

> I walk down the streets of the city witnessing the frantic activity of the underground mobilizing. Men and women – the soldiers of the AK (Home Army), who in a couple of hours are going to fight against the enemy – mix with the crowds of civilians so as to move unnoticed. The trained eye can recognize them by their brisk walk, boots, belts, berets, and trench coats that, almost give them the appearance of soldiers. Friends do not stop to chat. The air is heavy and electrified, just like before a storm.[66]

The electrified air would have also been heavy with the hope that the Allies would come to assist them. Poles staked their hopes on it as they knew that at the time Allied troops were breaking through the Normandy defences and the Red Army was coming ever closer to Warsaw's Vistula River from the east and to Lublin in the south-east. Some of the Germans in Warsaw seemed panicked and decided to leave and the German governor of the Warsaw district, Dr Ludwig Fischer (who was executed for war crimes after the war), left Warsaw before being ordered back by Hitler. Promises of help from the Allies for resistance to the Nazis filled the air.

As soon as the Uprising started on 1 August 1944, Hitler exploded with fury, although he had been warned that such an event was likely. The enraged Heinrich Himmler, head of the SS under the command of SS Lt General Heinrich Reinefarth, sent reinforcements to Warsaw consisting of SS police units and an especially sadistic unit known as the Dirlewanger penal brigade, who respected no moral limits and shot groups of people at random, women and children included. Direlwanger, an alcoholic, criminal and sexual pervert who had a doctorate in economics, encouraged every form of brutality. There were unusual non-German contingents in the German army – even an Azerbaijani infantry battalion on the German side (many Azerbaijanis joined the SS to escape the Russian Communists and stayed on in post-war Germany) and another RONA Brigade headed by Bronislav Kaminski, a opportunist and who headed a Russian Nazi party and whose forces constituted the twenty-ninth division of the SS.[67] Added to this were units of the Hermann Göering division and after a certain period, those of General Erich Von dem Bach-Zelewski, SS Obergruppenfuhrer and General of the Waffen SS, whose participation in mass murder of Belarusians had earned him compliments from Hitler, and who took command of all the German forces to suppress the Uprising. Enraged by the unexpected longevity of the uprising, Hitler, via Himmler, gave the crazed order, to kill all of Warsaw's inhabitants whether civilians or soldiers and to totally destroy every building, to level the historic city 'as an example' for others.[68]

The day to day progress of the battle is vividly described in an autobiographical account of a surviving soldier who was fifteen years old at the time. Julian Kulski managed to write up his account which was traumatically engraved into his memory after the war in *Dying We Live* (1979).[69] His perceptiveness and understated heroism are a 'voice' for the many child soldiers of that era including Bogdan, not to mention all who fought in this ill-matched battle – who had no chance to write down what they experienced. Norman Davies' *Rising 44* is also a detailed account of the battle to which considerable reference will be made as it reflects the outlook and mindset of the AK army of which my father was a part and which became a central memory for the remainder of his life.[70]

Many Poles think of Davies, an English-born Oxford-educated historian as 'one of their own', as regards his understanding of the Warsaw Uprising and refer often to his work on this. What follows draws on his well-sourced account and also on such memories as my father related to me, although in general, Bogdan did not speak about it at great length. It also includes some comments which Bogdan's cousin Janusz Bielski from Poznan (who had made his way to Warsaw) related to me. For Janusz fought with Bogdan on the streets of Warsaw in the same group of young soldiers within the Baszta Regiment (in the Baltic Battalion) in Mokotów.

The Warsaw Uprising itself lasted from 1 August until 2 October 1944 although sporadic fighting continued after this date.[71] About 200,000 were killed and 800,000 driven from Warsaw as the historic city was finally utterly destroyed, building by building, on Hitler's orders to Bach-Zelewski. No other capital city of Europe was destroyed as effectively as Warsaw was during and after the uprising. Around 500,000 were sent to various camps after the battle was over.

It is estimated that there were about 50,000 insurgents in the Armija Krajowa (AK) in Warsaw, of whom my father was one, and of whom 20,000 perished.[72] This is not to count the many ordinary Varsovians who assisted in a multitude of ways and those who were trying to hide from the Germans. My father related to me himself that all his schoolmates died in the Uprising, referring to his underground class

Monument to the 1944 Warsaw Uprising in central Warsaw. The Statue depicts young soldiers emerging from the sewers after 63 days of fighting in October 1944

A soldier emerging from the Warsaw sewers in 1944. From a photographic display in the Warsaw Uprising Museum in Warsaw

Schoolboys and girls joined the AK to fight the German occupiers in the Warsaw Uprising

of fellow high school students who, before they perished in battle, had risked their lives to attend high school classes in Nazi Poland.

The Commander in Chief of all Poland's AK forces was General Tadeusz Komarowski whose pseudonym was 'Bór' ('the forest') and who was known generally as Bór-Komorowski. The Commander of the Warsaw District Home Army forces was Colonel, later General Antoni Chrusciel, whose pseudonym was 'Monter'. He was also Commander-in-Chief of the Warsaw Uprising and gave the order to initiate it. These leaders moved around Warsaw among their soldiers during the fighting and while their names were known, not all knew their faces.

It comes perhaps as a surprise to know that while most within the AK were Poles, there were various other groupings as well, including some Italians, Red Army deserters and a platoon of Slovaks commanded by Lieutenant Stanko. There were people of many religious faiths – Catholics, Orthodox, Lutherans, Calvinists and Jews of Polish, Ukrainian, Byelorussian, Georgian, Armenian Azerbaijani and Spanish origin. There was even an armed platoon of deaf-mute fighters who defended their own building being assisted all the while by an elderly priest who served as their chaplain, helper and interpreter. Many joined forces in this final stand, wearing the red and white armband to identify them, in a motley collection of clothes. This was not a pan-nationalistic gesture, simply an expression of the age-old human desire to be freed from constant threat of oppression and death.

The Warsaw Jewish leader Isaac Cukierman (code named 'Antek') issued a proclamation on behalf of the Jewish Fighters' Organisation, urging its members to join the fight for a free Poland. About 1,000 joined and 324 of these were inmates released by AK insurgents in the course of the Uprising from Concentration Camp Warsaw. Those released included camp inmates from Romania, Holland and Hungary who, even in their weakened state, joined the battle.

Women were also part of the AK and many were messengers running through crossfire, as my father had done when he was a messenger, dodging bullets to deliver instructions from one part of Warsaw to another. One young Warsaw girl wrote:

> I was only fifteen years old. Two of us were told to deliver a message, and we had to cross Napoleon's Square. We were caught by crossfire on the streets. At that I was so terribly frightened that I just couldn't move. I froze – I was so frightened. There were two of us, because if one should be killed the other one was supposed to take the message and deliver it.[73]

The girl made it to her destination and survived to tell her story. Catholic nuns ran into the open wearing red cross bands and carrying stretchers but this sign of international peace had no meaning at the time and the Germans opened fire on them while they continued to give assistance to the wounded. This was a hell on earth where no norms of any recognisable humanity existed. Many religious nuns and priests died trying to save the lives of their compatriots. During these days filled with courage, death and dying, the AK members – whether soldiers, civilians, religious, volunteers – were shot indiscriminately after surrendering to the Germans as part of Hitler's genocide of unwanted peoples. No prisoner of war convention was respected during the battle.

Among the Home Army fighters in Warsaw there were officially 550 children aged 10-18 who belonged to AK units. After the uprising ended, they went into the POW camps in Germany – my father being among them. There were many other children in other cities who participated as scouts and messengers. In addition, this does not count the children who remained in Warsaw who would not have admitted to their young age and, perhaps like the Australian young men in World War I, tried to pass themselves off as adults. Bogdan at sixteen, a sensitive lad who liked reading and music, was one of the 'experienced' hands by that time. With many Poles of fighting age dead or in exile, and others in Soviet and German concentration camps, children took on the task. Many other children in Warsaw, not formally inducted into the AK, also fought and risked their lives helping the soldiers in countless ways. In a poignant tribute to these child soldiers, a statue of a boy in uniform, aged no more than five or six, stands in Warsaw at the official Warsaw Uprising Memorial near the centre of the city.

In the Warsaw Uprising each person was assigned a regiment, some of whose names were – Parasol (meaning umbrella), Baszta (battalion), Sokol (Falcon), Zośka (the girl's name 'Zoshka'), Rys (Lynx), Broda 53 (Beard 53), Dysk (Discus), Miotła (Broom) and Chrobry (Valiant). Warsaw was divided into districts and the regiments assigned particular districts to 'take over' from the Germans. District One took in the Old town Centre and District Two took in the area known as Zoliborz (Jolibord). My father Bogdan was a member of Baszta Regiment – in the 'Baltic' battalion – and fought in District Five in an area of Warsaw called Mokotów, south of central Warsaw. Like other AK soldiers, he was given a pseudonym or code name, in his case 'Zaremba'. Other groups – Wrack and Monopol – also fought in this area. There was a chronic lack of weapons in Mokotów as elsewhere and Norman Davies records of Baszta regiment:

> … on 1 August 1944, Baszta's 31 officers and 2170 other ranks possessed 1 heavy machine gun, 12 light machine guns, 187 rifles, 80 sub machine guns, 348 revolvers, 2

PIAT anti-tank rockets, 1750 hand grenades and 120 kgs
of explosives.[74]

This was hardly a match for machine guns, panzer divisions and
bombers that were soon to be sent to reinforce the German troops
in Warsaw. My father told me that his cousin Janusz Bielski, who
fought with him in Baszta, was the person in charge of his (Bogdan's)
immediate group. Janusz was the most senior at nineteen years of
age. This group of about ten young soldiers apparently only had one
gun among them although they had home made bombs and were able
to inflict some damage. Others like them, neophytes who knew little
about ammunition, budding poets and musicians among them, had
met secretly throughout Warsaw to learn how to wield weapons, how
to throw grenades and molotov cocktails in preparation for this hour.
A radio transmitter was set up by the young Stefan Korbonski, who
had escaped Russian capture in mid-October 1939. Korbonski, with
the help of an engineer, set up effective radio communication in 1941
which had to change locations on a daily basis as the Nazis relentlessly
sought to find the source of the transmissions. On the day prior to
the Uprising, Korbonski was set in his location near Marszałkowska
Street in central Warsaw, ready to transmit and hear hoped for news
of support from the Western Allies.

Songs amid terror

In what must seem the most unlikely activity under the circumstances,
there was a flourishing of poetry and song-writing in the years
leading up to the actual uprising among some AK members. Each
unit had its own battle song. Some might attribute this to a romantic,
heroic sense among Poles, deriving from memories of the Battle of
Grunwald and Piłsudski's legions, perhaps recalling the well-known
song 'Przybyli ulani pod okienko' ('the Ulan cavalry came to the

window') which recounts the cavalry of the Piłsudski years, knocking on the window of a house for aid, as they move forward to fight. However, the flourishing of song and poetry is not to be explained in any 'romantic-heroic' sense alone, as many have mistakenly tried to do. It is also primarily to be viewed as the fundamental human need to assert life amidst the macabre ruins of what daily reality had become. The young men had a sense of unmistakable realism when it came to their chances of survival. The songs were a sign that the cultural spirit of the country had not gone, for as variously as Poles might interpret the 'terms' cultural spirit, whether they were of the left or right or centre, they had a common enough sense of it to know it breathed some kind of freedom and by now, long unknown peace.

At this time, the young Karol Wojtyła, later to become Pope John Paul II, was hiding from Nazi searches in Kraków in southern Poland and forced into slave labour. In this crucible of subjugation and brutality, he had cause to wonder if anything of the cultural memory of his nation would survive as so many of its leaders had been killed. In what must have seen a strange activity at the time, he risked his life attending readings of Polish history and literature with fellow students in Kraków early in the war. This was before he entered the underground seminary there run by Cardinal Sapieha – for which the punishment was of course death – while doing long hours of forced labour for the Germans at the Solvay chemical plant near Kraków. It may seem inappropriate in war time to have such 'readings' but under Nazi occupation any attempt to preserve Polish learning or culture was a crime and meant one could be shot. Wojtyła relates in his autobiography that he saw his university professors at Kraków's Jagellonian university lined up and arrested in 1939 and placed in trucks to be taken to Sachsenhausen concentration camp.[75] He recalls the lectures he was attending the very day they were arrested and the conversations he was having as the order came for the professors to go to a 'meeting'. This was simply a ruse by the invading German army to gather the staff together to take them to Sachsenhausen where many died. Wojtyła escaped a similar fate by being put to forced labour near Kraków for four years. The Catholic University in Lublin where he was to lecture later, was also shut down during the war and used as a Nazi hospital, though it continued its activities in secret.[76] Wojtyła must have asked himself many times: What happens after an entire nation's culture is annihilated? What memories would survive after the destruction of such a war? What would remain after so many of the country's poets, artists, professors, intellectuals and students had been killed? Why was he trying to survive? How does a society survive an attempt to destroy it completely?

In the days of his living nightmare, he came to ponder long and hard on the essence of any country and culture. He came to realise that the means of survival in his current situation were essentially through keeping alive the culture and spirit of a nation, by whatever means this was possible. At risk of instant death if caught, Wojtyła entered Cardinal Sapieha's hidden seminary in Kraków, reading metaphysics while doing his long shifts of slave labour during the day. At that time no-one could have foreseen how momentous the consequences of his persistent thought and his decision to enter the seminary in Nazi occupied Poland would be on future history. His thoughts were to survive the ashes of the Nazi and Soviet years and to give voice to the surviving, dispirited Poles, who thought their best and brightest had been killed and many of whom felt that only a rump of the country remained. He came to speak in terms of universal human dignity of all after the 'bloodlands' of these times, to encourage the spark of spiritual greatness in all of us, thoughts which became a lasting legacy of his writings and of the 20th century in general. They certainly became a central force in the dismantling of Communism.

Under Nazi occupation, literature, songs and even plays were a reminder of the Poland that once was, sustaining morale and hope for the young soldiers soon to face a battle to the death. The songs were lyrical, short, and easy to memorise and especially seized upon. Perhaps the best known song of the time, one which Poles could sing at a moment's notice, and which I heard throughout my childhood, was that entitled 'Rozszumiały się wierzby płaczące' ('The weeping willows were trembling') in which, in poignant tones, a young partisan asks the willow 'not to tremble' and asks the young girl seeing him off 'not to weep'. He reassures the girl that in the group of partisans it is 'not that bad.' He hears the 'dance' of gunfire and come what may, he knows what he must do.[77] Another song written by young Krystyna Krahelska, a medical orderly of 'Jelen' division, who wrote in her song 'Hej chlopcy bagnet na bron' ('Hey boys fix your bayonets') – words that became well known to many of the young soldiers. She wrote: 'The dawn is unfolding, the wind is clearing our eyes …The road is far and long before us, We, the young, are going into battle for victory.' Krystyna was seriously wounded on the first day of the Uprising attending to a wounded soldier in Mokotów and died on the second day. Her song became one of the iconic songs of the Uprising.

With the best possible efforts at planning, morale among the AK fighters was high. In the first days of the uprising some crucial points were taken in Warsaw. The Kedyw battalion took the Kammler Factory within hours on the first day. German tanks were disabled by molotov cocktails thrown by young insurgents The disabled tanks provided useful cover where they remained in the streets. General Bór-Komorowski commander in chief of the AK estimated that nearly two-thirds of the city had been taken control of in the early phase of the Uprising and one soldier Wieslaw Chodorowski recounted: 'It was a glorious feeling …We did not feel hatred, just exhilaration in fighting for freedom.'[78] Bogdan would have shared this initial exhilaration, the first whiff of freedom after five years. Polish flags flew again from several buildings in the city.

However these initial hopes were not to last and the victories could not be sustained without outside help as more and more German reinforcements were rushed to Warsaw. The bridges across the Vistula and the airport remained in German hands. As Koskodan writes: 'The Poles assumed that Allied help, this time in the form of the Soviets, would be two to three days away. They in fact had been told this by the Soviets via radio broadcasts into Warsaw. With the Red Army already in the suburb of Praga, the AK had no reason to think otherwise.'[79]

However the Soviet army waited inactively as the insurgents fought on, for this had been the Stalinist plan all along, to watch the independence army be decimated while the Communists would pretend to be concerned for its fate. There was, furthermore, a worrying silence from the side of the Western Allies. Some Polish and other allied pilots in the British Air Force realised the precarious position of the Poles and some heroic individual sorties were made. These pilots tried to help them at great risk to their own lives, flying from Italy, and without much official support from their Allied confreres. The Soviet Union – an 'ally' of the West – had refused permission for any of the Allied pilots to land and refuel in order to fly on to help Poland. It is debatable how much pressure was exerted on them by the Western Allied forces, who were aware of Soviet displeasure at the Uprising's unexpected continuation. It hit an embarrassing note in the new geopolitical global narrative being forged, in which Poland as a nation was gradually being cast aside by the new superpowers. Given the embarrassment of a Polish resistance, and the enormous logistical difficulties of flying from Italy, the attempts by those pilots who did fly to Poland were nothing short of heroic. 380 pilots lost their lives in the attempts. This hastily organised 'Allied Warsaw Airlift', between 4 August and 18 September 1944, was conducted by Polish, British, South African, and American pilots flying from Celone and Brindisi, Italy. However, given the confusions of the embattled city under bombardment, only 45% of the dropped supplies ended up in the hands of the AK fighters. The Soviet government's refusal to allow Allied planes to land and refuel was a deliberate sabotage of the Polish efforts. Had they been allowed to land, this would have been of inestimable help given the long distances to be covered from Italy by the planes of that era. It would have changed the course of the Uprising.

The young soldiers, increasingly aware of the reluctance of the Allies to help them in their hellish battle, sent the following as a message on 24 August 1944, in poem form via the radio station set up for the period of the Uprising – 'Lightning Radio' – not asking for sentiment, but for concrete help, saying they would do all the fighting themselves if given some arms from their allies:

Why do you sing a mourning chorale in London
While here we have long awaited a time to rejoice
At the sides of their lovers, girls are fighting here,
And small children join them and their blood flows proudly.
Hello ... Here is the heart of Poland ... hear Warsaw speaking!
Throw the dirges out of your broadcasts;
Our spirit is so strong, it will support even you!
We don't need your applause
We demand ammunition!!![80]

The last line was more a 'begging' than a 'demand' but a silence ensued as the young fighters were increasingly mown down. There was a tendency of certain British press reports to refer to the 'brave Poles' in the hope that the battle would soon be conveniently over without the need to send much concrete help. Then eulogies could have been given and the chapter closed. Many among the British press and in crucial ministries were in thrall to the Soviet world view and with time became even more so and less inclined to believe Polish assessments of Soviet intentions which in the end, proved correct.

This had been eminently clear when the Poles had protested in the matter of the Katyń massacre. From the outset of the war, as stated in the previous chapter, no-one knew what had happened to tens of thousands of Polish officers who had simply disappeared in the Soviet roundups of 1939. When the German army uncovered mass graves of assassinated soldiers in 1943, each of whom had each been shot by a single bullet to the head, and had publicised the fact to the world, it became clear that their deaths were likely caused by Soviet action. However, no-one in the British press was willing or able to tackle what this massacre by an 'ally' signified. Few could 'go there' and face the unpalatable truth that the Soviet Union, their 'ally' was guilty of criminal acts. Referring to Western reactions to the Katyń evidence at the time, Davies says:

> Soviet guilt proved so unpalatable to the pro-Soviet prejudices, most preferred to feign confusion and to admit nothing. All Western information services were instructed to follow the Soviets and to describe Katyń as a German crime.[81]

Given the lies about Katyń, it is not surprising that strategic deceptions were in play concerning any proposed 'liberation' in the Warsaw uprising. Having assured the Poles and the Allies of support for the Home Army, the Soviet Army had done exactly the opposite.

Having relayed over the radio that 'the hour of liberation was at hand' the Soviet army came to the outskirts of Warsaw and waited on the banks of the Vistula River for the insurgent AK Army to be decimated by the Germans, so the Soviets could then walk in and claim they had liberated Poland. Some soldiers from the Russian side which included Poles from the east who joined to escape gulags or in the belief that they would help liberate Poland, desperately tried to help the insurgents and some crossed the river. The Soviets waited until the AK were largely destroyed by the Germans to deliver a few air drops, to placate Western protests In any case, they used no parachutes for the air drops and much of the food in them was destroyed when it hit the ground. However, the starving AK soldiers salvaged what they could in the final days of the battle. It was clear that any assurances from Moscow were nothing but deception. As for the Allies, they were caught between placating Stalin and watching the members of an heroic resistance being gradually bled to death.

Reactions to the uprising

If it was morally odious that the Soviet leadership deceived the Polish resistance after promising otherwise, the strange reluctance of the Allied powers to step in and help, despite the pleading of Anders' army and other Polish forces in exile, would have meant the dawn of yet another nightmare for Bogdan and his fellow soldiers. Suddenly the latter would have realised that their efforts did not matter and they were doomed fighters. The Uprising itself and later analysis of it by Western Allies caused not a little discomfort, a point examined in detail by Davies in his attempt to account for why the Home Army was virtually abandoned by the Allies to fight to the death when other resistance armies, such as that of the French, were championed and aided. Davies does not consider that it was a matter of being able to transport and weapons to the beleaguered fighters of Warsaw. It was rather that the geopolitical situation had shifted dramatically from the start of the war and there was a desire to see the Soviet Union as a sincere ally by Western elites and political leaders. The reality was that the AK, caught between two gargantuan armies and an evolving new world order, came to realise the truth that neither the Allies in the west nor in the east would come to their aid in any significant way.

The realisation that they were alone would have been deeply painful for the insurgents who expected they might be treated like their brothers and sisters in the French resistance. They, Bogdan among them, must have wondered what was going on. This certainly would have occupied the thoughts of the group led by Janusz Bielski in Mokotów and young Bogdan as these young men tried to process the reality of their desperate situation. Without help from any of the major powers – apart from the heroic airlifts from individual pilots in Italy and one flight from Britain, the battle continued even after the sense of abandonment. The insurgents continued for 63 days – beyond all expectations of survival – and kept creating havoc for the Germans who had expected to extinguish the uprising quickly.

One of the few voices braving the fury of the pro-Soviet British press commentariat in order to give some support for the Polish fighters in 1944 was George Orwell. He had lost his illusions about Communism during the Spanish Civil War and gave the 20th century its defining critique of it in his satiric novel *Animal Farm*. In an article published in *The Tribune* on 1 September 1944, Orwell attacked the 'mean and cowardly attitude adopted by the British press towards the recent rising in Warsaw' and challenged the elites who wanted to see the Soviet Union as saviours. Orwell recognised that this intervening Polish Uprising interfered with the conversions to Communism among the intellectual elites of the 1930s, among them the British Soviet spies, Kim Philby, Anthony Burgess, Donald MacLean, Anthony Blunt and John Cairncross, who were well connected with sectors of the Foreign Service and the press and had been spreading disinformation for years about Russia's actions. Given the disopprobium that any criticism of Soviet intentions caused at the time, it took considerable courage for Orwell to say the following in a London newspaper:

> What I am concerned about is the attitude of the British intelligentsia who cannot raise between them one single voice to question what they believe to be Russian policy, no matter what turn it takes, and in this case, have had the unheard of meanness to hint that our bombers ought not to be sent to the aid of our comrades fighting in Warsaw...their attitude toward Russian foreign policy is not 'Is this policy right or wrong?' but 'This is Russian policy: how can we make it appear right?' And this attitude is defended, if at all, solely on grounds of power.[82]

Davies' comments about attitudes in certain Allied sectors, as pungent as is Orwell's, was expressed many decades later, in the following comment:

> The selective sanctimoniousness of the Stalinophile lobbies in London and Washington ... was even more repulsive than their political stupidity ... even Britain's leading historian of Russia, Sir Bernard Pares, joined the international fray questioning the very existence of Poland as an independent country. His intervention was a good example of the strange phenomenon whereby all sorts of well-meaning Westerners, who had nothing in common with Stalin, nonetheless aided and abetted Stalin's depredations ... the British communists were ultra sensitized to failings of the

west but institutionally blind to Soviet horror – trained to believe 'the party is always right'.[83]

In his well documented analysis, Orwell gives an outline of the controlling forces of some of this ideological stranglehold on the press which resulted in the deep disappointment of the Polish insurgents and in many cases led to their deaths. He speaks of Christopher Hill who ran the Soviet desk at the Northern Department Foreign Office in 1944 and who was a Soviet mole and card-carrying communist.[84] Hill's colleague Smollet held a similar position in the British Ministry of Information was an active Soviet agent who had another colleague, the well known Soviet spy Kim Philby, who actually ran the Soviet Section of counter intelligence at MI6 under the Foreign Office. These pro-Soviet British spies and the networks surrounding them were in large part able to disable Britain's defences against Soviet penetration and assisted the press to strengthen its strident pro-Soviet contingent. They formed committees to soften up the public as regards Stalin's benevolence. Their contact/controller at the Soviet Embassy, Davies concludes, was probably Grigori Saksin who departed London in a hurry in September 1944. The British press had a vociferous pro-Soviet contingent and Orwell, Arthur Koestler and very few others wrote sympathetically of Poland. The beleaguered Poles fighting to the death in Warsaw, outnumbered by Nazis, betrayed by the Russians, largely forgotten by the Allies, were only to learn of this later, and then made 'sense' of the Allied silence.[85]

In contrast to the tone of Soviet appeasement in sectors of the West, a different assessment of the situation came from John Ward, the sole British journalist who remained in Warsaw during the uprising and transmitted reports back to Britain, despite the extreme danger to himself. Part of a radio dispatch on 4 September stated:

Poland is our oldest ally in this war. Despite all she has

suffered at the hands of the German invaders, she has remained always an active power against the enemy. Polish troops fought in France in 1940; later Polish pilots took part in the battle of Britain, her troops fought at Tobruk, and are still fighting in Italy and France. The Home Army in Poland itself has now risen and is also fighting openly as it has fought under cover during the whole war. Poland is a country which I, as an Englishman, am proud to call an ally. She produced no government to co-operate with the Germans. The only government she has acknowledged is the one in exile in London. To end I would like to make an appeal to the British Nation. It is short: HELP FOR WARSAW.[86]

Ward's appeal for help added to the many being made by the Polish government in exile in London, by Anders' army, by the combatants themselves, and by the Poles who had fought in the Battle of Britain – all of whom stared on in disbelief.

Nearing the end

Meanwhile back on the streets of ever more severely bombed Warsaw, there was street to street fighting, then house to house fighting. Members of the resistance groups were separated. As the Uprising wore on and Radio Lightning still kept transmitting, and messengers kept crossing Nazi occupied sectors, there would have been less and less food and an increasingly exhausted force continuing to fight. It is extraordinary that a printing press and Radio station continued in such circumstances.[87]

Despite the sense of abandonment by Soviets and the pro-Soviet influenced politicians among the Allies, the unity which had strengthened the insurgents during the five years of occupation held them together amid this increasing destruction. The unity of purpose had been exemplified in countless ways prior to the Uprising on such occasions as when an anti-Nazi activist was stopped by a Gestapo agent on a Warsaw street. The Gestapo agent asked, 'Where have you been?' and the Pole replied, 'To the dentist', seeing the brass plaque of a dentist on a nearby building. In reality he had been meeting his resistance group. The Gestapo agent immediately knocked on the door and questioned the dentist to check out the story. The dentist, never having seen the supposed Polish 'patient' in his life, immediately supported the latter's story and thus saved his 'patient's' life. But mostly no questions were asked and people were rounded up or shot at random.

The longer than expected duration of the uprising gave the Nazis the chance to replenish their arms. At one point during the uprising a priest, Father Rostworowski, was confronted by a German soldier asking why a particular hospital in Dluga Street (in central Warsaw) had not been burned to the ground. The priest explained there were wounded inside. The SS commanding officer whose name was Kotchke then gave the order to execute all the remaining wounded within the building. The priest hurriedly walked in with tears in his eyes praying and giving Holy Communion to each person at the hospital while the SS officer shot each patient in rapid succession. The priest tried to help some of them crawl out and escape but the Germans grabbed these men from him and shot them in the head, poured gasoline over them and burned them. Then when the priest's turn came to be shot, the SS officer noted with annoyance he had run out of bullets. That is why we have come to know the story.[88]

Another Warsaw inhabitant, Wanda Lurie, was in an early roundup of the Dirlewanger Brigade who indiscriminately killed doctors, nurses, patients and civilians wherever they found them. As she was

A cross stands in destroyed Warsaw

Women and children were killed indiscriminately by the Germans. No conventions of war were respected during the Uprising

Every part of Warsaw is systematically bombed

Warsaw – previously called 'Paris of the East' – totally destroyed on Hitler's orders

herded into a group to be shot Wanda recounted, "I went in last and kept back, always lagging behind in the hope that they would not kill a pregnant woman." She moved forward and then recalled, "I saw a heap of bodies about a metre high." She then saw her children die one by one: "The first salvo hit my elder son, the second me and the third, my younger children." Wanda fell wounded but was able later to dig herself out from the pile of bodies. She later gave birth to a healthy baby. The only reason the killing slowed on 6 August was that there was a temporary delay to the supply of bullets for the Germans.[89]

Julian Kulski, the 15-year-old soldier who wrote his account soon after the war, was in 'Zwiciel' regiment fighting in the Zoliborz district of Warsaw. He wrote of his experiences in the years of German occupation and after the war, noting the following, in his recollection of the events of 5 August 1944:

> The Germans are attacking the Old City with airplanes, tanks, infantry, and all available artillery. From Zoliborz one can see quite plainly the dreadful pall of smoke hanging over the Old City, and hear the unceasing explosions of bombs and artillery shells. Every hour enemy Stukas fly over Zoliborz from the Bielany airfield, dropping bombs on the city before returning for a new assault. It is outright slaughter; we do not have one antiaircraft gun in the entire city.[90]

Later in the same day, he recalls:

> The westernmost suburb of Wola evidently has received the brunt of the first attack, and it is reported that the Germans and Ukrainians are giving no quarter to anyone in their way. They are taking no prisoners, and are killing men, women, and children on sight. According to

eyewitnesses who have reached Zoliborz, the entire staff (as well as the sick and wounded) at the Hospital of Saint Lazar on Leszno Street has been massacred. Babies were swung by the legs and their heads split on the corners of buildings; women were raped before being shot; and hundreds of civilians were herded by the Germans in front of tanks attacking the barricades. Polish fighters cannot open fire on these innocent civilian shields, and some of the enemy's successes have been due to this tactic.

Were it not for what has happened during the last few years, and what happened to the Ghetto little more than a year ago, nobody would have believed the Germans capable of such barbarism.[91]

In another entry dated 1 September, he describes the insurgents moving away from the from their encircled position via the sewers:

Leaving only token guards on the barricades, platoon after platoon, company after company, formed a long line. Then, with perfect discipline, the armed men descended one by one into the stinking, swift-flowing sewer. The trip took four hours through waist-deep sludge and poisonous fumes. The human chain, each link holding tightly to the next one, snaked its way underground. Everyone had to move slowly, in total darkness and in silence. Those who slipped and fell in the deeper parts of the channels and had no strength to get up were drowned. The others could not spare precious time or reserves of energy to search for them, and without lights it was a hopeless task anyway.[92]

Thus many of the insurgents moved beneath their German attackers in the sewers beneath and in this way – for some time at least – escaped to other parts of Warsaw.

From the outset of the uprising, the Germans often commented on the ingenuity and ferocity of the fighting. The battle for one Warsaw apartment house went on for 24 hours. The battle for St John's Cathedral in the Old Town took two weeks and was fought over at one stage by Germans in the choir section of the church and Poles downstairs. Some insurgents lay frozen, playing dead for several hours when caught in German machine gun fire.[93] Priests and religious sisters helped the wounded, attempted to rescue artwork from churches amidst gunfire and even said Mass in the ruins for anyone able to attend with artillery firing around them. Nazi snipers at times tried to pretend they were Poles and, once among them, shot Poles at random.

One nine-year-old boy, Stanisław Florczynski, whose father was forced to work in the 'Gazownia' – the station supplying power to sections of Warsaw – climbed up several stories via the stairs of the Gazownia building in which he was forced to stay throughout the Uprising. He came to a window and looked out onto the battle below, with the dark clouds, the incessant noise and explosions. The day he looked out from his high position, he saw groups of terrified civilians forced out of apartment buildings – men, women or children – who were quickly shot one after the other in rapid succession by the German soldiers at point blank range. Stanisław's father warned his son never to crawl to his high vantage point again as he might be seen and place them all in danger. While in forced labour at the 'Gazownia' they all had some chance of survival.

My father Bogdan was one of the 4,500 soldiers assigned to the Mokotów area and the German offensive began there in earnest on 24 September with captured soldiers executed on the spot. One of the main aims of the Mokotów group was to capture the school building on Woronica street which had stores of German weapons. My father was assigned to take the section of Mokotów known as Krolikarnia. He related that at one point during the siege – it must have been towards the end of the relentless bombardment – that he was cut off from the remainder of the group and holed up in the cellar of a house, with Germans firing all around him. He had to lie still and breathe silently. He had already been twice wounded – shot in the leg and the upper arm but he was still conscious and able to move when he had to. Strange to say, the place where he was hiding had a yard with a chicken which laid an egg each morning. Here in the midst of a bloodbath was a surviving chicken. My father risked being shot each day, by leaving the cellar of the house and crawling quietly across the yard to grab the daily egg, and then crawling back. This egg was his food for the day, fresh and raw. And the chicken continued to lay the egg, amidst the volleys of gunfire surrounding the house as houses and streets were fought over. At some point after a few days, however, during an exchange of gunfire, the chicken got shot by a German and was presumably taken away. My father recalled years later how distressed he became as his last source of food was gone. He expressed no complaint at being shot in the arm and leg, but the disappearance of the chicken was a real blow. He now saw only a period of slow starvation till he died, unless a German bullet found him first.

Final act and surrender

Bogdan, however, did not die. At some point after this episode in the house, he was reunited with some of his group, and moved with them carrying his bullet wounds. There was no time to tend the wounds and he limped on as best he could. He recalled that the young men knew that either death or surrender were near. They took turns doing guard duty, allowing the others to rest briefly, trying to keep up some semblance of order in the disintegrating situation around them. They had one gun left between them and whoever was on duty kept it. My father told me that one of the group was a young man of 17 who had had the extraordinary experience of escaping from Auschwitz, and had vowed never to be captured by the Germans again. How he escaped from Auschwitz I don't know but there are such recorded events and he was one of very few to have done so in the early years of the concentration camp.[94] What happened during his 'watch' at Mokotów, in these latter chaotic days of the uprising, also remains a mystery. He disappeared along with the only gun the group possessed. He must have thought a similar fate to his previous experience in Auschwitz awaited him. It was suspected that he killed himself somewhere, rather than face the horror of another German capture. He was never seen again. Whatever his state of mind during the Uprising, it cannot have been helped by the memories of Auschwitz and the thought of impending capture.

Some Mokotów defenders tried to escape through the sewers to the City centre but as they emerged they found themselves in German territory and were all immediately shot. There had been mass hangings and shootings after random street roundups for the past five years, so the young fighters knew what fate awaited them if caught. Given that so many soldiers were shot on capture during the uprising and that there was little reason to believe anything the Germans said was true, the eventual communication by General Bach-Zelewski promising that the Geneva Conventions would be observed if the Poles surrendered must have taken some time to take on trust. The General was a Nazi guilty of many mass killings and while some might say he was not in the same league of criminality as Direlwanger whose group respected no combatant rights and killed without mercy, there was not much to distinguish them in the end. He had already had his share of ordering mass killings in Belarus and elsewhere. The AK Commander-in-Chief, Bór-Komorowski, got a message to Bach-Zelewski insisting on such rights before any surrender would take place. Would he, the ruthless killer, act according to the Geneva Convention as the rumours stated? Julian Kulski recalls receiving the information that the AK was ordered to surrender by its commanding officer. The text which he heard and which my father Bogdan would have heard read as follows:

> Soldiers!
>
> I thank you, my dear comrades, for everything you have accomplished during these two months of fighting with the enemy, for your efforts, pain, and courage. I am proud that I had the honor to command such soldiers as you. Remain such in the future and show the world what a Polish soldier is, he who will sacrifice everything for his country.
>
> Soldiers!
>
> An hour ago, as ordered by the Supreme Commander of the Armed Forces, General Bor-Komorowski, I signed the surrender document of our group ... We are surrendering to the Wehrmacht as a regular army, and we will be treated according to the Geneva Convention.
>
> I thank you once more for everything. God be with you![95]

These sombre words marked the end of the Uprising and all that awaited the Poles was surrender and an uncertain fate. The AK did surrender and took on trust the words of General 'Bór' that they would be treated as regular army POWs, though they had not been treated as such during the entire course of the Uprising. My father would have emerged on or after 27 September, as that is the recorded date of surrender, in the area of Mokotów, and in his wounded, emaciated state, believing that the captured Home Army members were to be treated as POWs, he would have lined up to march to the assigned point. He had suffered tuberculosis, malnutrition, been shot at, lost his childhood friends, lost his father, did not know of the whereabouts of his mother, had been without anyone to care for him since he was 12, except for contact with his much loved little sister Alicia. She was living in an orphanage and was also running from building to building in the bombardment of the uprising as religious sisters took care of their young charges. The sisters would run to less bombed places followed by the children, seeking some temporary respite. Alicia and Bogdan would have dreamed of the time when they might meet but it was not to be for a long time – in fact not for three decades.

On 4 October, General Monter issued his orders to the Special Battalion which was to stay behind to keep order during the evacuation. Radio Lightning which had kept operating throughout the Uprising under near impossible circumstances, made its final broadcast on that date, farewelling the soldiers and wishing them well. Then the transmitter was smashed with a sledgehammer. The last issue of the Information Bulletin, number 102, appeared, and on it appeared the words, 'The battle is finished.' Gen Monter took the salute at a farewell parade amid the ruins of Warsaw, now a smouldering extended graveyard, watching his exhausted soldiers, the majority of whom were overpoweringly young, march silently four or six abreast, in long columns to designated areas for the post surrender plans of the Germans. After 63 days of fighting there had been no liberation. My father related to me that even in their exhausted state, one German officer had said to the Poles that they were good fighters and – crazy as this may seem – invited them to come and fight for the Germans. One reason for this may have been an ill thought out attempt to swell the ranks of the German army to further stem the Soviet advance. When the Poles were told of this 'offer', my father recalled that the Poles gave the German a reply in unrepeatable words and sign language. After the soldiers marched by, a long stream of civilians then followed.

> Two vast streams of humanity, each several hundred thousand strong, wound their weary way towards the two German transit camps Dirty, exhausted, starving, and bewildered, they had 15 to 20 kms to walk without assistance. Woman clutched babies and children. Men carried the aged and infirm on their backs ... emaciated, blinded, bleeding, bandaged, or limping, the wounded clung to each other.[96]

General Bór-Komorowski, dressed in civilian clothes, was joined by other generals and driven in German staff cars to sign the surrender. One can only imagine what thoughts they went through their minds, after the heroic efforts, massed deaths and destruction of the past years. General Bór was taken into captivity, and never saw his country again, finally ending up in Britain for the remainder of his life.

The Führer was elated at the surrender of Warsaw. Then in a frenzy of hatred, he ordered the systematic destruction of any of its remaining buildings and artwork, in addition to its already destroyed state, hoping to irreparably damage the country for all time. The destruction had to be total. Brandkommandos or fire squads bombed the ruins in rapid succession, street by street, building by building, literally razing a once beautiful pre-war city to the ground (the old city centre was later restored, as someone had preserved a plan) systematically checking the progress of the destruction before retreating. This city of pre-war creative life, with its writers, thinkers, priests, poets, songwriters, professionals and many ethnic minorities who evidently had loved living there, was obliterated in a way that reflected a pathological hatred towards the Poles.

Meanwhile the Soviet Army had expediently marched into Lublin in July 1944, before the Uprising, and had set up a 'provisional government', setting Poland firmly in the grip of the Soviet regime for the next 50 years. As previously stated, their entrance into Poland was a further military incentive for the Uprising, to make a stand for a free independent Poland. Disinformation had already started on the Soviet side, not only questioning the Home Army's courage but also questioning its very existence and motivation. Wild stories started to be spread, such as the one that General Bór-Komorowski had been in league with the Nazis along with other confusing rumours. The Soviet divisions, which had waited on the outskirts of Warsaw, had bided their time to be able to enter the city, to promote themselves as 'liberators'. Again George Orwell said of these developments in *The Tribune* of 6 October 1944: 'No, the Lublin Regime is not a victory for socialism in Poland ... it is the reduction of Poland to a vassal state ... Woe to those in a vassal state who want to maintain their independent views and policies...'. When stories of Soviet arrests of any AK soldiers left behind filtered through to the West, the press,

> ... simply refused to believe bad news about the Soviet system when it stared them in the face. Mesmerised perhaps by Soviet power and deeply committed to an ethos of team-play, which the Soviets did not share, they shied away from playing their own powerful cards, fearful of provoking a negative reaction. Hence Stalin's own cynical view of a sphere of influence was installed without protest and democracy was doomed.[97]

To add to the starkness of the capitulation, the Polish premier of the Government-in-exile in London, Stanisław Mikolajczyk, went with Churchill to Moscow. There he realised that Poland's boundaries had already been decided several years before by Stalin and Churchill at their meeting in Teheran from 28 November to 1 December 1943. No Polish leader had been informed and, according to many historians, Churchill played a role in the deception. Davies says, 'Churchill, shame-facedly admitted his fault, but later turned his rage on the Polish premier whom he had so inexcusably misled.'[98]

This secret reorganisation of the borders of Poland and the surrounding eastern European countries involved the loss of the old Polish city of Lwów (which means 'city of lions' and was alternatively known as Lviv and Lemberg) which the premier learned about for the first time to his utter shock. This loss of Lwów had come about because of a misunderstanding of where that part of the border of Poland termed the Curzon line lay. At the Teheran Conference, the Russian Foreign Minister had handed the British delegation a copy of a telegram dated 25 July 1920, stating the latter's support for the Curzon line. However, the British were unaware of the fact that this version of the Curzon line was one which had actually been accidentally modified by an official in the Foreign Office some time before, placing Lwów in the Ukrainian/Russian sphere of influence. On offering them this erroneous version, the Russians realised that the British did not recognise the mistake. The British did not check their original map and the Soviet delegation capitalised on their confusion insisting they take Lwów. The British simply agreed. In general, Western leaders simply fell for the Soviet hard line and signed away a third of Poland. Thus the failure of the Uprising resulted in the loss of much Polish territory and also in the handover of several nations of Eastern Europe to a new era of Soviet tyranny. Bogdan and his surviving confreres were victims of systemic breakdown of the Grand Alliance which was to affect the lives of millions in Eastern Europe and those who were displaced after the war. Again, Davies observes on this point:

> In January-February 1945, the Yalta Conference took place. Western leaders abandoned all effective influence in Poland and Eastern Europe in return for Stalin's co-operation in Germany and in the Far East. This outcome would have been unthinkable if the Warsaw Rising had succeeded. Shortly afterwards, 16 democratic leaders from the Polish Underground, who had lived through the Rising and who would have formed a crucial element in the political system proposed for Poland at Yalta, were arrested by the NKVD. Their show trial in Moscow in June coincided with the formation of the so-called Government of National Unity in which they might otherwise have participated. The Chief Defendant, General Okulicki – Bór-Komorowski's sometime deputy and successor as Commander of the Home Army, who had originally been flown into occupied Europe by the RAF – was not broken by his interrogators and delivered a defiant speech from the dock. He subsequently died in the Lubyanka. His British allies, whose Ambassador was present at the trial, did not protest.[99]

In the midst of the geopolitical rearrangement of Europe most of the insurgents were sent to POW camps at Murnau, Bavaria, Sandbostel, Saxony, Woldenberg and Brandenburg. The women were sent to Erfut, Thuringern or Oberlangen on the Dutch frontier. However many of the Warsaw civilian survivors of the uprising did not fare so well. For despite the promises of POW treatment of the arrested AK soldiers, many were still shot and over 100,000 civilians were sent as labourers to the Reich and, in contravention of the capitulation agreement, tens of thousands were sent to concentration camps or to Soviet gulags where the majority perished.

5

Soldiers in cattle wagons

After his arrest by the Germans, Bogdan, feverish, emaciated by hunger and weakened by illness, walked in orderly procession through the ruined streets of Warsaw with his fellow fighters who were likewise battered, desolate and exhausted. They must have thought they were living through apocalyptic events in history or perhaps they were too tired to think. Weakened as they were they walked to the transport point which would take them to their destination as prisoners of war. Along with the survivors Bogdan was finally put into a cattle wagon which was to take them on a long ride to prisoner of war (POW) camps in Germany. His group were listed to be taken to a POW camp in northern Germany. Being taken as a 'prisoner of war' was not a guarantee of survival and many of the insurgents must have thought they would be killed. In my father's case, however, the 'Geneva Convention for prisoners of war conditions' applied here though, as it turned out, the Germans did not apply it to all insurgents and killed many of them. Bogdan's journey by train from Poland to his prison camp in Germany was described to me by his cousin Janusz Bielski who had also fought alongside my father in Warsaw at the 'senior' age of 19 and whom I met when he visited Australia several decades later, after Bogdan had died. When both Bogdan and Janusz were put into cattle wagons with numerous other arrested soldiers, Bogdan was in a feverish state on the floor with bullets in his arm and leg. As the train set off and was headed for the Polish-German border, Janusz began to plot his escape, asking Bogdan if he wanted to take a chance with him, offering his help. As they hurtled on into the countryside, time was getting short and an attempt would have to be made at the next stop because it might be the last chance before the border. Janusz recalled that my father was semi-conscious and could barely move in his wounded, emaciated state. He understood what was at stake, however, and in his feverish tones, not knowing if either of them would survive for long, Bogdan urged his cousin to make the attempt. As he, Bogdan, was unable to make a move, he thought it better that at least one of them should survive, so he hastily bade his cousin goodbye and wished him luck, not knowing if he would ever see him again. (In fact he never saw him again, though I was able to meet him and hear the account of these events from him).

When the train stopped at a certain point not far from the border Janusz peered cautiously over the open top of the rail car and saw that there was a soldier assigned to guard each car. After glancing back at my father, he took his chance, quickly crawled up and jumped out, running as fast as he could across the clearing, aiming to get to a small forest about 100 metres away. As he ran, he was fired at by several guards, but he zig-zagged so wildly every shot missed him and he survived.

Janusz kept running and finally made it to a wooded area and continued deep into the forest to lose his pursuers finally reaching a spot where two women happened to be walking together. They would not have been too perturbed by the sound of gunshots as this had been nothing unusual for the past five years. Janusz quickly pushed himself between them, and out of breath, shaking and holding each woman by the arm and said he was an AK soldier who had escaped from a train – could they help? The women immediately treated him as their 'brother', ready to declare he was so if challenged by any German soldier. After some time in hiding, with a little food and change of clothes and appearance, Janusz left the village. With great difficulty he made it back to his girlfriend, Krystyna (Krysia) Bielska, who ended up as his wife. Thus it turned out that he stayed in Poland while my father went to Germany and Bonegilla. After the war, Janusz evaded the hostility of Soviet-controlled Poland – not daring to mention his involvement in the Uprising. He managed to study medicine, working and living most of his life in Poznan in western Poland and became a professor of medicine. He obviously hid the fact that he had been in the resistance successfully, as he was never deported to Siberia as happened to some insurgents who took their chances to hide in Warsaw rather than surrender. Being short of stature he could no doubt pass himself off as younger than he actually was and so did not arouse the curiosity of the new Soviet rulers.

My father meanwhile lay semi-conscious in the cattle car which crossed the border and went ever further into German territory. That journey to the prison camp near Hamburg where he did forced labour as a POW in the latter stages of the war was a point of no return. It was another 'beginning' point of the journey to Bonegilla among so many other beginnings. All hope of returning to Lublin, to his sister, his family, his former life, to his own land ended when he crossed the border. Ironically, as a prisoner of war for almost a year, Bogdan said he fared better in German hands than those soldiers who ended up in Soviet hands.

Those Polish soldiers who had been arrested by the Soviet army, which was designated an 'ally', never received the status of prisoners of war and were sent to Soviet concentration camps and most were never heard of again. Such was the fate of the extraordinary Witold Pilecki, who had volunteered, with the help of the underground, to get into Auschwitz to obtain an eyewitness account of the camp for the world, then escaped and wrote his report. This brave fighter of the Nazis was an example of the collateral damage of Yalta. After the war he ended up in Soviet hands.. The Soviet torturers did their work relentlessly for 10 months and then shot him in the head and threw his body away. To this day no-one knows the whereabouts of his remains.

Post-war realities for the AK

After the war's end, the very existence of the AK, the Home Army, was a source of confusion in the post-Potsdam, post-Yalta world. The new Soviet wordgames and geopolitical narrative demanded by Stalin centred on the notion that Poland's only army now was that put into place by the Soviet Union – the Ludowe Wojsko Polskie, the so-called Polish People's Army. Bogdan and his fellow fighters in the AK had no place in this narrative and this became a problem for the Western powers who wished for good relations with the Soviet Union. At the same time the very concept of nationhood underwent re-definition in the east and west in new post-war realignments. While Western Europe went along with the Russian reinvention of Poland, the AK survivors, my father included, slipped into a kind of non-existence and no-one quite knew what to do with them.

Who is to say what these survivors thought as they watched the joyous London victory parade to mark the end of World War II? The Polish pilots whose squadrons had willingly served the Allied cause found themselves excluded, having been feted as heroes of the Battle of Britain a few years before. For they and the Home Army survivors in Britain, who had been allies all along, even designated 'First Ally' by the British, now were not allowed to march in the victory parade. In fact no Polish soldier (as indicated, they had been the fourth largest Allied army) was permitted to march in the victory parade. After helping the Allies on air, sea and land, after the efforts of General Anders' Allied Polish army in exile, and the countless acts of self-sacrifice on the part of the Poles for their allies, this seemed a particularly hard final blow. The reason for this was the appeasement of 'Uncle Joe' by potent sectors of the British media and leadership, not to mention by the powerful US ally Franklin D. Roosevelt, and the acknowledgement by them that Poland was now no longer the nation it was before the war and would remain indisputably under Soviet control. There was widespread reluctance to upset the new status quo.

An article in the *British Financial Times* of 5 July 2005 comments on the Poles who fought in the Allied cause. Written 60 years after the end of World War II, it describes a modern day attempt at restitution of the situation the Poles found themselves in at the end of the war:

> Among the veterans who will march along The Mall on Sunday in a parade marking the 60th anniversary of the end of the Second World War, few will participate with the same pride as a contingent of elderly Poles.
>
> For the Poles and their military standards will be present for the first time in a British victory parade. Even though Poland made one of the largest contributions to the Allied war effort and there were thousands of Polish troops stationed in the UK at the time, the country was excluded from the original London celebration in 1946. Stalin, who had established communist rule in eastern Europe, indicated that he did not wish Poland to be represented and the British authorities agreed for fear of offending their ally. Now Britain is making amends by putting the Poles at the head of Sunday's parade.[100]

The same article notes a recent British report by a committee of British and Polish historians, detailing Polish contributions to the Allied efforts. Perhaps one that has been better known is the first breaking of the German Enigma code cyphers in 1932-33 by three mathematicians: Marian Rejewski, Henryk Zygalski and Jerzy Różycki. They later smuggled their discoveries to the West where they formed the basis of the work of Britain's code-breakers at Bletchley Park. Other contributions referred to in the British report are the: the supply of information by Polish spies regarding Hitler's invasion of Russia; information about the Germans' secret weapons including the V1 and V2 rockets, crucial information on Nazi defences in France in advance of the D-Day landings. The report says that 43 per cent of all the reports received by the British secret services from continental Europe in 1939-45 came from Polish sources. Of particular note was the contribution of the Polish pilots (whose story is recounted in Olson and Cloud's *A Question of Honour: The Kosciuszko Squadron. The Forgotten Heroes of World War II*, 2003). Flying aces such as Jan Zumbach, Witold Urbanowicz, Witold Łokuciewski and Miroslav Feric (a Czech who stated he was a Pole by choice) played a crucial role in the Battle of Britain, leading some to state that the Kościuszko 303 Squadron was the most formidable unit of this battle. The surviving pilots who had given all for the Allied cause, watched the victory parade from the sidelines.[101]

The actual day of liberation would have been a painful, bitter-sweet occasion for these 'non-existent' uprising survivors and the Polish Allies. The latter were still to process fully that Stalin, Roosevelt and Churchill had sealed their fates at Yalta in 1945 when they had acquiesced to the Soviet takeover of much of Eastern Europe. Britain formally withdrew the recognition of the legality of the Polish Government-in-exile on 6 July 1945 (although this government continued to operate in Britain until Poland was freed of Soviet rule in 1989 and only resigned formally once the new freely elected post-Soviet government took over). However, in the immediate post-war years, the charade of 'free elections' in Poland was to follow with the imposition of Communist government, the exile and death of former AK soldiers, the deliberate degradation of the Polish economy and the perpetuation of the advancing 'Cold War.'

While victory parties echoed on, the people of Poland, Hungary, Romania, Czechoslovakia, the Ukraine and the Baltic states passed from one criminal regime to another, to a 'reign of state terror which has no equal in European history.'[102] Having had a twenty-year career of terrorising nations, Stalin was determined to apply his version of reality to the already shattered Poles hence the insurgents of the AK were to be non-persons, eliminated from any immediate historic consciousness in Poland. For decades it was a illegal to mention the AK's existence. The Warsaw Uprising survivors in the West found themselves in this confusion amid the over 10 million dislocated persons in Germany, among them many Germans who had fled former homes, now located in Soviet territory. In immediate pragmatic terms the AK, who were among these millions, fell into a kind of military limbo, belonging as they did to a world and regime that had all but vanished.

The more immediate and pressing problem facing the Allies and the United Nations was what to do with these 'displaced persons' such as Bogdan, who could not return to Poland, and who were under no illusions as to their certain imprisonment and death if they did so. They were 'displaced' but very evidently present in Germany. They existed but did not exist. People commended their bravery but no-one knew what to do with them. The British army found a solution and transformed my father, along with his AK peers into the role of 'warden' in association with the British army, no doubt pleasing the Poles in asserting their 'existence' and pleasing the British in having found an innocuous sounding title that could offend no-one politically. The 'wardens' were paid a small amount of money as well as being given food and accommodation for which they were immensely grateful. Bogdan was placed in Schleswig-Holstein in Saxony and, as I understand it, he and his confreres helped the British in 'mopping-up' operations after the war. My father related that there were some conflicts with Nazis refusing to surrender even after Hitler had committed suicide on 30 April 1945 during the Battle of Berlin, and after the surrender was signed in Reims on 7 May and ratified the following day. Bogdan stayed in the British zone of influence and ended up on guard duty.

In one photo taken at the time, he is in a group of other similar wardens doing guard duty of German POWs at a place called Rantum Sylt which was a former municipality on the island of Sylt in the district of Nordfriesland, in Schleswig-Holstein, northern Germany. The photo is dated 29 November 1945 and hence Bogdan would have been only 17 at the time. Another taken in Rantum Sylt shows him smoking a pipe, which must have been an untold luxury for the times and would have made him feel very 'grown up'. In yet another photo, dated simply Christmas 1946, he is with a group of 'wardens' in Neumünster, no doubt most of them separated from their families and trying, during the Christmas period, to put a brave face on their situation as displaced persons.

The insurgents in post-war Germany heard horrifying stories of those AK fighters who had been left in Warsaw being sent to Gulags by the Russians where many of them, after enduring the horrors of the Uprising, lingered and died. A Catholic priest who was sentenced to the gulag in Vorkuta in northern Russia six years after the war ended, was amazed to find a group of some 250 insurgents from the

Bogdan after release from prison in Germany immediately after the war,
ready to assist the British Army in his 'warden' uniform

Bogdan in late 1945 with Polish survivors of the Warsaw Uprising in Rantum Sylt in northern Germany (Schleswig-Holstein) where he and his fellow Polish 'wardens' guarded German prisoners of war. He is second from left in the front row

Bogdan (second from the left in the back row) with fellow Poles celebrating Christmas in 1946 in Neumünster

The family who were left in Poland (circa mid-1950s). Rear left is Alicia, Bogdan's sister, who spent much of the war in an orphanage. Next to her is Zofia (whose husband Antoni Tydda left Poland in 1939, joining the ground crew in the Polish-British Air Force. He was never able to return to Communist Poland). Alicia married Zofia's and Antoni's son Janusz who had remained in Poland. In the front are their children, from left to right, Wojtek, Janusz and Andrzej. On the right at rear is Wanda Maria, Bogdan's and Alicia's mother, survivor of Ravensbrück concentration camp. All lived in a two-room apartment in Naruto-wicza Street in central Lublin. Alicia's husband Janusz took the photo

In post-war Lublin, a few streets away from Alicia's apartment stood the Catholic University of Lublin (known as KUL) where a professor named Father Karol Wojtyła regularly lectured during the 1960s and 70s, before he became Pope John Paul II (Photo from the Catholic University of Lublin Museum)

Warsaw Uprising, all young men and women, some still wearing the
tattered remains of their grey scout uniforms which they had worn
in the battle. A young man from the group offered him his meagre
rations saying that as the rest of them were dying 'you must live in
order to return and to tell the world.'[103]

If the story of the Warsaw Uprising insurgents had been suppressed
on both sides of the Iron Curtain, even more sobering is the story
of the hundreds of thousands of Russian prisoners of the Germans
who had fought against the Soviet Union. These Russians suffered a
particularly cruel fate for they were simply handed over by the Allies
to the Soviets as the Soviet regime demanded, in effect for immediate
execution or imprisonment in Siberia, for Stalin did not want any
anti-Soviet Russians in his totalitarian empire. Anyone who had been
imprisoned outside Russia was suspect, for they had seen another
world. The facts of the situation and the immense distress on the part
of the victims, caused by this unparalleled act of political expediency
on the part of the Allies, were suppressed for decades after the war
and few historians knew about them. Some British officers involved
in the handover were traumatised by the orders they had to follow,
in some cases seeing the soldiers shot within minutes of their being
handed over. But not all were traumatised and some just 'followed
orders' as is the case with human nature.

Solzhenitsyn took up the details of this unjust handover and
described it in his great testimony of the Soviet tyranny, *Gulag
Archipelago* (1973), for he had met some of the very few that survived
this massacre which occurred while the rest of the world was rejoicing
in victory. When Western archives relating to this event were at last
available to historians, two remarkable books quickly appeared: *The
Last Secret*, 1974, by Nicholas Bethel, and *Victims of Yalta*, 1977,
by Nikolai Tolstoy, both chilling, detailed accounts of what had

happened. Historian-documentary film maker, Jeremy Murray-Brown, relates that one piece of film footage showing some of the gruesome handover survived in the National Archives in Washington but was not made available to the public for decades. Of the 'handover', Murray-Brown says:

> To carry out the repatriation order, American and British servicemen often had to resort to deception and brute force. No one doubted what was in store for the Russians once they were in Soviet hands. Many were executed on the spot. In some instances, Allied guards responsible for turning over their prisoners could see their bodies hanging in the forests where the exchange took place. Some were transferred on the same boat that had brought the British delegation to Yalta a few months previously. They were shot behind warehouses on the quay side with low flying Soviet planes circling overhead to help drown the noise of the rifle fire. Many returned prisoners were tortured before being shot. The remainder disappeared into prison camps for long sentences, receiving the worst treatment of all the Gulag's inmates.[104]

While many in the West simply thought the Soviets were a 'bit extreme' at times, those who had ever lived at close quarters under them did not want to return for they recognised a criminally pathological regime for what it was, even if Western Communist leaning academics did not. Migration was never strong in the Soviet Union's direction, it was always the other way – history had given ample evidence of that. In this way the Allies were complicit in the deaths of many innocent Eastern Europeans who had helped them throughout the war and it was part of what Bogdan assimilated day by day in the new world order and tried to understand.

In these post-war years, my father mingled with British soldiers and German civilians. Like most Poles he could make a clear distinction between the Soviet-influenced members of the British elites and the ordinary British with whom he made friends. He was genial and intelligent by nature and from his youth was a witty story teller, despite all that he had endured. As a young man, however, he already had an underlying seriousness, having been a witness of that reality alluded to as the 'heart of darkness' by Joseph Conrad. Little by little, Bogdan learned to move from the life of trauma to a more 'normal' existence, if such is the right word. His contemporary Julius Kulski, who had been a child soldier and survived a prisoner of war camp, recounts that some of the AK soldiers actually died in captivity after what they had endured. Kulski himself had recurrent nightmares of the most horrendous episodes of the Uprising. As with the holocaust survivors emerging from the concentration camps, the knowledge of the extent of human evil now had to be interwoven with a more quotidian post-war life. The burden of knowledge was too great to bear for some. Holocaust survivor Primo Levi (1919-1987) had never known such manifestations of evil as he saw in the camps, evil which he described in the post-war world in the following way:

> … for the first time we became aware that our language lacks words to express this offence, this demolition of a man … Imagine now a man who is deprived of everyone he loves, and at the same time of his house, his habits, his clothes, in short, of everything he possesses: he will be a hollow man, reduced to suffering and needs, forgetful of dignity and restraint, for he who loses all, often easily loses himself. He will be a man whose life or death can be lightly decided with no sense of human affinity … on the basis of a pure judgement of utility…[105]

In a similar way psychoanalyst Viktor Frankl (1905-1997), a contemporary of Levi, a survivor of Theresienstadt, Auschwitz, and Dachau, also tried to come to terms with the abominations he had witnessed. He gives harrowing descriptions of the camps. in his widely read work, *The Search for Meaning* (1946, 1971) which focuses on his time in Auschwitz. Frankl explores the apparent meaninglessness of the evil he confronted saying that no explanation was ever given for such evil or suffering in the psychoanalytic literature in which he was educated, concluding that it was gravely deficient in ignoring the extent of the capacity for human evil.[106] Nor did he later revise his views in the booming post-war 1960s, 70s and 80s when the more positive 'humanistic' psychology reigned supreme. Frankl's account certainly resonated with ordinary people. His book sold over nine million copies and was translated into over thirty languages.

As researchers of trauma now know, there is the additional trauma in a traumatic event, in that victims realise that few can understand what they have been through, even if they wish to listen. There is an abyss which words alone cannot bridge. This is something well known to psychologists dealing with traumatised individuals in a wide range of situations And thus a knowledge of unspeakable things was carried in silence by Bogdan and many of his fellow DPs as part of the journey to Bonegilla years later. The existence of Bonegilla cannot be understood without it.

Waiting for the next move

Having been assigned a 'warden' for the British army, Bogdan threw himself into the duties given him and dealt with his situation as best he could. With time, a new pattern of life asserted itself. His job guarding German prisoners of war and his nascent hopes for a future would have given him a sense of some kind of identity, even if AK survivors were not supposed to exist. He learned to speak fluent German and English. He even learned to play the piano in his British army 'warden' quarters and to sing songs such as the Andrews Sisters' 'Boogie Woogie Bugle Boy of Company B' and the other hits of the times. I think the Andrews Sisters and Vera Lyn particularly caught his attention and that of millions of other fans. Bogdan had a natural musical talent, on top of his talent for languages and interest in mathematics, history and literature. He explored all these, in various ways, for the remainder of this life as a genuine scholar, though never having formal qualifications. He picked up the details of playing the piano accompaniments of the songs of the day relatively quickly and played for many British-Polish get-togethers around the piano.

In later life, amidst the seriousness of his nature, he could suddenly sing, dance and tap his feet as he recalled the songs and they forever remind me of him wherever I hear them. It is not the songs themselves or the fact that he sang them that are the issue here but rather, the sense of Bogdan's being a survivor of a 'death-in life' trying to live again after what he had known and lost. However cheerful the songs, they could not mask entirely his inner tendency to be a thinker who contemplated history, war and human nature. His memories of war did not draw out the bitterness in him. He had faced the abyss of evil and remained human and sought the remnants of good beneath each episode of destruction. He was under no illusions about human nature, but his early experiences with suffering and death did not extinguish a true capacity to love. When Bogdan did relate something, it was without any trace of anger. Rather he told it with a searching inner eye, trying to see below the surface of things with equanimity, a term he always liked. That equanimity was part of the 'riddle, wrapped in a mystery, inside an enigma' of the life of many DPs in Bonegilla.

Bogdan stayed on in Germany, making some friends, reading, learning music and hoping for a country to live in. As well as singing the Andrews Sisters' hits, and doing the post-war dances, he could whistle or sing a part of Mozart's 'Figaro', and then turn to listen to a Chopin nocturne. For him, it was more important to preserve the memory of beauty and goodness, realising its power to transform reality and console the human heart. As with many of his generation he did not spend too much time relating his wartime experiences and this is why I had to do my own journeys to where he fought, to where he ended one life and began another. It is why I had to read and listen to others' accounts to put words on the silent stories he was already telling me in my youth in Bonegilla, for his silence ended up causing me to go on journeys criss-crossing continents, searching for those beginnings which had started long before the meaningful silences began.

In all directions

At one point during the five years he spent in Germany, Bogdan was contacted by a member of the Polish government-in-exile (which continued until the Soviet era of Poland ended and the first leader of a free Poland was elected in 1991) and was asked if he wanted to go to Britain and play a role in this government. News of his abilities must have reached some of the members of the existing government-in-exile group. Bogdan considered it for a while but he told me that he refused. The Polish government-in-exile, though it continued to function in some way, was of course no longer recognised as Poland's official government. While he admired all the wartime heroes who had done their best in horrendous circumstances and loved the country of his birth, he knew the world he had once known had been forced into a new narrative and he did not know how he could fit into it.

For others, staying in Britain was an option and around 200,000 Poles were taken from the German DP camps to live there. Bor-Komorowski, Anders and other leaders of the Allied and AK forces stayed in Britain and frequented Polish circles in the post-war era in London. The last wartime leader of the Polish government-in-exile, Prime Minister Stanisław Mikołajczyk, who was given empty promises by the new Polish regime, returned to Poland. However he realised his situation there was hopeless and escaped dramatically from Poland in 1947 ending up in the USA. The former Commander-in-Chief of the AK, General Monter, went to Washington DC.

Some ex-insurgents who had done daily radio broadcasts under very difficult circumstances during the Uprising, ended up as employees of the BBC. And when talent was sought for a radio station directed to broadcast to countries of the Soviet bloc, it was often from the ranks of the Polish section of the BBC that the talent was found. Novak, an ex-insurgent, was appointed director of the Polish section of Radio Free Europe in Munich. Of this man's work Davies writes, 'No amount of Soviet jamming could hold (it) back' and he adds that Novak became 'in all probability the best-known and the best-loved voice' in post-war Poland.[107] Other ex-insurgents made their way as best they could – even though in Britain they were not considered eligible for the modest pensions paid to those Poles who had fought under Allied command. Some were helped by the Polish Catholic Mission, by British friends and sympathisers, but it was not uncommon for generals to end up working as waiters, ex-judges and professors to end up on factory lines – in particular the Cherry Blossom Boot Polish Factory and the National Coal Board.

One of the Polish flying aces of the famous British air force Kosciusko Squadron 303 mentioned in a previous chapter – Jan Zumbach – ended up trying his hand at many varied business exploits after the war. Some of these involved African politics. Because of his flying renown, Zumbach was hired to head the Biafran Air Force with its hastily renovated B-26 bomber. With the Air Force's sole plane and Biafran air crew, Zumbach, who sympathised with the Biafrans, flew his bomber in 1967 and bombed the Nigerian planes standing idle thus delaying any hostile attacks on the smaller country. He recounts his various exploits in Africa in *On Wings of War* (1975, Zumbach died in 1986).

There were many stories of resourcefulness and ingenuity in the post-war era. Many of these Polish heroes of the forgotten battles, however, lived on the margins of society, having missed opportunities for education in younger years. Some succumbed to mental illness after what they had seen, others lived quiet, isolated lives in continual poverty. Antoni Tydda, the chief technical controller of the Aircraft Factory in Lublin, who had escaped with his son Jerzy from Poland after the invasion by Germany in 1939, and who had been a member of the British Air Force throughout the war, tried to run an electrical repair shop in London and lived in near penury, never being able to be reunited with his wife Zosia who lived out her days in Poland. These were the quiet forgotten stories buried under the new harsh realities and post-war 'boom'. Many families were never reunited, many were traumatically changed after the events and many simply had no idea what awaited them from day to day and tended to live in a state of either hyperalertness or numbing despondency, suppressing thoughts and emotions which if given an opening might overwhelm them. For some it was easier to focus on immediate needs than to make sense of the changed moral and political universe around them.

Perhaps one of the most difficult things to swallow was the lack of any prosecution of Nazi war crimes related to the Warsaw Uprising at the Nuremberg trials, which often condemned Nazis for similar actions in other contexts. Perhaps most galling for the Poles was the appearance SS leader Erich Von dem Bach-Zelewski at Nuremberg who was put in command of the German assault on Warsaw during the uprising. He appeared in the court as a witness but not as someone examined for his role in numerous atrocities. He tried to paint himself in a 'mild' light which earned him the furious insult of 'Schweinhund Verrater!' from Hermann Goering himself who sat in the dock at Nuremberg, and who evidently was all too aware of Von dem Bach's true role in the murder of innocent civilians on the eastern front.[108]

The complexities of the post-war realignment of powers, the ironies, the travesties of justice, the relegation of persons to 'nonexistence' were carried as an entire universe within him as Bogdan walked under the eucalyptus trees in Bonegilla. The realities of this universe were etched on his face and transmitted as spiritual legacies sensed in my childhood as I walked and played along the streets of Bonegilla camp with this serious young man. Even his occasional joy seemed transfused with sadness. It was as if he saw profound injustice at the heart of all existence, carried within us all in some half-apprehended sense, in some hidden realm of consciousness, only waiting to be revealed by confrontation with evil. Bogdan understood betrayal for what it was, but valued beyond measure its opposite – that is being an unfailing ally to another in a time of darkness and that is why he came to Australia and Bonegilla with such immense hope and reached out to its welcome.

As the Australian Immigration records state, Bogdan boarded the ship *General Hahn II* on 25 January 1950, and arrived in Port Melbourne on the 19 February 1950.[109] He boarded the last leg of the journey in Naples having previously travelled to Naples from Germany by ship. He was only twenty-two when he stepped ashore in Port Melbourne on the other side of the world. The *General Hahn II* carried 1,301 DPs in total and the passenger list included Lithuanians, Hungarians, Latvians, Ukrainians and Poles. My father is listed in one of the papers of the time as 'ex-Gen Hahn no 325' and his nationality as 'Pol', with an accompanying photo of him in post-war warden uniform capturing his gaze, a faint smile and the sense of some hidden knowledge. He told me there were some celebrations, cheering and singing on board as the ship passed the equator and there would have been much curiosity and no doubt immense joy as it approached the Australian coastline. Here before them lay the new world, the welcome to a new life, the balm overlaying previous suffering. At some point during the processing in Melbourne, Bogdan would have realised he had finally 'arrived' in his new country, even though he was officially listed as 'alien', and like the other newly arrived migrants, would have boarded the train, either for Wodonga or for Bonegilla siding, to his new mysterious destination, far away in the bush, where a new journey, new landscapes, new sights and new dreaming began …

6

Valerie before Bonegilla:
a place in eastern Latvia

My mother's Valerie's story of escape and emigration as a DP has a different origin, different details and nuances. Valerie (in Latvian, Valerija) was dark-haired, brown-eyed and intense with a dreamy, reflective nature from childhood. Her path to Bonegilla began in a little known town, in a little known province of eastern Latvia called Latgale. This little eastern province was in a country further north than Poland, not far from the northern climes of Estonia and Finland, the place of landscapes covered in pine trees sprinkled with snow. As with my father in Lublin, Valerie spent her childhood years in a border area that was situated near Russia, in fact too near Russia for comfort. By using the word 'eastern' every Latvian would automatically know what this meant. It meant being 'not far from Russia', for eastwards meant towards Russia. And to be born in that location already gives a very bold outline to anyone's life history, to any portrait of a life.

Latvia has been called 'the land of the blue lakes' and is one of the three Baltic countries, all of which lie on the Baltic Sea, the others being Lithuania and Estonia. It has a population of around 2.29 million and spans an area of 64,589 square kilometres, sharing borders with Russia and Belarus (or Byelorussia) as well as Lithuania and Estonia. While most people may have heard of Riga, the capital of Latvia, few have heard of its eastern areas – Latgale, Rēzekne

Rēzekne, Malta, Feimane, Ludza or Karsava. It is in these unusually named places that Valerie spent her youth. These towns and other towns of the border province, with names strange to pronounce for English tongues, even for Slavs, had their own legends, unique culture, memories and a different language – Latgalian – from the rest of Latvia, different from the Russian Orthodox and Swedish and German Protestant influences in and around the province. It was determinedly Latgalian and its people were conscious of their unique place in Latvian history.

Valerie was born in a town of wooden houses, church spires, squirrels, apple trees, rivers, rich black soil, wide lakes and a little station which was situated on the line running north to Leningrad (the former St Petersburg). This Latgalian town was called Malta and was situated near the much larger town of Rēzekne. She was born on 1 June 1926, which was early summer, a time of year always replete with flowers, festivals and young men leaping over bonfires on St John's Day on 24 June, an interesting interpolation of the Catholic feast of Saint John the Baptist and an ancient pagan fire-jumping ritual, still celebrated by Latvians with great enthusiasm each year. I witnessed young Latvians jumping through just such a St John's Day fire in the Sydney suburb of Sutherland a few years ago in the backyard of Gundega Zarina, daughter of Latvian emigrants who had invited everyone along to sing, eat, drink and jump. They do it to this day.

Latvia, like the other Baltic countries – Lithuania and Estonia – was, and is, a country particularly given to extolling nature in poetry and song. This is not simply a nice statement but refers to something deep in the Baltic psyche. You can quote poetry over a cup of coffee with someone you have just met. Children and adults sing about trees, flowers and almost every aspect of nature and have annual song festivals in which school children participate. It is not uncommon to see young girls with wreaths of flowers in their hair, whether in national costume, jeans or punk gear. With its 1.5 million recorded folksongs, Latvia has more songs per person than any nation on earth and most of them are about nature. These folk songs were collected in the 19th century by an indefatigable enthnomusicologist named Krisjanis Baronis, who has streets named after him in just about every city, town and village in Latvia. Those songs are part of the Latvian 'dreaming' and thread all the occasions, ceremonies and celebrations of life. Their importance can be gauged in considering how Latvians celebrated after years of Soviet rule. Of course they held an enormous Song Festival in the capital city in 1990 at which over half a million people sang well known songs as a sign of national unity. The songs had been a thread of continuity under Soviet rule and now the continuity of the culture came into its own. The valiant conductor managed to keep the massed choirs in rhythm and it is an extraordinary sight to see this mammoth 'singing revolution' especially the singing of the national anthem. This harked back to first Latvian National Song Festival which was held in 1873, the beginning of a long-standing tradition with strong national overtones which continues to this day.

To indicate how far this propensity for folk singing goes and what it means to the people, the past president of Latvia, Vika Freiberg, who had degrees in political science and psychology, also wrote a book about Latvian folk songs. No one thought it odd that a politician would write such a book, although if an Australian politician were to do so, it would without doubt arouse considerable comment. Folk songs are inextricably bound up with Latvian history and culture and are as much about the history of Latvia, as they are about folk songs. Valerie would have sung such songs all through her childhood – at school, in church and at home at family gatherings. Someone just needed to intone the melody and the song would be taken up and verses were part of the common memory. Some would elicit tears, some laughter, some sighs. And from my earliest years, I recall my mother singing songs about hay, horses, springtime, love and loss – even among the gum trees of Bonegilla and later as she drove along in her car in Sydney. While I did not understand all the words, we sang about Latvian oak trees floating down rivers and the eternal significance of this, driving past the car yards, grevillias, banksias and shop fronts on Parramatta Road.

Being born in the inter-war years, Valerie as a child witnessed the surge of hope and development in an independent Latvia, as Bogdan had in Poland. It was an atypical period for this tiny nation, coming after centuries of Russian occupation. This had come after centuries of German domination, with periods of Swedish and Polish influence in between, the latter not being seen in the same light as the superpower domination. Decisions about Latvia had often been made in the past in Berlin and Moscow, but this was not so in the years when my mother lived there. The following account of the cultural, historic and political milieu, is not a detailed one of those years but, as with Bogdan, it presents in some historical and social outlines what Valerie carried with her to Bonegilla. In the end it is only a fragmentary outline of all that she experienced and all that happened, filaments of the long trail of a complex history. But even pieces of memory reveal something of sights and sounds of places lived in long ago, of mysterious depths, of tones of the soul, of the intangible aspects of a life from which the Balts like Valerie came, as they walked along the road leading to the ships taking them to Bonegilla and other destinations.

Living in Latvia meant and means taking the existence of snow seriously. Latvia might as well also be called the land of snow and cold for, while its springs and summers are green and flowery, it can get to minus 40 in winter and this is serious cold, for which you must plan or you can die. Much art reflects the annual dusty flakes of snow of pine trees, frozen still rivers and snowed in houses which are entirely transformed in spring by the gradual riot of coloured flowers and trees everywhere. However, of all the seasons, one could say the country, like others around it, is most resplendent in its autumns, where an ethereal pageant of yellow, amber, orange and brown leaves fill the entire land, sending poets into lyrical frenzies or melancholic reflection on the fragility of beauty and time. Old brown round-towered castles rise above the fir trees in places with strange names such as Sigulda and Cesis where, in the past, Livonian knights lit their fires, gazed over plains to watch out for any threats to the land, made their plans and dreamed their dreams. The castles are still there for tourists to see. Latvia along with Lithuania and Estonia has been 'rediscovered' since its years of being buried under the Soviet regime and increasing numbers of people, including myself, have gone there.

Valerie, a pert, intelligent young girl, would have sat in school in the town of Malta in an area called Rozentova, named after a magnate who had once lived in this particular part of the town. The school was located opposite the wooden church, with its mix of Byzantine-style icons, onion domes and Latinate gothic architecture, the centre of many religious feasts and processions. Among the neat rows of desks, she would have sat serious-faced, as inhabitants of the northern Baltic states tend to be about any task. She would have learned something of the past along the lines of what follows – which may be subject to dispute among historians – but which gives general outlines of the world she knew.

What Valerie learned in youth

Valerie would have heard and read that the ancestors of the current Latvians, the proto-Balts, arrived around 2000 BC. She would have learned that the area had already been inhabited by Finns, who via Estonia had come down from further north and intermingled with some of the proto-Balts. These people became known as the Livs and were a group living alongside the proto-Balts. The territory inhabited by these Finnic Livs living in Latvia was called Livonia, although this word came to have another designation with time, referring to the lands controlled by a Christian militia called the Livonian Order. The Livs had a different language from the other Latvians and are a never-ending source of fascination for linguists, for they incorporated both Indo-European (from the proto-Balts) and non Indo-European (from the Finns and Estonians) features in their language, and this is extremely rare, if not unique in Europe. My mother would have learned something about the Livs' idiosyncratic and fascinating customs, about the history of her area, Latgale and about other Latvian provinces. She would have learned that one such province Kurzeme even had colonies overseas during the 19th century.

In class, she would have learned, as schoolchildren there learn now, that because of its location Latvia became a well traversed trade route from the land of the Vikings to the Greeks, and that it is mentioned in ancient chronicles. It was a major stop on a kind of 'northern silk road', as it was known, except that it would more properly be called an 'amber road'. These trade routes from Scandinavia, through Latvian territory along the river Daugava, to ancient Russia and the Byzantine Empire, carried the treasure of amber, which was known in ancient Greece, in the Roman Empire, and up to and during the Middle Ages, being considered more valuable than gold in many places.[110]

The pagan tribes of the area, previously mentioned with regard

to Lithuania, had a pantheon of over two hundred gods and
goddesses and, like the other Baltic countries, resisted early efforts
at Christianisiation in the tenth and eleventh centuries. However,
Latvian schoolchildren would have learned that this all changed with
the arrival of Albert von Buxhoeveden in 1199 (from Bexhövede in
Lower Saxony, c.1165-1229). Albert was a stalwart German missionary
and started his grand project to convert the Latvians. He was told by
his uncle Bishop Hartwig of Bremen that he could have the bishopric
of Riga if he could convert these particularly unruly heathens. He
succeeded in making some headway in his mission by about 1206
and was named as a Bishop at Ikšķile near the Daugava River, where
the first western church in the territory of Latvia was located. Thus
Bishop Albert continued the slow process of conversion of these
wild northerners and with the arrival of other missionaries, the
campaign proceeded in earnest and a first hand account of this little
known aspect of history can be found in *The Chronicle of Henry of
Livonia* (1961).[111] In 1201, as Valerie would have learned with all her
classmates, Bishop Albert began building the city of Rīga, Latvia's
capital, near the mouth of the main river, the Daugava.

In time Rīga grew into a solid impressive centre and became the
largest and most powerful city on the southern coast of the Baltic
Sea. The founding of Rīga was the beginning of urban history in the
entire Baltic area. Bishop Albert also set up a military order in 1202,
based on the Knights Templar, known generally as the Militia of
Christ of Livonia, sometimes known as the Brothers of the Sword,
consisting mainly of German warrior monks, and this group had
significant influence on the development of the area. These events
were occurring at the time when the larger Fourth Crusade armies
were entering Constantinople.

Where exactly was Livonia? The territory of Livonia took in the eastern coasts of the Baltic sea, of present day Latvia and Estonia, – the Gulf of Riga and the Gulf of Finland in the north-west, Lake Peipus and Russia to the east, and Lithuania to the south – quite a considerable area to convert! After the initial conversions to Christianity, a Papal legate whose name was Philip of Modena was sent to set up a Livonian Federation, a loosely organised confederation which that existed from 1228 to the 1560s. It was an attempt to ensure co-operation between the powerful Livonian order and the Church. Although both groups were led by Germans, such co-operation did not always proceed smoothly. In time, the knights tended to defer less and less to the bishops and do things 'their way'.

The order's headquarters were located at Viljandi in Estonia where the walls of the grandmaster's castle still stand, and other strongholds included Cesis, Sigulda and Aizkraukle in present day Latvia, where the ancient castles previously referred to, still stand. The Livonian Order took on the rules of the Teutonic Knights from 1236 onwards although they retained their own administrative areas and procedures. The order declined in the 16th century and was secularised under the last grandmaster of the order, Gotthard Kettler, who with the group, converted to the Lutheran faith.[112]

Sitting on her wooden bench in class, my mother would have heard all this. She would have known from a young age the difference between the 'Liv people' in Latvia and the military 'Livonian Order' and would have seen the stone remains of Livonian castles, even in her far flung 'eastern province' of Latvia, which was somewhat looked down upon by the other provinces as it was a bit far away from the more developed coastal areas. The eastern province was also spurned because it was Catholic and had not gone the path of the other three provinces in converting to Lutheranism during the Reformation. The other provinces – Kurzeme, Vidzeme and Zemgale – were more 'progressive' while Latgale, staying with its Catholic heritage, was regarded as 'behind the times', though Latgalians saw themselves as 'the true Latvians'.

Valerie would also have learned that there always had been threats from neighbouring Russia, even though locals got on well with individual Russians who came across the border seeking farm work and to engage in trade. There was no need to spell this out too dramatically. For everyone knew what had happened in Russia during the revolution, hoping it would never come to Latvia. Riga was the place after all, where the treaty was signed on 11 March 1920, an act which marked the end of Russia's attempt to re-take Latvia after it had gained its independence.[113] The Treaty of Riga loomed large in the thoughts of most Latvians for it signified the end of the Soviet occupation of their country and the end of the Polish-Soviet War, referred to previously, in which Marshall Piłsudski had stopped the advance of the Soviet attempt to take over Western Europe.

Perhaps less known to Latvians would have been the killing of the Ukrainian peasants during Stalin's Five Year Plan from 1927-1932 which occurred in the inter-war years. As many as five million Ukrainians died as Stalin deliberately denied them permission to till their land and sent Soviet teams to take possession of any food they had. These horrors proceeded virtually unknown to the outside world, even to inhabitants of nearby countries as the Soviet government countered attempts to get information on it. If some news did filter out to the Western media it was denied, if known about, by Western sympathisers with Communism.[114] Hints got through the wall of silence but the neighbouring countries found it hard to verify or assimilate such facts, as later, many would find it difficult to process the realities of what transpired within Nazi concentration camps. While Valerie lived in a peaceful Latvia, the horrors beyond the borders were unknown or if some knew of them they must have seemed too unbelievable. For if a few knew, they would have thought with some justification, 'Why would Stalin kill so many of his *own* people?. Why is he killing so many Ukrainians? Why? This is the 20th century after all, isn't it?'

In the context of a history filled with powerful influences from Russia, Germany, Sweden and Poland, Valerie would have learned that she was living in a special time in her country's history and that there had been past events, which despite former subjugation, indicated a wealthier past. There was a period, during the colonial era, in which this small country itself held colonies overseas, as previously noted, a fact which surprises many newcomers to Latvian history. In the 1600s, the western Latvian Duchy of Kurzeme or Courland, experienced a notable economic boom. The most successful ruler in the Duchy was the Baltic German Duke Jacob Kettler (1610-1682). During the long period of his rule (1642-1682) Courland became so successful in trade, with a navy of considerable size, that it rose in status as a regional power and established two colonies overseas: an island in the estuary of the Gambia River in Africa, and Tobago Island in the Caribbean. Both were successful ventures until the end of Jacob's reign, when the Duchy's navy fell apart as did control of the colonies, no doubt to the relief of the Gambians and Tobagans. However, in what must be one of history's greatest curiosities, the Latvian Couronian place names from this period are still evident in those former colonies today such as Courland Bay in Tobago.

The period of the Lithuanian-Polish Union, also mentioned in previous chapters, had a significant influence on Latvia. For centuries, missionaries were sent from Poland to Latgale, in particular, where Valerie lived, and rather than falling under the Swedish Protestant influence during the Reformation (as had the surrounding provinces) this province retained its adherence to Catholicism. When the urban coastal province, Vidzeme, came under Swedish Protestant Lutheran rule, the nation's capital Riga (which is located within this province) at one stage overshadowed Stockholm as the largest and most developed city in the Swedish kingdom. Riga was economically and culturally part of a growing urban network linking the major states and cultures of western, eastern and northern Europe and was part of the Hanseatic League. Vidzeme was known as the 'Swedish bread basket' because it supplied the larger part of the Swedish kingdom with wheat. The Latgalians in the east, from the perspective of Riga and its burgeoning economy, looked a more backward place, compared with the Swedish influenced provinces and the latter did not hesitate to inform the Latgalians of this on every possible occasion. However, the province of Latgale remained proud of resisting Swedish influence and retaining its pre-Reformation Catholic faith and traditions – to the chagrin of the Swedes, the Russians and the Protestant Latvians. Thus there arose among the Latgalians the sense that they were different, that the authentic cultural heritage of Latvia had been somehow preserved there. However, inter-provincial rivalry never overcame the greater good which was the underlying sense of national unity – all Lutherans, Catholics, Jews and Baptists could sing the national anthem together with great gusto – and this perhaps was due to the small size of the country and the ever-present threats to Latvia's existence.

In the early 18th century, Latvia came under the political and territorial ambitions of Russia, not for the first nor last time. The Great Northern War broke out, largely as a result of the Russian Empire's desire to expand its territory aiming to secure another port on the Baltic Sea. In 1710, the Russian Tsar Peter I achieved his aim in conquering the area of Vidzeme, giving the Russians Riga as a valuable port. This was a launching pad for further incursions into other parts of Europe and in 1772, when Poland was partitioned, Russia gained control of Latgale which had been under the considerable friendly influence of Catholic Poland. More Russians moved into the area and in reorganising its new territories, the Russian government abolished the notion of Latgale as a separate province, dividing it according to Russia's own plans into separate districts and incorporated it into the Russian-dominated Polotsk province.

It would been common knowledge in my mother's high school history classes that by the end of the 18th century, all of Latvia's territory was under Russian rule with the once mighty Courland (Kurzeme) becoming part of the Russian Empire in 1795. Serfdom still existed and was not abolished in Latvia until the 19th century (and not until 1861 in Latgale) during which time there was a revival of nationalist fervour. Literature, the arts and social life flourished as never before. The first newspaper was started, and after a move for independence in 1905, Latvia actually gained full independence as a country in 1918, after the signing of the peace treaty between the Latvian Republic and the Soviet Union in 1920. November 2, 1918, became Latvian Independence Day and would have been a sacred day for my mother and her family. Many songs, flag-raising ceremonies, serious speeches and national anthem singing would have been central to the day. It must have also been a momentous occasion for those of my grandparents' generation, who had survived Russian occupation and witnessed the first independence day they had ever experienced. It was a restoration of justice after centuries of Russian rule. The ceremonies, the music, the dancing and of course the singing would have remained long in their memories and they would have thought this new era would last forever during that hope-filled interlude of the inter-war years. For the effects of Russian rule had been long evident in the suppression of education and even the national language. My grandparents, even though they spoke Latvian and Latgalian, had been forbidden to learn to write their own languages and altogether forbidden to use the Latin alphabet. Only the Cyrillic one had been permissible under the Russian occupation. And now they found themselves free to speak their own language in public, to write in it, to sing, to recite poetry in it. History such as the facts related above could be taught freely during the inter-war years in Latvian schools.

Heady days of freedom in the inter-war years

In those heady days of newly found Latvian freedom, my grandparents would have seen the future as one of unbounded hope, faintly aware of the abyss of evil growing around them. My grandfather Jazeps Klučnieks (1880-1948, pronounced Kloochniks) was a tall, sturdy man with a brown, bushy moustache and a genial, generous nature. He worked in the Latvian Railways in the early decades of the 20th century, living in Rēzekne and in several other smaller towns in Latgale, Malta, Aglona, Feimani and Vishki among them, moving to them as needed as a station master and bridge builder. He knew the area like the back of his hand. He lived in the brown wooden cottages in the grounds of each station, with their solid wooden furniture and curtained windows. These cottages adjacent to the stations were supplied to each station master as a matter of course, wherever they were sent. He also spent considerable time in the large provincial town, Rēzekne, a focal point in the area.

A town called Rēzekne and beyond

Rēzekne is a junction town in which you see many signposts to well-known Russian destinations – trains pass through it as they head from west to east from Riga to Moscow. They also pass through as they go from south to north from Warsaw to St Petersburg (Leningrad). The first railways, in fact, came to Latvia in the 1850s with the commencement, in the Latgale province, of the Warsaw-St Petersburg line. One cannot avoid noticing the two main stations in Rēzekne, at opposite ends of the town and called 'Rēzekne I' and 'Rēzekne II'. The former is on the railway line to Saint Petersburg and the latter is a significant stop en route to Moscow. For an Australian, or any traveller from outside Latvia, to wander the streets here and read the names is already to be in another world, far from the eucalypts of Bonegilla. The distance from Rēzekne to Moscow is 685 kilometres which is really not that far away. The distance from Rēzekne to St Petersburg is only 450 kilometres, and to Warsaw 860 kilometres, in each case also closer than Sydney is to Melbourne.

In recent years, having travelled to Latvia a number of times, and having seen the railway lines, I came to understand that where he lived, my grandfather Jazeps must have seen thousands of trains pass by to their destinations before the war – to Moscow and Saint Petersburg, to Warsaw and Riga. He saw the journeys, checked the timetables, monitored the stops, awaited further arrivals – his whole life revolved around the journeys of so many people passing through this eastern town, with their baggage, hopes, anxieties and anticipations. In the pre-war years, dressed in his well-cut uniform, he would have pored over the rail timetables, checked arrivals and departures, talked to his colleagues and felt part of Latgale's developing future. Perhaps unusual in a land of serious temperaments, he liked nothing better than discussion and some laughter. Not that there was any habitual levity in his nature, but perhaps he had learned to smile and laugh in the manner some respond to deep suffering for his father had died at an early age and he had supported his mother and other siblings from his youth. In any case, he cut a fine figure in his Latvian Railways

Jazeps Klučnieks, Valerie's father, with his fellow Railway workers in the early 1920s in Rezekne in Latvia

The Klučnieks family home in Garkalne near Rezekne in the 1930s. It was totally destroyed in World War II during a battle between Nazi and Soviet forces

Jazeps and Julija Klučnieks with their three children – from left, Valerie, Zenia and Bronia

Latgale street in Rēzekne

uniform and even wore it on his wedding day in 1923 when he married my grandmother Julija Lepere (1899-1972) a tall girl with wavy dark hair and brown eyes and a typically serious Latvian nature. Jazeps had met her in the wooden church at Feimani, in south-eastern Latvia, where her family lived and where he was no doubt stationed at the time. Julija was a good deal younger than he was – he was 43 and she was 24 when they married – but everyone was delighted at the match and thought Julija had married a man of status and means. To work in the railways in this era was to be at the cutting edge of modernity. It was a happy marriage and Julija enjoyed her life as the wife of a high ranking, popular, station master. They had a shared history and mutual hopes. Like other Latvians of that time, Jazeps saved money to build a home in Latgale and for his wife and three daughters, Zenia (short for Eugenia), Valerie and Bronia (short for Bronislava).

Expanding towns, growing hopes

My grandfather along with his wife and daughters would have walked along the main streets of Rēzekne (Rēzekne in Latvian, pronounced Reyzekne), the major town to which people in surrounding areas came to transact business. He had great ambitions for all his girls and sent his oldest, Zenia, to a high school in Rēzekne, where she boarded with a family during the week. Jazeps was sent to run Rēzekne II station (the Moscow line) several times and also Rēzekne I (the St Petersburg line) and was familiar with its ethnic mix and thriving Jewish community and the constant movement across the borders. Rēzekne was typical of many towns in Latvia whose growth was boosted by the coming of the railways. The town now has a population of about 38,000. It has a university, cultural museum, libraries, various churches, some surviving pre-war buildings (some with bullet holes still visible), schools and a music school. Its history reflects some of the major events of European history. One travel guide describes this central

Latgalian town as follows:

> Rēzekne itself is noted for its unique location among seven hills in the very centre of the Latgale region. The town is built on the Rēzekne river, and in its southern section is the lovely Lake Kovsa. Apart from the scenery, Rēzekne is noted for Latgale Street, the town's oldest, lined with buildings constructed on the plans of Catherine II of Russia at the end of the 18th century.[115]

In Rēzekne and the surrounding areas, Valerie mingled easily with people from many ethnic backgrounds. For a provincial town Rēzekne had (and still has) a cosmopolitan feel to it, in the sense of the visible mingling of people from different countries, reflecting its border location and historical influences. There have always been Latvians, Poles, Byelorussians, Ukrainians, Jews and Russians among other nationalities living there, and they had done so for a long time by the time Latvia gained independence in 1918. In the pre-war years, there were several Latvian, Polish and Jewish high schools and the townspeople slipped into one language after another, according to the needs of the situation. They did not think it unusual to acquire several languages – it was a natural feature of the life there, a necessity, not an onerous task. My mother, grew up speaking the provincial language of the area, Latgalian (with currently about 150,000 speakers in the world), as well as Latvian, Russian, German and some Polish. The Latgale area, though considering itself a bastion of ancient Latvia, was as multicultural and multi-religious a community as one could find anywhere in eastern Europe. Within the space of a short walk one can easily even now encounter a Catholic cathedral, a synagogue, a Lutheran church as well as a Baptist, Russian Orthodox, Old Believers Russian Orthodox church and several other churches – all of which would have had sizeable congregations prior to the Second

World War. The vibrant co-existence of these communities would have threaded Valerie's life and growing maturity but above all she knew she was Latvian, and what is more, a Latgalian.

There has been a long-standing Russian presence in Latgale and my mother recalled meeting many Russians in her childhood. The Russian Polotsk principality and the merchants of ancient Novgorod had established trade relations with Rīga although they found difficulties there, as they were restrained by the regulation of the Riga Merchant Guilds which had long been part of the Hanseatic League. A greater proportion of Russians lived in Latgale where they worked on farms (my grandfather employed some Russian seasonal workers on his farm in the inter-war years). Many who established themselves in the area had fled from religious or political persecution in Russia. While there were some expected tensions, these did not erode the everyday community interactions and constituted a totally different kind of co-existence from the forced political russification of later eras.

There had also been considerable influence in this eastern province, as previously noted, from the Polish-Lithuanian Commonwealth to the south. This was evident in the sizeable Polish populations which once lived in the area: As the Latvian Institute explains:

Poles have been directly involved with Latvian-inhabited lands since 1562, when the weakened Livonian states, under threat of an invasion by the troops of Russia's Tsar Ivan the Terrible, sought protection from the Polish king. Thus began the so-called 'Polish Era,' which lasted in Riga and Vidzeme until 1621, in Latgale until 1772, and in the Duchy of Kurzeme, which was under the vassalage of the Polish king, until 1795. In Latgale the Polish cultural influence continued, and the Polish landed gentry remained even after the region became part of the Russian Empire. In this predominantly Catholic region, the destinies of the Latvian and Polish nations were most closely intertwined. The first book in Latvian was published by Polish Jesuits in 1585.[116]

Thus the 'Polish' era ended in 1772 but its influence continued long afterwards. In this ongoing 'intertwined' destiny of the Latgalians and Poles, it happened that some of the Polish nobility in Latgale consisted of polonised descendants of former German Knights of the Livonian Order, but many were also landed gentry from Poland and Lithuania. The Poles were active in both 19th century nationalistic rebellions against Russian rule, especially that of 1863, when an armed Polish unit engaged Russian army troops in southern Latgale. After 1863, the Russian authorities repressed any expression of Latgalian or Polish nationalism. However, Poles continued to play a significant role in Latvian life in spiritual and cultural terms and particularly in Latgale and they were represented in the first and subsequent Saemas, that is, the first governments of Independent Latvia. They established schools, social organisations, Polish language newspapers and took part in every area of Latvian life.

During the post 1772 era of Russian rule, the Latvian, Latgalian and Polish languages and Catholicism were suppressed to such an extent that, even though the use of the Latin alphabet was forbidden for the latter half of the 19th century, this did not destroy the personal relations between older Latgalian and Russian inhabitants. Communication between them tended to be cordial, as long as politics was kept at a safe distance. For both Latgalian and Russian traders, the immediate tasks of everyday life were much more interesting and profitable than the affairs of 'big men' and their 'plots'. Politics though ever present was looked on as something distasteful compared with personal human interaction. And so it was with the various other groups which permeated and enriched the life of the border province. Thus their churches and meeting houses stood side by side in streets, and people moved in and around each other as the generations lived and died. Rēzekne's Russian Orthodox church, opposite a Catholic church, was a source of pride to all its inhabitants. In it there were and are large icons of Christ and the Virgin Mary and extraordinary paintings in the cupola and ceiling vaults. These were gifts given by Tsar Alexander II due to his gratitude after having survived serious train crash in 1888 in Borki – and all the townspeople of Rēzekne, both Latvian and Russian, would have been honoured by the Tsar's gift. A local Rēzekne pamphlet from this Orthodox church says that 'there is a small stone repository devoted to [the] successful survival of Alexander II in the train catastrophe' – the catastrophe and the generous gift to the town being been part of the community memory. This age-old personal Russian interaction is a very different story from the later Soviet military and ideological repression of the entire country.

In Rēzekne, there has long been an 'Old Believers' Russian Orthodox church of Saint Nikolai, different from the main Orthodox church. The Old Believers church belongs to an 'unreformed' branch of the Orthodox church which refused to accept the reform of the liturgy in 1658. Its Russian adherents fled from the hostilities facing them to wherever they could. A considerable number came to Latgale where they were allowed to pursue their beliefs in peace. In addition, the pre-war synagogue in Israel Street, would have been familiar to the townspeople. There had been a Jewish community in Latvia since 1591 and before World War II this group comprised nearly 8% of the whole population.[117] As regards Latgalian Jews, the Latvian Institute website explains:

   … the majority of Jews arrived only in the middle of the

seventeenth century as they fled the pogroms organised in the Ukraine and Belarus by Bogdan Khmelnytsky. These Jews spoke Yiddish, as was common in Poland, and they were more strict in their observance of orthodox traditions than were German Jews. Most of them were small tradesmen and craftsmen, but some were farmers. Until 1844, Jewish communities in Latgale had their own local government officials – kagali – who collected taxes, enforced the observance of secular and religious laws, and maintained order.[118]

A high proportion of Jews had lived in Rēzekne and the nearby town of Ludza in the pre-World War II years. In fact most craftsmen and many shop owners in those towns at that time were Jewish. In the pre-war years, all the various groups lived not only side by side, but in a constant interchange which they had done for hundreds of years. However, most of the Jewish population of pre-war Latvia lived in Riga, Daugavpils and Liepāja. The majority perished in the Holocaust, in one of the more vicious extermination campaigns by Nazis and their collaborators – if one can call any part of the extermination more vicious than any other. The Einsatzgruppen ('task forces') played a leading role in the destruction of Latvian Jews, according to information given in their own reports, especially in the report of SS-Brigadeführer (General) Stahlecker, the commander of Einsatzgruppe A, whose unit operated on the northern Russian front and in the occupied Baltic republics. His account covers the period from the end of June up to 15 October 1941 and describes the brutal killings with cool detachment.[119]

After the repression of the Nazi and Soviet regimes and their collaborators, some Jews returned to Latvia and according to census data there are around 15,000 Jews still living in the country. A Jewish community still exists in Rēzekne and the cemetery has tombstones noting deaths of Jewish inhabitants during the past twenty years. While some Latvians lamentably co-operated with the Germans, others did not and the lives they saved are noted in the Jewish Holocaust Museum in Riga which has photo displays of the thriving life of Latvian Jews in the pre-war years. The Museum explains that two eminent philosophers hailed from Latvia, Isaiah Berlin and Yeshayahu Leibovitch, and that Jānis (Žanis) Lipke (1900-1987) was a Latvian rescuer of Jews in Riga during World War II, among many others noted in a section of the display dedicated to rescuers.

In a history filled with persecutions from powerful neighbours, perhaps an indication of the keenness for Latvia's independence can be seen in briefly considering the fate of a statue in Rēzekne's main street, Liberation Avenue (in Latvian, Atbrīvošanas Aleja). It is a tall statue called 'the Mara monument' which stands in the centre of the town at a roundabout and has great symbolic significance for the townspeople. It is a sculpture larger than life of a young girl gazing into the distance and was done by Leons Tomasikis and named Latgales Mara. Valerie would have certainly seen it many times and reflected on its significance. First unveiled on 8 September 1939, as a monument to the liberation of Latgale from Soviet Bolsheviks in January 1920, the statue would not have been popular with the Soviet regime over the border, especially as the young girl held up a cross, the sign of the Christian character of the country. So, when the Soviets re-entered Latvia in November 1940, they removed the statue. Not to be deterred, the local population restored the Latgales Mara statue on 22 August 1943, but the Soviets destroyed it again after June 1950. They should have known by that time that the Latvians had a determined streak to them and would not leave matters as they stood. In the end the Latvians had the last word for the statue was rebuilt after the Soviet Union fell and was unveiled on 13 August 1990 where it still stands today. It was one of the first things pointed out to me when I returned many years later. Valerie and her family would have heard of it being unveiled in 1939 and must have pondered the past history of their country and wondered what the future held.

7

The War and Latvia

The resurgent Latvian nationalism of the inter-war years changed forever in 1939 for Valerie, her family, her nation and millions of innocent people. Prior to the war, my grandfather Jazeps planned his retirement from Latvian Railways to pursue the farming life. He was already nearing sixty and had saved his money carefully to realise his plans. Over several years he built the house of his dreams in 1935, a large wooden house, a little upmarket for the times, surrounded by flowers, just outside of Rēzekne. It was in a leafy area called Garkalne, dotted with pine forests, apple and chestnut trees. Jazeps had used his savings from his working years to purchase the land, plan and build the house. Previously he had had to live in allocated station masters' houses in places with exotic names such as Aglona, Feimani and Viski, where he was appointed station master, along with his wife and his children Zenia, Valerie and Bronia. Now he had a permanent place to live and the future loomed bright; he would have put his heart and hopes into his little paradise on earth.

The house at Garkalne was large enough for all, with ornate, wooden carved window sills, solid wooden furniture, a wall cuckoo clock, embroidered tablecloths, lace curtains with surrounding barns, sheds, stables, orchards and a well – all in good use. A quiet country life proceeded within its walls and around it for the years immediately preceding the war. There were horses to take people where they needed to go – to the town, to relations or to the station for, while the trains took people to 'big' destinations, horses were commonly used to move within areas and towns. At Garkalne there were also farm animals of various kinds and milk was in plentiful supply for the making of cheese, butter and buttermilk. There were plentiful apple trees and vegetables grown on the land. Jazeps turned his thoughts to his daughters' education. When his two oldest daughters reached high school age, he sent them to board near their schools. In Zenia's case it was probably 1939 and in my mother's case around 1940, already after the beginning of the war. Jazeps wanted each of his daughters to receive a good education, despite what was happening around him, and used his retirement savings for this purpose. In my mother's case, he thought that she should start high school at the famed agricultural school at Malnava about 60 kms from Garkalne. It was my grandfather's hope that Valerie would acquire the skills to manage a farm and that her sisters would also learn such skills along the way. She boarded at this school as did many of the young Latvian men and women whose parents envisaged a similar life for their children.

Of course, Jazep's – and everyone's – dreams were extinguished when Latvia increasingly became the pawn of Soviet and Nazi ambitions. People heard radio bulletins and spoke to each other, wondering what awaited them. In 1940 the Soviet Union annexed Latvia, along with Lithuania and Estonia, and thus dragged these tiny countries into its version of totalitarian reality.

Valerie would have witnessed the attempt at Soviet subjugation of Latvia. She would also have seen that this was interrupted by the beginning of the German-Soviet War in 1941 and the rapid invasion of Latvian territory by Nazi Germany's armed forces. By 10 July 1941, German armed forces had occupied all of Latvia which became a part of Germany's Reichskomissariat Ostland, the Province General of Latvia. Thus after a brief period of freedom, Latvia was again an occupied land. While some in Latvia mistakenly considered the Germans as their saviours from the occupying Soviet regime, anyone who disobeyed the occupying German regime, as well as those who had co-operated with the former Soviet regime, or were even suspected of having done so, were killed or sent to concentration camps. Camps were constructed to exterminate the Jewish population of this small country, people who had lived there for many centuries and had successfully conducted schools, organisations and businesses.

Latvia's population perished not only in cross-fire or on the battlefield. During the years of Nazi occupation, special campaigns exterminated approximately 70 000 Jews, 18 000 Latvians and 2 000 Roma inhabitants among others – in total about 90 000 people.[120] Jewish and Roma civilians were eliminated methodically according to the crazed Nazi theories of racial purity. In the case of the Latvians, those who were killed were mostly civilians whose political convictions were unacceptable to the Germans, those who assisted the Jews to escape, or who were simply in the wrong place at the wrong time.

As with many near the Russian border, Jazeps and Julija, living in Garkalne, had the misfortune to be caught in the crossfire of the Nazi and Soviet armies. Soldiers of both armies fought on Jazep's land. In what all thought was a lull in the fighting, Bronia, the youngest child, was for some reason at Garkalne standing in the gardens around the beautiful wooden house. Her parents were in the nearby town of Malta and were due to return to their place later in the day. It was the time when the Germans were pushing forward to Russia in Operation Barbarossa in June 1941. She recalls the very moment in that year when, out of the blue, gunfire and explosions started again. She was alone surrounded by two groups of soldiers hurling bombs and shooting at each other. She desperately ran for cover. Several bombs rained down on the area around the house and several fell on the house. Bronia told me many years later when I visited her that while at first she just stood terrified and numb for a while, she then ran for the trees and then turned again to see the ever-increasing explosions. She saw the largest bomb fall on the family home, as if in slow motion, watching the pieces of wood, its doors and windows go in all directions, moments of destruction frozen in time. The life she knew was disappearing in front of her. The house was totally destroyed as Nazi and Soviet armies fought each other from all sides.

As Bronia sat cowering behind the trees, the young terrified girl was so traumatised that she wanted to scream but was unable to. She opened her mouth but no sound came out. Try as she might, she was unable to say a word for six months. My mother Valerie was in boarding school in Malnava, but she and her schoolmates were now victims of the new realities and were turfed out of their school as the building was requisitioned by the Germans and used as a Gestapo headquarters. Zenia was in Rēzekne living with a banker and his family and attending school when the bombing started. Bronia recalled that Zenia rushed home to her parents, all the way to Malta, probably getting some lifts on the way as it was quite a distance for a young person to walk. Zenia told Bronia and her parents of the dead bodies she had seen floating along the river she had crossed on her way home. A very few out of the Jewish population managed to escape, some were helped to escape, but most perished. At this time there were regular round-ups of Jews and others who were taken to forests and shot at point blank range. The new realities terrorised the population and this was the intention of the occupiers.

Jazeps and Julija stayed in the nearby town of Malta. Not long after these dramatic events, my grandfather, in a lull in the fighting, returned one night with three male friends to Garkalne where his dream house had once been. Out of the wreckage of the house he

Byzantine onion domes on a typical eastern Latvian wooden Catholic church in Feimani in Latgale

Valerie (wearing glasses) with high school classmates in Malnava in Eastern Latvia. The school was soon taken over by the Gestapo and the students sent home

*Rezekne railway station, a junction on the Warsaw-St Petersburg line.
Jazeps worked here and at Rezekne II, on the Riga - the Moscow line*

*Stanislaus Lepers (left) brother of Julija (author's grandmother) shortly after his return
from Siberia circa 1956 . On the right is Alexander Lepers who helped Valerie and Zenia
escape from Latvia on the last ship to leave Riga*

picked up usable pieces and built a one room shelter on his now bombed land. Perhaps he thought he could assert some semblance of order in the midst of moral and political chaos. The family stayed at times in that one roomed shelter. Meanwhile, at Malnava, where Valerie was at high school, the Germans ordered out the students and teachers for use as a headquarters. My mother Valerie came home and my grandfather considered what to do. He still clung to the idea of an education for his girls and that the war would be over soon. Perhaps there were other schools – perhaps a boarding school in another area might be safer – for some parts of the country tried to maintain a semblance of normal life. He found out about another boarding school still operating in a province further south towards Lithuania in a town called Bebrene.

After much discussion he sent Valerie there by train to complete her high school education. Zenia continued her schooling in Rēzekne, again boarding with the family she had come to know well and Bronia, being younger, attended the local school at Malta, not far from Garkalne. The teachers must have tried especially hard to maintain a degree of normality and continue teaching their subjects under conditions of occupation, uncertainty and threatened destruction of the country. My mother's final year of school in Bebrene in 1944 was cut short as teachers and students knew the new Russian advance was well on its way and that quite simply, they could all die. The principal announced to the teachers and staff that the 'school year' would end sooner than expected. Exams were held and graduations done in a hurry. The staff counted the expected arrival of the Soviet army in weeks and then days. My mother was in her final year at school and a good student aiming to attend university, if universities still were to exist in the next year. Leaving certificates were handed out in June 1944 not July as was the custom. The students were urged to go home and each wished the other well. Life was now totally precarious and punctuated with fear as the Soviet Army strengthened in the east and approached closer to the border each day. Jazeps along with most Latvians realised in 1944, with a sinking feeling, that another occupation awaited them after this German one and, as a landowner, even if a small one, he would be an 'enemy' of the Soviet regime.

As with many Latvians, secret plans were being made to escape from the country – at least 'for a while' – many holding the hope that 'things would improve'. Thus it was decided at some stage in late June, that Zenia and Valerie, the older sisters, would go ahead to Riga and the rest would follow. After the truncated, agitated conversations the idea was that the family would move in stages to arouse less suspicion. The two older sisters boarded a truck in Malta in the pre-dawn darkness and hurtled their way to Riga in advance of the others, sitting pressed against people in the open back section. Their mother Julija had given them 'sveistmaize' – that is, sandwiches, wrapped in a handkerchief, waving them off – as it turned out – for the last time. In what was a defining moment of their lives, Valerie and her sister, Zenia, still teenagers, were cut off from their parents and younger sister Bronia for the Soviet army marched into Latvia shortly after they had left and there was no chance for others to escape. The Soviet occupiers stopped all further movement of the local population and Jazeps, Julija and Bronia did not make it to Riga. Valerija and Zenia were among the last to leave Malta heading west, aiming, as they vainly hoped, to come back as soon as things got better.

So fast was the advance of the Soviet army, my grandparents did not have time to even pack a suitcase. So they were left behind with Bronia, their third and youngest child, not knowing what was to happen, but not imagining in the wildest dreams that they were never to see the older girls again. Before the Soviet prohibition on all movement, there had been a panic and as many as could get away to the Baltic coastline and out of Latvia did so. Keeping a few steps ahead of the Soviet advance (there were memories of the deportations to Siberia in 1940) they moved in convoys or small groups, terrified they might not succeed. For their fears of the Soviets were well grounded. In 1940 about 35,000 people had been deported in cattle trains to Siberia. This is a large number to take in a few weeks from a country with as small a population as Latvia.

As a memorial of that time a single wooden freight car stands in Riga at Tornakalns railway station. One can see it from any suburban train which passes through there to go to Jurmala and Tukums. No toilets within, no food, no drink within the small cattle cars, just moaning voices emanated from trains carrying their human cargo east, most never to return. It was just as the Poles had been taken in 1939, many of whom had already died. An account of this time of deportation is given in Latvian Ilmars Salts' *A Stolen Childhood: Five Winters in Siberia* (2008) in which the author recalls the arrest of his father in 1940 when he was a young boy and the subsequent long journey he, his mother, grandmother, brother and sister made over several weeks to an unknown fate in remote Mizgirevka in Siberia. The children are left orphaned after their grandmother and mother die (their father had been killed) and they have to learn to fend for themselves in the harsh realities of the Siberian environment. They learnt to pick berries, to fish and to beg and do work for locals. Despite all their efforts they came to know every variant of hunger and cold. Ilmars 'made' some shoes out of cloth and had no coat for the severe winters. However, he took care of his younger siblings, taking on the role of both parents. At the end of the war they knew the children knew they had survived but did not know if anyone knew of their existence. After a time they were returned to Riga in a train full of orphans.[121]

As if to vindicate the fears of the escapees from Latvia, between 1945-1949, another 100,000 Latvians were deported to Siberia, my great uncle Stanislaus among them.[122] Latvia lost about 35% of its population through death, deportation or people fleeing in fear which had an acute impact on this small nation. With most of its Jewish population killed by the Nazis, now all other political undesirables, such as those who owned a piece of land, or who had in any way worked for the Germans, whether forcibly or not, were now the target of deportation and extermination by the Soviet forces. My grandfather realised he had no chance of holding on to his land or little wooden semi-detached cottage in Malta so he willingly relinquished all ownership quickly to the Communists to save the life of his family. It seemed to work at the time. However, this would not have been enough as things turned out, for his name and that of the entire family were on a deportation list to be taken to Siberia for the 'crime' of ever having owned land. The Soviet enforcers would have caught up with him in the near future. It made no difference what one's individual story was.

Here a strange element enters into this story for it is extraordinary how the remaining family very narrowly escaped deportation. Not only were Jazeps and Julija to be deported to Siberia but also brothers, sisters, cousins and the extended family. They only learned of their escape from this fate later. To explain it, a little detail of family history is relevant at this point for it was because of this detail – or rather a person – that they nearly all evaded deportation. It so happened that my grandmother Julija's mother, a woman called Onufrija Lepere, was the second wife of her husband, the first wife having died some years earlier. In fact when Onufrija came to marry, she inherited two step-sons from her husband's former marriage. One of these was named Juzuks Lepere and must have had some Communist leanings as he ended up living and working in Moscow from the time of the revolution onwards. Bronia related to me that Juzuks worked in a 'public' ministry in 1944-5 and saw their name of his entire family on a deportation 'list' for Siberia. Or perhaps someone informed him of the fact. Whatever his Communist sympathies were, his family ties seemed to loom larger, and he literally saved them by removing them from the list of those to be deported. How he did this in the crazy milieu of Stalin's regime was not related to me – I was simply told that it had happened. Like many family stories which are told and re-told, perhaps some vital factors have been lost in the re-telling but the most important thing was that Juzuks managed to do this. Thus, whether he used some personal influence or secretly had the names removed in some other way, it is hard to say. In whatever mysterious way he did it, he saved the family remaining around Rēzekne from deportation.

All escaped that is, except for one – my great uncle Stanislaus (Julija's brother) who was 'denounced' by a local resident and despite Juzuk's efforts was arrested and sent to Siberia for nearly 10 years. He would have been there longer except that he was released through the persistent efforts of his brother Alexander Lepers and son Janis, who left no stone unturned in their efforts to rescue him. Eventually their efforts paid off and his sentence was shortened a little. When Stanislaus returned to Latvia from Siberia by train, he came off the train a living skeleton. Every rib protruded on his emaciated frame and even years afterwards were visible as a testimony to what he had endured. He walked to his brother and son waiting on the railway platform and did not say a word – he simply embraced them. He would not have lived much longer in the sub-Arctic camp he was assigned to, doing forced labour each day. Valerie heard about this story many years later when she was in Australia, long after she had passed through Bonegilla, and some letters from her family had begun to flow. She related it to me in tones of horror. Apart from her sorrow for her uncle Stanislaus' suffering, she had cause to think of what her fate might have been if she had remained in Latvia. For even if names were removed from a deportation list once, there was nothing to prevent a Soviet official placing them on it again.

8

Germany and surviving the bombs

As they sat huddled amongst other people on the back of a truck which was speeding on its way towards Riga in 1944 with the Soviet Army advancing not far behind, Valerie and Zenia thought their journey was a temporary separation from their parents and the world they knew. The two young women reached Riga in July 1944 and found their way to the apartment of their Uncle Alexander (their mother's brother and the brother of Stanislaus who was to be sent to Siberia) who was to help them. Uncle Alexander had worked in Riga both as a director of a boarding school and in the Latvian public service, keeping a low profile. He had to work out what to do with the 18- and 19-year-old girls who had suddenly appeared at his door. As matters turned out, when Valerie and Zenia were walking to Uncle Alexander's apartment on arrival in Riga, they had a chance meeting that would set the course of their futures.

All of a sudden, amidst the fearful atmosphere of the capital city, on the very street on which they were walking after they alighted from the truck, they met their young 10-year-old cousin Veronica Tjarve and Veronica's mother Anna Tjarve (also a sister of Uncle Alexander). Veronica and her mother Anna were also in the process of trying to escape from the advancing Soviet army and had come up in similar fashion on the back of a truck from the town of Feimani in Latgale (about 60 kilometres from where Valerie and Zenia lived). They all embraced and learned they were all placing their hopes in this highly admired 'Uncle Alexander' who lived nearby and seemed to know his way around paper work and overcoming obstacles.

The Tjarve family – that is Veronica and her mother Anna – had little chance of survival because of the circumstances of their lives. They lived a fair distance away in the country town of Feimani in western Latgale and their lives had taken quite different twists and turns in the course of the war. Living in the countryside was no protection. Anna Tjarve and her daughter knew they were 'dead men walking' so to speak, as far as the Soviet regime was concerned. The reason for this was that Anna's husband and Veronica's father – Jed Tjarve – as a former businessman and former Latvian policeman was hated by the Germans because he had helped Jews escape and now was hated by the Russians because he simply had been an official. He had spent much of the war in hiding. Jed knew he had no option but to disappear.

In fact, as Veronica herself related to me, he had spent most of the previous years in hiding in forests and in narrow escapes, on one occasion hiding in a cupboard when visiting his wife and daughter in Feimani, as the house was searched by Germans. They did not find him on that occasion. Earlier he had been ordered to participate in the arrest of Jews but instead had warned the Jewish townspeople to escape and helped them in whatever way he could. He tried to play the role of an incurable drunkard (which he was not) on occasion to save his life and was taken in his 'drunken' state to a killing field and either fell or was thrown into a pit which contained the bodies of Jews who had been shot. How Jed crawled out I do not know but he did and again he went into hiding. It became known to the authorities that he did not die and so the searches for Jed continued relentlessly and the lives of his wife and child were hung on a thread.

Jed planned the escape of his wife and daughter. He had considered it too dangerous to come to Riga with his wife and child in 1944 as he was wanted by all sides of the conflict. At least if he was killed, his wife and child would survive, or so he hoped. He worked out a safe means to get Anna and Veronica to Riga. As for himself, he decided to go it alone and escaped via a complicated series of forest routes, as Veronica later related to me – heading for Germany to meet up with his wife and child at a pre-arranged place, if he survived the journey.

In the atmosphere of panic and terror which had seized the people, Veronica and Anna spoke hastily to Zenia and Valerie on the streets and at Uncle Alexander's apartment. They persuaded Zenia and Valerie to come with them to Germany 'until things get better'. It was left up to my uncle Alexander to help find some places for them on the next boat leaving Latvia, not an easy task in wartime. Thus a group of four – Valerie, Zenia, Veronica and her mother Anna – all boarded a ship near Riga, amidst the crowds of fleeing Latvians, looking back to the place they were leaving as the ship sailed out of the port. They saw the fading lights of Riga and wondered if the fate they were going to was worse than the one they were leaving. As the pine trees, sandy shores, spires and dark wooden cottages of the Latvian coastline receded into the distance, they sailed out into the cold waters of the Baltic sea and even colder uncertainty of their future fates. How could they have known as they clung to each other in 1944 that they were being catapulted to the other side of the world, that the threads of a new journey were being spun, that they were heading for places they had never heard of, among them battlefields in Germany and Bonegilla Migrant and Reception Centre near Wodonga in Australia, and that they would never see Latvia again.

Later in Australia, Valerie recalled that fateful journey to Germany and how she saw a blood-red coloured sky above her that evening.

She had a premonition she would never see her country again – which turned out to be true. Like many others she disembarked at Hamburg and was taken to a camp for displaced persons already in existence in the chaos of Germany sliding to its final phase of destruction as it was bombed by Allied forces.

After disembarking, the group of four women ended up in Göttingen and were then assigned to various kinds of forced labour for what remained of the Third Reich. While the Allied attacks on Germany continued, forced labourers and concentration camp survivors had to contend with bombings from all sides. When the bombs fell, people ran for shelter. In fact, during the next year Valerie spent a good deal of time running in and out of bomb shelters and trenches, nearly getting killed several times, caught in the crossfire between Germans and the Allies. Just as my father ran to avoid German sniper fire in Lublin, and Wanda Maria my grandmother avoided bombs in Ravensbrück concentration camp, Valerie was having her share of near death experiences in northern Germany.

She related to me that she was seriously wounded in one bombing attack during this period, not far from Göttingen and in fact very nearly died. She heard the signs indicating an air raid and, like the others, scrambled to find some protection in the nearest bomb shelter. A bomb fell above the shelter and in the eerie aftermath of the attack Valerie, wounded and semi-conscious, realised there was no movement nor sound around her. Had everyone died? Was she dead? She sensed the liquid trickling down her back in many places and wondered about what to do. She realised that all around her had been killed and she was not far from death herself. She had wound rosary beads around her wrist and prayed that something might happen. How long this continued she could not say as she lapsed in and out of consciousness. However she did crawl out from among the dead bodies and lay wounded on the roadside for what seemed a long time with a large piece of metal shrapnel piercing her back. In one of those strange anomalies of war, when people resume their daily business, once the bombing is over, a German country woman happened to pass by the scene of destruction in a horse-drawn cart some time later as my mother related to me (whether hours or a day later she could not recall). She must have been the only person on the road for otherwise the German woman might not have heard the faint whimpering coming from somewhere nearby. She turned around and heard my mother's groans, coming from a bleeding, moving human figure on the ground amidst the other bodies. She would have seen the rosary beads wrapped around my mother's arms and perhaps heard some words of prayer interspersed with the faint sounds.

The elderly woman stopped her cart and realised this moaning came from a body that was not a corpse like the others. The lady managed to pick Valerie up, heave her onto the back of the cart and take her home amidst whatever other produce she was transporting, probably potatoes. My mother must have passed out for she did not remember much of this journey – the piece of metal shrapnel still stuck out of the diagonal wound which extended from the top of her shoulder blade to just above her hips. At this village farmhouse, the metal pieces were removed by the farming folk and the remaining gash was deep. Valerie, who had finished school not long before, and had had so many hopes, now lay on her stomach for several months unable to move. She was cared for by this kind stranger's family, not knowing where her parents were, where her sister and cousin were. Because of her injuries, she could not move her back or body at all. At one point she said someone did visit with an offer of medication – it ended up being one aspirin – for which she was very grateful. She bore a deep diagonal scar across her back for the rest of her life.

There were no effective painkillers anywhere to be had and she just lay and recovered until she was able to move again. With time she became strong enough to leave and having thanked the woman for saving her life, Valerie returned to the displaced persons' camp where here sister and cousin were living, telling them all of her experience. They were relieved to see her again, thinking she must have died.

Assimilating the new realities

As the geopolitical groundshift reorganised Europe, my mother would have sat at nights talking to her relations, looking at the sky wondering if she would see her parents, Garkalne, Rēzekne and Malta again, whether she would see the orange leaves of the country roads of Latgale, whether she would see her school friends with whom she had discussed her dreams. She could never have foreseen the dramatic changes which lay before her. As previously mentioned, at the Yalta meeting of February 1945 attended by Churchill, Roosevelt and Stalin, much of eastern Europe was ceded to the Soviet regime and this included the Baltic states.[123] When the end of the war came there was little joy for her and for other Balts who saw ever-increasing Soviet control of their countries and little hope of return. The Balts who had been displaced, like millions of others, lost their connectedness to their family and the places they had once known. They were now adrift in an uncertain chain of events and lived from day to day. But their 'dreamings', their narratives of a once better social, cultural and political life were not yet extinguished.

It would have dawned on Valerie that she could not return to Latvia and that she was now a 'non person' in the eyes of the Soviet regime. At some point, absorbing the new post-war realities of this time, she turned her mind to do something useful – hoping she might study. She still had her Leaving Certificate with her. In fact, my mother had wanted to be a doctor all along in school. Back in Latvia, while she was studying agricultural subjects which her father had encouraged her to do, she wondered how to break it to her parents that she was irresistibly drawn to the study of medicine. Towards the end of her final year back in Latvia, she had spoken to her parents just before her final rushed exams and asked if they would much mind if she tried medicine instead of agriculture. They were pleasantly numbed with surprise at the interest their daughter had for medicine and encouraged her. Later I was to learn that on my grandfather's side of the family there had been several doctors across the generations.

My mother's younger cousin Robert Klucnieks studied medicine in Soviet-controlled Latvia and to this day is a forensic psychiatrist practising in Riga, and her grand-nephew Valerijs (the male form of the name Valerie) Sumkins was to study medicine in the future at Riga University. In the future journeys to 'see' where Valerie had lived, I was fortunate enough to meet both of them, neither of whom had met my mother but who were interested to hear of her journey to Bonegilla. I have no doubt that Valerie's experiences of war and seeing the horror around her, propelled her into the direction of medicine as well as her having a natural propensity for this field of study. She said as much to me and often recalled in later years that what she witnessed during the war changed her forever. When she finished high school in Bebrene, before the Soviet Army entered Latvia, she had actually been accepted as a medical student at the University of Riga, which still functioned at that time. She was all set to attend medical lectures in 1945 but given the fact that the family was on a deportation list, it is doubtful she would have ever been accepted there in post-war Soviet controlled university quotas – nor whether she would have even survived.

Seeing that there was no imminent hope of return to Latvia, Valerie,

Zenia, Anna and Veronica realised there was nowhere to go but to stay put in chaotic Germany, amid the millions of displaced persons like them. Worse still, they could not even inform their families in Latvia they were alive for if one did write from the West to anyone in Soviet countries, this could endanger their lives. Families in the Baltic countries were deported on the merest hint of having contact with someone in the 'capitalist, decadent West' and a letter with stamps from a capitalist country was a dead giveaway to anyone appointed to observe a street or neighbourhood and report strange letters to the authorities. There are always people in each country who profit out of being informers for the prospect of some money, food or immediate gain. I was told on my later visit to Latvia that my grandparents cried inconsolably at nights wondering where Valeria and Zenia were – how could they know? Jazeps used to cry and call out, 'My girls, my girls, where are you?' as his wife and remaining daughter Bronia (who told me of this) wept with him and tried to console him.

Despite the Soviet suspicion of 'overseas' mail, my mother devised a way of telling her parents that she and her sister were still alive. She concocted the plan to write to an old school friend Bronia, from her earlier boarding school days. Bronia (not her sister but her friend) lived with her family near Malnava in a place called Karsava. Valerie decided to take a punt and write to her in a coded way with no return address on the envelope, knowing that Bronia could just declare it was a mistake. This friend fortunately received the letter and understood my mother's veiled request to let her parents know she and Zenia had survived. Writing this letter was a fortuitous move, as Bronia had a relation in the Communist Party and was thus fairly immune from any repercussions for having received the letter with a foreign stamp. Bronia wrote back to the coded address given by Valerie in the text of the letter, assuring her she could write back to her – of course with

few giveaway details – saying she would personally deliver any news
to her parents. So it happened that Bronia the school friend then
travelled by train from Malnava to Malta – it was 1947 – to where my
grandparents now lived renting a room, in a semi-detached cottage
they had once owned. My grandfather Jazeps had bought this cottage
on his retirement for his daughter Zenia even though the family lived
in Garkalne which was now just a pile of rubble on the ground. In
this small semi-cottage, there were three other families allocated to
share this limited space. In the one room in which Jazeps and Julija
lived, Bronia my mother's friend read out the letter from Valerie in
hushed tones, the precious letter which told them the news that their
girls were alive and safe in Germany. This resulted in days of tears
of gratitude mingled with tears of desolation in not being able to see
the two girls again. This form of roundabout contact was to continue
for several years and Bronia was able to write to my mother with
some guarded pieces of information about her parents and sister.
As a young child I remember my mother's conspiratorial attitude in
opening the 'letters from Bronia in Karsava' which continued for
decades and her telling me of her friend who had risked so much for
her.

At some point in 1945 my mother, armed with her Latvian high
school graduation papers and 1944 letter of acceptance to Riga's
medical school with her, tried her luck in enrolling at a German
university to fulfil the aim of becoming a doctor. Like other DPs in
camps around Germany she had picked up fairly fluent German. In
fact it was the only way that Hungarians, Poles, Latvians, Lithuanians,
Estonians, Romanians and Germans could communicate with each
other in the medley of languages surrounding them. To her immense
surprise Valerie was accepted at Bonn University in the latter part of
1945. She moved to Bonn where she managed to find a room to rent

in the house of an elderly lady, Mrs Esch, whose kindness she recalled all her life. She then worked feverishly on her German language skills and studied Latin (a requirement for medicine in those days) at some classes run at a high school in Bonn called the Beethoven Gymnasium. Even as a child I used to wonder how she could turn her mind to studying Latin in a situation of loss, physical pain (her back injury) and utter poverty but then this may have been what helped her cope. I once heard from a Latvian that a Lithuanian philosophy professor, who was an inmate of a concentration camp, had conducted classes in philosophy there to anyone who wanted to listen and who had not yet been killed and that pondering the problems of philosophy had occupied the minds of many of the suffering souls who listened to him.

Valerie enrolled for her five-year medical course with the assistance of a 'Red Cross' scholarship. This gave some minimal support but she also did part time work for a Lithuanian literature professor at Bonn University for whom she would copy out swathes of quotations in Russian (in which she was fluent) so he could use these passages in his lectures. Though she obtained a little money from this, and perhaps the Lithuanian professor had given her this work out of kindness to a fellow poor Balt, she told me she sometimes went to her medical classes on an empty stomach. She was helped by the occasional free food handed out at the University and at some point in her studies, met a young German girl studying dentistry at Bonn university – Ria Blömeke-Stake – a young Catholic woman from Münster, who became a lifelong friend and helped Valerie where she could. Valerie had the gift of making friends at a deep level of the soul and had a strong sense of the spiritual all her life. She also had extraordinary determination to get through her course even while enduring the loss of her family, a determination enabling her to focus on current tasks without demur. She was fortunate in that her sister Zenia at the same time enrolled in dentistry at Bonn University although not in the same year as Ria. Valerie and Zenia themselves related to me in later years that they could hardly believe they had done these courses in such difficult circumstances. Zenia finished her course shortly before my mother and met her future husband Lazar Kulic in Germany. Lazar was a handsome dark-haired Serb who had fought in the Royalist Serbian Army and was now also a DP. He was enrolled for a degree in Agricultural Science studies at Bonn University and was bowled over by the beautiful Zenia. He and Zenia decided to get married and see where they could be accepted as DPs. When they were accepted for Australia they looked to their new country with great hope and awaited their departure in 1949.

Meanwhile aunt Anna and cousin Veronica whom Valerie and Zenia had met in Riga and with whom they had escaped from Latvia had had a most dramatic time. They had met up with Anna's husband Jed at the pre-appointed place in Germany. Jed had fled Latvia overland and had nearly been killed several times as he crossed several countries in the hope of meeting up with his wife and child. As previously explained he was an 'undesirable' for both Nazi and Soviet regimes. His crime with the Germans was that he had helped Jews escape. His crime with the Soviet Regime was that he owned his own house and had run a small shop with his wife and made a small profit in business. He was a 'non-person' many times over. Anna, Jed and Veronica knew that their home in Feimani in eastern Latvia had been bombed long before. Jed finally arrived in Germany one day at the agreed-upon-meeting-place in a bedraggled state, not communicating much about what he had endured to get there. One can imagine the meeting after a long absence. Anna and Veronica said when they saw him again, Jed had one sock on one foot and one shoe on the other after his marathon journey. At last the family was united and its members could try their survival skills in a new setting, for they would need them in devastated post-war Germany.

Living in the displaced person's camp in Emden and later Göttingen, Anna, Jed, and their child Veronica engaged in some post-war trade among the ruins. They had a talent for business, as some people do, and having had past experience, they quickly used their skills in the frenetic barter economy which sprang up whereby one could trade potatoes for cigarettes, stockings for milk, butter for ham, coffee for sugar, in fact anything for anything. Veronica, who was younger than Valerie and Zenia, was a handy courier and recalled that after attending school in the DP camp, she then used to ferry all kinds of goods from one side of town to the other on a borrowed bicycle. She became an adept businesswoman and organiser at a very young age. She also attended a school for young Latvians which was set up in the displaced persons' camp and played basketball amid the ruins and debris of German streets with her schoolmates.

Her parents Jed and Anna were caught up in the interviews of the displaced by the IRO (International Refugee Organisation), were accepted for Australia and awaited the journey with immense gratitude and hope At that stage, when speaking to the Australian Immigration officers, they probably still did not realise where Australia was and would have tried to draw maps or borrow them to gain some impressions of their future country. In May 1950, they found themselves travelling by ship to the great Antipodean land of dreams, where they were sent to Greta migrant camp, not far from Newcastle, smaller than Bonegilla, and the setting of the movie *Silver City*, which tried to re-create the stories and setting of the post-war DPs. Soon after their arrival Jed and Anna were informed they were to be sent to Dalby in Queensland where they were appointed to work at the Gas Company to pay for their ship's passage. Poor Veronica, by then only 16, was separated from her parents and felt lost without them. She decided to take matters into her own hands, escape from Greta and join them up north. After what she experienced in war-time Latvia and in her post-war trading career in Germany, escaping from Greta was probably no big deal. Being enterprising she somehow got together enough money for a train ticket and went north on a seemingly endless journey to Brisbane which may as well have been to Patagonia or Timbuktoo, as much as she knew about it. She got to Brisbane, changed trains for Toowoomba and then finally made it to Dalby. The parents were overjoyed to see their daughter in Dalby where they all stayed for several years. Veronica did her training as a nurse at Dalby Hospital. She was one of Calwell's Balts, who being very attractive, caught the attention of many in the town. Later, after several years work in Dalby, the family moved to Sydney to live in Maroubra.

Meanwhile, after finishing their studies at Bonn University, Zenia and her new husband Lazar Kulic from Serbia, had also boarded a ship as part of Ben Chifley's Displaced Persons' program and sailed for Sydney in 1949. From there they were taken by train to Bathurst Camp, 172 kms to the northwest, where they lived for two years and where their son Michael was born. In fact Bathurst became the site of some unique events among the DPs – it was here that the very first New Australian Opera Company was formed which performed *Tosca* for the residents of the camp and for the wider Bathurst audience. It was also the place where the Polish DPs published the first edition of the *Tygodnik Polski*, a Polish Catholic weekly newspaper which survives to this day. Bathurst, smaller than Bonegilla, was also an ex-army camp and operated until 1952. Lazar had a job within the camp and paid back his 'passage' in this way.

Zenia had a most interesting time during her stay for while her dentistry degree from Bonn University was not recognised by any Australian authority, this did not prevent people learning about the fact that a newly graduated dentist was in the camp. It must have been a sensation for she got many enquiries. For wherever one goes in the world, there are people who have problems with their teeth. And in Bathurst there were camp dwellers with sore teeth and an inability to explain it all in English. And here in front of them in broad daylight was a beautiful newly arrived Balt who was a dentist and could speak German – the common language. It was clear that Zenia's skills were in high demand. Zenia related that somewhere in Bathurst (the camp was located outside the town), she found a second-hand foot-pedalled dentist's drill. How she and Lazar got it into the camp without anyone noticing no one knows but if they had survived World War II, why wouldn't they be able to smuggle a dentist's drill inside Bathurst migrant camp? And so while she was there, Zenia practised her newly found dental skills on the camp's inhabitants and saved a few extra pounds that way. Not that she demanded any fees. People were happy to pay a modest price for such service.

No one in authority ever found out, the patients were evidently happy and relieved that someone skilled could take away their pain. And Zenia would have accepted a lot less than the dentists beyond the camp. There was the extra bonus of Zenia – apart from the German she knew – speaking several languages and being able to communicate with patients in their own tongue. All this dentistry in Bathurst was to prove very useful when she finally moved with Lazar to Sydney for it helped pay the deposit on a house (albeit an old one with rotten floors needing many repairs) which was an unheard of thing for the DPs of that era. As things turned out, Zenia was never to practise dentistry again after this period in the camp, as her qualifications, like those of so many others, were not recognised and future ill health prevented her from ever taking matters further. I remember, however, seeing her second-hand dentist's drill in Sydney as she brought it with her as a prize possession when she and Lazar moved out of the camp. I never once complained of a toothache for fear she would call me to check it out for the drill did look an imposing machine. I think in our times it would be a definite antique of great value.

With her relations gone from Germany, my mother Valerie studied hard and finished her medical degree at Bonn University in mid-1950. She was the last of this family group of escapees from Latvia to board a ship in late 1950 – the *Skaugum IV* – on completion of her medical studies. She had been offered the chance for further studies in Canada, but felt that she should stay near whatever family she had, since returning to Latvia seemed ever more remote as the Stalinist years wore on. She signed her papers in Germany and received vacuous assurances that her medical degree would be recognised in

Valerie – third from left in the second row, standing with Latvian fellow refugees in Germany (Bremerhaven?) circa 1949 shortly before coming to Bonegilla in Australia

Australia (it was not, as many DPs who were doctors were to learn). My mother's years of medical study had ended in success and she even won an anatomy prize.

The day the results were put up she longed to celebrate with someone – but her parents were on the other side of the Iron Curtain and her sister and cousin were in Australia. With no Skype, internet or mobile phones at the time there was no-one to share her joy. There was not even the remote possibility of affording an overseas phone call as the sister and cousin had no phones in Australia and Valerie would have been too poor to contact them in this way, even if she knew how. So she stood alone near the exam board at Bonn University, read the results, and was ready to walk away to celebrate alone when some German medical students saw her, spoke to her, realised her situation and took her off to celebrate with them.

Then came the time for Valerie to pack for Australia and begin the journey to the mysterious place called Bonegilla. She bade Mrs Esch, her landlady in Bonn, an emotional farewell promising that she would keep in touch with her. In fact she did so for the rest of her life and sent her letters from Bonegilla as soon as she arrived. Then Valerie went to the port of Bremerhaven to board the ship bound for Australia in late 1950 with her old brown suitcase carrying all her worldly possessions and an old small guitar given to her by Mrs Esch as a keepsake. The threads of her journeys were taking her across seas further and further from her childhood land of happiness in Latgale. Now she was going on the longest voyage, across a great expanse of water and there seemed no going back. Her excitement would have been tempered by sadness and apprehension as she set out for Melbourne.

At the end of 1950, Valerie, along with long queues of DPs would have walked up the gangplank of the *Skaugum IV* at Bremerhaven and heard the ship's siren as they sailed away from Germany to the Antipodes. In fact, she was seasick a lot of the way and could not remember certain parts of the trip. During the voyage, however, she met some kind Latvian people, the Ludborzs family, who had also escaped from Latvia, having had many harrowing experiences to relate. As the Russian front advanced into Latvia, the Luborzes had tried to keep one step ahead. Lidija Ludborz, who was a young girl at the time had left her hometown of Karsava in eastern Latvia with her mother and two-week-old brother, and had actually traversed the entire country on foot and by horse and cart, finally reaching the Baltic port of Ventspils in the west in 1944.[124] Lidija recalls that the terrified Latvians she was with travelled in convoy, sleeping in forests, gathering what food they could until they reached Ventspils on the Baltic sea, and registered there with the Red Cross who happened to have an office there. In most parts of Eastern Europe the Red Cross was simply ignored or not allowed to see those it wanted to see most – the concentration camp inmates and those in gulags – but there happened to be a Red Cross office in the coastal town of Ventspils. Lidija and her family were all taken aboard a German transport ship and ended up in a DP camp. Once within Germany they were moved from place to place – the story of so many of the DPs. Lidija recalls the bug-infested beds and getting ill there. She also recalls what would be a momentous event in retrospect, and one without which she would not have survived to tell the tale, namely, leaving Dresden the day before it was destroyed. She related the following:

> We actually left Dresden on the night that the allied bombing raids razed the city and I very distinctly remember the long snaking train moving out at a snail's pace as the sky was lit up with flares for the bombers.[125]

Lidija actually could remember seeing Dresden burning from

a distance and gazed on it after it had been destroyed. Her father had escaped separately, and, after near brushes with death, arrived emaciated and hungry in Germany and was later reunited with his wife and children.

Carrying its human cargo, all with extraordinary stories of survival, the *Skaugum IV* sailed into Port Melbourne on 11 December 1950 and the DPs walked ashore with their old suitcases, tentative steps, no doubt with tentative smiles and hungry eyes, taking in the details of this strange southern place. They would have walked in orderly fashion to the train that was to take them north to the strange sounding place called Bonegilla. They came as hopeful adoptees of a sunburnt country and bearers of memories of war, loss and a past whose contours were etched into their hearts and souls, and from whose horror they had formed their understanding of life, and from whose ashes they hoped to start again and give something to their new land.

9

And on to Bonegilla

Bogdan arrived in Bonegilla on 21 February 1950 and Valerie on 11 December 1950. They were part of the ongoing groups being transported to Australia. A few years before, the first group of displaced persons to arrive by train in Bonegilla in December 1947 consisted of 839 men and women solely from the Baltic countries of Estonia, Lithuania and Latvia whose numbers rapidly increased in subsequent movements. They were aboard the *General Stuart Heintzelman II*, the first ever ship carrying DPs to Australia. These Baltic survivors of war must have lined the decks in fervent anticipation, scanning the horizon for their first glimpses of their new home, eyes rising and turning, gazing at water, sand, horizons, trees and the unknown. Was this the moment the journey would begin anew or was it a point among the uncountable, inaccessible threads leading to other yet unseen endings? Was too much written into the souls and fates of the DPs already, for this to be a true beginning or was the previous horror a template which would threat its way into the future lives they were to live?

Whatever the DPs thought as they drew nearer, their hopes knew no bounds and they expressed great willingness to adapt, and to do what settlers in Australia had done long before them, to engage with its newness and to try to understand the mysteries of this great south land. After seeing Hamburg, Bremerhaven, Gottingen, Berlin and

191

Bonn and many places in Europe en route, nothing would ever have appeared quite the same as Bonegilla siding – framed by grass, reeds, gum trees, squawking magpies and clear blue sky as far as the eye could see. Trucks were sent to pick up the new arrivals to take them to their new home, that strange looking, ex-army, tin barrack town which gradually appeared in outline surrounded by eucalypts and goannas.

The new arrivals disembarked from the trucks at some point and, as a photograph from the times shows, they walked two by two through the bush in orderly formation carrying their suitcases to their first room and first bed in their new country. Here was a welcome and a home after so long. These were Calwell's 'beautiful Balts' with their strange names and strange stories – the 'first wave' – those with no home, no country, no papers other than the designated ones which called them 'alien' residents as part of the 170,000 displaced people Calwell had agreed to accept.

Calwell and the Singing Balts

When this first group of Balts had arrived, the Albury newspaper, the *Border Morning Mail* of 9 December 1947 carried the headline 'Attractive Girls from Baltic countries'. What was striking about the new arrivals was their youth. Their average age was 24 and the oldest among them was 32.[126] Groups from Albury and Wodonga, such as volunteers from the Lutheran and Catholic churches, the YWCA, the CWA, Rotary and Apex arranged welcomes and provided some support. Members of the organisations took the new arrivals shopping, some taught them Australian idioms such as 'she'll be right mate', yet for others it would have been a strange meeting of different worlds.

Some of the newly arrived Bonegillians applied themselves as soon as possible to cleaning their rooms, and must have had myriad thoughts as they settled down to their first night's sleep in Australia. The next day the process of adapting would have begun in earnest – they would have learned the times of their language classes and acculturation lessons which had been prepared for them. After all, this was Bonegilla Reception and Training Centre – the new immigrants had to be trained and prepared to adapt to Australia. They were part of the Australia's new revolutionary approach to migration, in the largest planned intake of immigrants which had ever occurred in its history thus far.[127] While the British had been the immigrants of first choice, the influx of East European DPs introduced a variety and mix of peoples to Australia which was changing the country in unforeseen ways. In fact they did change the country in bringing their perceptions of another world and their impact may have played a part in the abandonment of the White Australia Policy in 1972.

Meantime, Arthur Calwell planned his moves in the context of this policy, which in effect was pro-British, and he was keen to assuage any fears on the part of Australians that they were being invaded by strange non-British foreigners. Not long afterwards, he visited Bonegilla on 18 December 1947 and toured the facilities. He was treated to songs in Estonian, Latvian and Lithuanian. Of course, with their propensity to sing, the Balts had already formed themselves into small choirs and were to form choirs in various capital cities once they moved out into the community (choirs which still exist to this day). He must have looked approvingly, however, on the 'new' songs which the group had learned under the careful direction of an Australian teacher. There was 'Three Blind Mice' – which no doubt ended up as 'Sree Blind Mice' and what must have sounded even more interesting – 'It's a Long Road to Tipperary.'! In the various tones of Baltic accented English ('It's a lonk rot to Tippeh – rairy'), this might have been the most unique rendition of the latter song ever done in Australia. It is a pity no recording was made of this event. Calwell listened to the singing in Bonegilla, and was delighted, taking it as a measure of the success of his new immigration program. He wished the newcomers well in their attempt to make a new life in their adopted country. A new era in Australian migration history had begun.

The international town grows

The ex-army huts, the streets, tracks, dormitories and surrounding eucalypts echoed with the strange tones of Lithuanian, Latvian Estonian conversation and the ubiquitous German, the 'lingua franca' the refugees had learned in the DP camps and which they could use to communicate with those of differing languages. Bonegilla was rapidly becoming a 'little Eastern Europe' in the Australian bush whose residents were most keen to learn English. Soon immigrants from Hungary, Poland, the Ukraine, Yugoslavia, Czechoslovakia among other nations followed. This first wave were unique in that they had been truly displaced, they were the global homeless and did not leave a country which was 'theirs'. There were no comparisons to be made with a former land, no return journey possible to the home country if unhappy, no path but the one of adaptation to the society of post-war Australia.

Bonegilla was designed to hold up to 7,000 people at any one time with the possibility of 100 more being accommodated in tents. The layout of the camps was such that there were 24 blocks and 30 or more huts made up one block – which is a fairly spread out area when one imagines it. It would certainly take a long time to walk from one end of the camp to the other – the entire area of Bonegilla took up 130 hectares and some aerial photos of the time still survive and are on display in the Bonegilla Migrant Experience Museum. As previously stated the individual dormitories and rooms had unlined

Entrance to Bonegilla (From the Bonegilla Collection at Albury Library Museum)

Arthur Calwell with young Balts on a visit to Bonegilla camp in the late 1940s
(From the Bonegilla Collection at Albury Library Museum)

Bogdan Skowronski up a gum tree near Bonegilla shortly after arriving as a DP in 1950

Typical barracks which provided accommodation in Bonegilla
(From the Bonegilla Collection at Albury Library Museum)

School time in Bonegilla
(From the Bonegilla Collection at Albury Library Museum)

A photo of Bonegilla arrivals
(From the Bonegilla Collection at Albury Library Museum)

tin walls and there were ventilation gaps between the wall and the ceiling, and this would have surely puzzled the DPs who had come from colder climates where insulation was taken seriously.

In each block there was a mess hall, kitchen, pit toilets and supervisor's office. Each of the huts held about 26 people, dormitory style, and each person was allocated linen and grey woollen blankets as well as crockery and cutlery and a cup. The centre's facilities eventually included a large hospital, three churches, a movie theatre, library, primary school, canteen, butcher, barber, police station and three banks. The administration area provided a paymaster, social services, CES, customs, alien registration and information centre.[128] Bonegilla residents had to apply for permission to leave the camp. The initial Bonegilla arrivals were initially registered as 'aliens'. As the National Archives website explains of the designation:

The threat posed by world war during the 20th century twice caused the Australian Government to require all 'aliens' (i.e., non-British subjects/foreign nationals living in Australia) to register with local authorities. Registration was required between 1916 and 1926, and again between 1939 and 1971. Alien registration forms may include information on the ship and date of arrival, date and place of birth, occupation, marital status, a physical description or photograph, and addresses in Australia but this policy did not persist past the first few years.[129]

With their Alien registration forms, the DPs set about trying to find work and plan a stable future. The first talk as a group that the new arrivals would have heard would have been from the first overall supervisor of the camp whose name was Commandant ex-Major Kershaw. As Glenda Sluga explains in her account of the

period in 'Bonegilla Reception And Training Centre: 1947-1971',
the infelicitous term 'commandant' which the new arrivals would
have heard clearly enunciated to them, was changed to 'director'.
According to Sluga's account, Kershaw did have something of a
no-nonsense, gung-ho commandant about him and gave rousing
speeches to the newly arrived migrants as if he were an army chief
addressing his troops before battle. He even told them all how lucky
they were, and how his own grandmother had not travelled by train
with padded seats in them as they had from Melbourne, but had to
go on foot to destinations in her youth. One wonders how much he
knew of the recent war experiences and backgrounds of the people
before him and the successive traumas they had endured.[130] In the
circumstances, it must have seemed quite sinister to some of the
new arrivals who had themselves survived or had family members
endure concentration camps to hear of a 'Camp Commandant' as
their immediate authority. Likewise it would have seemed strange
to be segregated into men's and women's groups on arrival, without
knowing what was to happen next. The first DP group had much to
reflect on in what they saw. With time, however, when these details
were altered and other staff came on the scene, the inevitable dynamic
of Bonegilla's international society took over. Subsequent directors
were ex-Sgt Dawson (from 1952) and Colonel Guinn (from 1954).
The latter had previously been in charge of Bathurst Reception
Centre and could not quite let go of his military background as his
words indicate:

> For thousands of years the army has provided the answer
> for the best system of handling large numbers of human
> beings, covering accommodation, feeding, transport,
> etc. Having commanded a brigade enforcement centre
> in addition to an Infantry battalion I had more than the

necessary experience to control and supervise a Migrant Centre.[131]

In this 'ever onward and forward' atmosphere, in the constant stream of arrivals, departures, talks, job placements and classes, people were sent all over Australia to wherever the needs were greatest at the time. Glenda Sluga explains that within a few days of arrival the newcomers would be taken to a centre where they matched with job vacancies. There was a payment of twenty-five shillings made to each person on arrival. After one week, one pound was deducted from this weekly amount and each person was left with five shillings, enough to buy a few supplies and stamps. Hence, most were keen to take on a new job and begin a new life, wherever fate led them. The employment allocation out of the first group, as Sluga records, included: 25 employed at Keira Dam, 10 in the timber industry, 200 as fruit harvesters, 100 as forestry workers, 65 in railway constructions, 16 in salt harvesting, 15 in flax production and 12 in the newspaper industry.[132]

Stories and first impressions

There are many stories of 'first contact' with Bonegilla some of which have been recorded. The Migration Heritage website has gathered some of the stories of the new arrivals such as that of Elizabeth Mergl, of Hungarian origin, who arrived with her husband in 1949:

> The SS *Nelly* sailed from Naples. It was so crowded – I think 1,600 (passengers) – we had almost standing room only. I was seasick from the first minute to the last; it was a very long journey because I was continuously sick. The journey was four weeks. We arrived 13 November in Melbourne. The first impression was[of] some wharfies

on the dock and a man had big lettuce under his arm, breaking the leaf off and eating it. That's what we had seen first. That was shocking to us. I had never seen that before!

We didn't care much about anything, just getting off the ship. Then we got herded to some train, which was also very crowded. We made a couple of friends on the way. We still have one person who came with us; she is now 92, older than I. They had brought us to Bonegilla and we were [there] for two or three weeks. It's a camp where it's a big room and just beds, and that was your home, the one bed. For meals you had to go in a dining room and they fed us whatever they cooked. It was strange to us because we (had) never eaten lamb before and it didn't taste nice; probably it was mutton. It was food, we didn't complain, we had a place where it was supposed to be peace. We had a wonderful, wonderful 50 year peace here.[133]

In this passage there is some irony in the fact that an refugee from Soviet-controlled Hungary sets eyes on a wharfie – who may well have had glowing ideas of Communism – and that the worlds would have been separated not only by geography but also by an abyss of understanding, one knowing at close quarters what Communism was capable of and the other seeing it from a safer distance. There seemed little way of communicating the realities of the Soviet world to Antipodean sympathisers who were never likely to come up against them.

Sometimes organisational details at Bonegilla fell through the cracks but were dealt with stoically by most newcomers, in the way the previous years of hardship in German displaced persons' camps had been dealt with. The following account is of a Slovenian refugee Anton Potocnik who stayed a short while at the camp:

I migrated to Australia on the *Skaubryn* in May 1951. When we boarded the ship (in Bremerhaven) we were lined up in a single line, trousers down, and there was [sic] doctors and nurses walking past, checking for diseases. We had to work on the ship. My job was to keep the showers and toilets clean. It was a mess on that ship. We only had a Captain, First Officer, not many engineers and in the kitchen there were only two chefs. There were roughly 1,400 of us on the ship, which was very crowded. That ship wasn't a passenger ship. It was a converted cargo ship, especially for refugees. In the room where I was in, there were 48 of us. There were some families on the ship, but the majority were young single blokes like myself …

I knew nothing about Australia before I arrived. All we saw in school books in Slovenia was a map of Australia; sometimes with a kangaroo in the middle of it, sometimes an Aborigine with a spear. That's all I knew about the country. We arrived in Melbourne on 26 June 1951 and spent the night on the ship. Next day we boarded the train to Bonegilla migrant camp where we stayed for roughly two weeks. We were again searched on arrival at Bonegilla. When we got to the camp we were given aluminium plates and two blankets. Some got packets of Aspros, some packets of Bex. We got to the barracks – five beds in there. Three had mattresses, two didn't. I had a bed which didn't, so I used the blankets on top of the wires. Because of this I had nothing on top of me. In June 1951 it was very cold in Bonegilla, ice outside. We slept in our clothes. I never took my clothes off all the time I was in the camp.[134]

In the early shock of adaptation, Bonegilla residents have all kinds of first memories, some similar to these quoted above, some positive, some negative. Where my father Bogdan was concerned his recollections of the first days were perhaps piquantly Australian. He told me that he got a short term job chopping wood at or near the camp shortly after arrival. In a photo of the time he stands on a sturdy branch, having climbed up high on one of the eucalyptus trees, and posed for a photo taken by one of his workmates. He is only twenty-two. His hair is swept back, over his high forehead and high cheekbones, and he exudes energy, looks meditative, with hope triumphing over the enigma in his gaze, though his clothes hang on his too thin frame. One working day, he brought some bread with him to have at break time. Carefully he put it down on a fallen tree trunk on which he sat and looked away for a few seconds. Soon afterwards he was surprised by a light flurry of noise and then saw a possum making off into the scrub with the entire loaf of his recently purchased bread. He was dumbfounded, stared at the scrub and took a few seconds to ponder the devious ways of this thieving marsupial. He never forgot this early introduction to his new country. He told me it took some getting used to seeing possums in and around the camp – they came into one's room at night or ran all over the roof – a very iconic initiation to Australian fauna.

Others experienced continual struggle in their efforts to adapt. Denise Hutchinson (née Kraus), the Australian-born daughter of Stan and Marta Kraus (of Czech, Ukrainian and Polish background), who arrived in Bonegilla in 1951, recounted her parents' story to me. Stan and Marta sailed to Australia on the *Liguria* which broke down in the Indian Ocean and was towed to Fremantle. They then changed to the ship *Nelly*, and went on to Melbourne, sometime at the end of January/early February 1951 from where they caught the train to Bonegilla. Denise who was born at Albury Base Hospital and later became a medical doctor, recalls:

I thought they stayed there (i.e., Bonegilla) a long time because it was so much talked about but apparently it was only a couple of weeks ... Dad was assigned some spray painting job, and Mum was sent to the Toora Hotel as a housekeeper, with her Polish friend Jozefa. Apparently they ran away after 3 months, they weren't being paid properly by the owner, an ex-AFL star, and went to Melbourne where Mum married Dad, and went back to Wodonga with him. They lived in a little farm house at Barnawartha, a hamlet near Wodonga. and when she was about 5 months pregnant with me, a bush fire swept through and they ran away with only a suitcase. After that they lived in a garden shed, at the back of a house in Tallangatta Rd, Wodonga, owned by a nice Lithuanian couple called Bartasius, and this is where I spent my first few months. I remember mum telling me she was drying my clothes in front of a kerosene stove, a single burner where she also cooked, and Dad worked on the roads. Dad and about another 6 Czechs were swindled by another Czech entrepreneur Mr Mucha (Mr Fly) who got them all to work for him for nothing for 6 months promising them all a share in fabulous riches when he built up his garage business. He even offered to 'invest' Mum and Dad's bush fire relief money, till mum kicked him out.

Stan Kraus, a lively, intelligent, genial and kind man, a born raconteur who was ready for all manner of unpredictable events, then moved to work on the Snowy Mountains Scheme which involved extended periods of time in the Snowy Mountains. It must have seemed to him and to Marta that they were back in Europe when they saw the snow beginning to fall there. After these initial years and the earlier disruptions and adventures surrounding Bonegilla, Cooma and Cabramurra, the family moved to Canberra where they finally settled and where Denise lives with her husband Michael and sons, Henry and David and where Marta still lives at the time of writing, Stan having passed away several years ago. The brief stay in Bonegilla and the years of work on the Snowy Mountains scheme left indelible memories of pioneering adventures and the family always vividly remembered this period of their lives.

The prospect of being separated from the family weighed heavily on some of the newly arrived migrants given what they had gone through in the Nazi years. Bruce Pennay recounts the story of 'John Z' from Czechoslovakia who came to Bonegilla in 1949:

> John Z, aged 7 … remembered his father lost his social service benefits because he refused to go to Cooma. His father did not want to be separated from his family again, as he had been when he was sent to a Nazi work camp. When the next job offer did not provide sufficient family accommodation, he negotiated a foster agreement in Latin with the local priest for John to go to an Albury couple. They used Latin to make the arrangement.[135]

In contrast to most people who stayed in Bonegilla only a few weeks, Bogdan and Valerie, arriving separately in 1950, managed to obtain jobs in the camp itself, which gave them a different kind of experience. There was not the same sense of urgency or immediate need to pack and leave that other new arrivals experienced. Bogdan and Valerie knew they would have to stay put to serve out their labour contract for the next two years and so Bonegilla became their world for the next seven years. After his stint at chopping wood, Bogdan got a job in the local camp hospital as a medical orderly although this was a general description of a job that entailed other duties. Papers of the time, just before his departure six years later list him as a 'senior medical orderly' but he also helped patients with interpreting and translating due to his skill at languages and friendly nature. He was gifted with a desire for precision, and found pleasure in spending time searching for 'just the right word' when translating. His social facility and ability to listen enabled him to learn English rapidly. Within a few years he spoke with the fluency of an ABC news announcer, and in later years could pepper his conversation with quotations from Shakespeare, Orwell and George Bernard Shaw. He never became a professional translator, except that he was always asked, even in his eventual workplace at the Sydney Water Board, to translate technical documents. Just out of interest he once translated a book from English to Polish (a work about Talleyrand), keeping the longhand written pages in a folder. Like many immigrants who missed out on years of formal education, he read widely and in the process developed an extraordinary inner life and applied his mind to all he encountered. As a child I recall he often quoted lines from Shakespeare's *The Tempest* to me, standing in semi dramatic pose, as if he were an actor at the Globe Theatre saying with deep feeling: 'We are such stuff as dreams are made on, and our little lives are crowned with a sleep.'

As is well documented, the educational qualifications and abilities of the new post-war arrivals made little difference as to the initial jobs they received. They were all 'labourers' or 'domestics' in all the varieties of meaning these words took on, even if they had previously been professors, lawyers or doctors This disturbed some arrivals, but others took it more philosophically. My mother, Valerie, obtained work in the Bonegilla camp hospital, ostensibly as a nurse, a 'domestic', but in reality, as time went on, she was entrusted with medical tasks by the doctors working there, though she was never formally designated as a doctor. This was part of the colliding worlds of virtual reality in which many of the DPs lived. The doctors working at the hospital treated her as a colleague, even if she was only paid the same as every other DP worker.

It was during this work at Bonegilla Hospital that Valerie met my father Bogdan. They must have seen each other a lot in the hospital amidst the comings and goings of the patients. They would have had much to share regarding their previous experiences. They were both alone and single and would have been able to share the difficulties of getting news from their respective families in Soviet occupied Eastern Europe. They would have shared views on the Soviet takeovers of both their countries and the news of the gulags, something shared by most residents in the camp. In the time off work they evidently enjoyed dancing, as a photo of the time shows them waltzing in what must have been a dance organised at the camp. The dress Valerie is wearing has frills, and she must have had it made by some of the enterprising seamstresses in the camp, for few could afford to pay for new clothes sold in shops at Albury or Wodonga.

My mother was a dark-haired beauty, with brown eyes and a slim waist. She had a wistful, dreamy air as a young woman according to the Lidija Ludborz, who had travelled with her on the ship to Port Melbourne and who called her 'an angel'. Valerie would have spoken to my father in German as their common language. Bogdan would have kissed her hand on meeting her, a habit which many of the East Europeans kept from the old world. With time they became engaged and were married in 1951 in the Catholic church in Bonegilla itself, a corrugated iron structure with simple benches inside for pews, a simple altar and cross and some wooden steps outside the front door. Father Auburn from the Wodonga Catholic parish officiated at the ceremony. My mother's wedding dress and my father's dashing bow tie stand out against the stark simplicity of the surroundings. There were a few camp friends at the wedding and my mother was again in a frilly white dress, which again must have been made by one of the local camp tailors or borrowed for the occasion. As they had virtually no money, there would have been nothing available for a honeymoon and no doubt they were back at their jobs soon after the wedding. They were allocated a room in the camp near the hospital which was a step up in the world from the original dormitories which held anything up to 20 people. Sometimes when there was an overflow, tents were set up outside the camps.

Identity and trauma

It is of interest to note the effect of non-recognition of prior education would have had on many DPs, a situation different from that which came into effect several decades later. Those DPs who arrived in the post-war years, with European university qualifications, have stories to tell of the non-recognition of degrees in Australia, having been assured otherwise in Germany. This would have compounded the recent experiences of trauma on persons who had, in many cases, lost their families, their country, former lives and indeed their sense of identity. In fact, writing of the sense of dislocation among the post-war refugees, as early as 1966, James Jupp, following up some post-war arrivals, notes the 'high rate of mental and marital breakdown amongst East Europeans which continues into the present, some fifteen years after most of them arrived. War experience is a major factor in mental collapse.'[136] This was the sad fate to be faced by many of the camp inhabitants, an as yet unknown legacy of the wartime experiences which many tried to but could not overcome. Thus the beginnings in the new land could not always overlay what the DPs had endured, for trauma and loss have their own dynamic and impact on a person's life. Of course, the longer term effects on the DPs were largely not evident in the hopeful young arrivals during their time in Bonegilla and other reception camps; and people differ in their ability to assimilate traumatic experiences into their lives, some having more constitutional vulnerability than others. Sadly it was to be an important issue in the years to come in many DPs' lives, as I was to see in various ex-refugees, but in the meantime the young arrivals lived on hope, planned their futures and did their best to integrate their past dreamings and more recent nightmares into their new bushland life. In any case, the mental health of the arrivals was largely a non-issue in the Australian migrant camps, apart from cursory reference in speeches, and organisations such as STARTTS, which directly deals with the effects of trauma on individuals, was not even on the horizon and was not established till 1988 in Fairfield in Sydney.

During the DP phase of migration, post-trauma research was not well known, nor had much of its longer term effects been studied. Post Traumatic Stress Disorder was not included into the Diagnostic Manual (DSM III) until 1980, in response to the Vietnam war veterans' insistence on the deleterious effects of trauma. While there had been some study done on Holocaust survivors and other victims of the Second World War, (e.g., by H. Krystal in *Massive Psychic Trauma*, 1968), it would take a number of decades for researchers to deepen their understanding of trauma and its insidious longer term effects.[137] As a young child happily running around Bonegilla with no idea that I was a future 'psychologist in the making' there was much to observe then even from a child's perspective, though often the 'sense' did not come to me till many years afterwards.

Bogdan getting about in Bonegilla on a bicycle

*On his wedding day, Bogdan stands with his best man
with Bonegilla huts in the background*

Bogdan and Valerie on their wedding day in Bonegilla's small Catholic church in 1951

Valerie (first on left) with her fellow nurses and doctors of Bonegilla Hospital in the mid-1950s

Valerie (third from the left) with medical staff at Bonegilla hospital standing amidst the hills of Albury

Bonegilla Camp Hospital, children's ward. (Original in the Immigration Photographic Archive, 1946 – Today, held at the National Archives of Australia in Canberra)

Given this post-war psychological context, it must have come as quite a shock to some of the educated new arrivals to hear their qualifications described by Commandant Kershaw as bogus, as a commentator of the time observed:

> The group that I travelled with contained two doctors, a veterinarian, several lawyers and other professional people, who were given a reception address by the camp commandant in which it was stated that it was no use their showing diplomas to employers, etc, because everyone (in Australia) knew they had been bought on the black market in Europe.[138]

I think Kershaw had left by the time my mother arrived, but one can only imagine the thoughts of people hearing this appraisal of their years of effort at university. The effect of such talks must have dispirited some greatly, but other professionals, realising they had little choice, just got used to the fact that they had to do menial jobs on arrival in Australia. It was not uncommon for labourers to address their fellow labourer professionals as 'professor' or 'doctor', passing a brick saying 'For you Herr Doctor' or 'Take this Herr Professor' – perhaps a sign of respect for their peers who had been so obviously robbed of professional recognition and identity, but also a carry over of the European habit of addressing a professional person by his or her profession's name, instead of using the surname. Thus one might be called 'Mr Engineer' if one was an engineer or 'Mr Dentist' if one was a dentist. I heard these titles often in my childhood, even if the recipients worked as labourers, clerks and cleaners. But these titles were not insisted on and with time their use faded away – there was a sense of 'being in it together' and facing the challenges of life in a new country. As regards the difficulties of the DP doctors in adjusting to their new situation a book was written on this very subject in 1975 by Egon Kunz entitled *The Intruders* which details the enormous and varied difficulties facing the medically qualified new arrivals.[139]

In my mother's case, I think she decided that staying in Bonegilla was as good a start as any she might have in her new country and some initial experience in the hospital might even help her in the future. She was only twenty-four on arrival and had her Bonn University medical degree papers with her when she came to Australia, unlike others who lost their degrees and identity papers during the war, or others who were deprived of a university education because of war. There were, according to Kunz, nearly three thousand medical doctors among those displaced in post-war Europe and the IRO (International Refugee Organisation) set up a board to help verify the credentials of those who had lost their papers. But even if they did recover their papers, it turned out that their degrees were mostly not recognised in Australia (as with dentists, vets and pharmacists) and the consequences of this exclusion by local professional groups caused a great deal of suffering. Of course some people were like my enterprising Aunt Zenia, Valerie's sister, who, as mentioned, happily plied away as an 'underground' dentist in Bathurst camp, with eager patients in dental pain at her door.

Some others among the DPs had had their university studies interrupted by the war and were never able to take them up again. Bela Haffner, of Hungarian and German background, who found he was alternately living in Hungary and then Yugoslavia during the war, fled the Soviet advance just before he was to do his final exams in medicine in Serbia. He did not have the chance to do the exams again after he migrated to Australia and worked at various jobs, including a period in the NSW Railways, as he had to provide for his wife and child. This story is similar to that of many other highly educated people who arrived and had no chance to do the required exams in their new country.

Where Valerie was concerned, perhaps the Bonegilla medical experience helped, as it gave her time to consider her options. Photos of the time in Bonegilla show her wearing a white coat and stethoscope around her neck. After she left Bonegilla, Valerie was later able to have her degree recognised in Sydney, after doing some exams and clinical work because of the assistance of a kind doctor she met. She worked for several years in her chosen profession at Marrickville District Hospital and as an assistant in various surgeries, before serious illness overtook her and cut short her professional life. Despite this, she did at least have the chance to put her medical skills to use for a time and work at her chosen profession. So many others never had the chance to put their degrees to use, a great loss of talent which could have been used at the time but which was sacrificed for the pressing economic and political narratives of the time.

Adapting to day to day camp life

As youthful Bonegilla residents, Bogdan and Valerie mixed with others in the camp after their working day. There were get-togethers in the camp where people dressed up in such evening clothes as they could muster together, to pay a visit to someone else's room. I recall going to other rooms for social visits and to the 'Mess' with my parents to eat at nights, though eating there was voluntary. As I recall there were wooden table which seated eight or more residents who sat eating the camp fare in such communal rooms. The food was cooked in bulk and because of its ready availability it was often mutton. This was an object of mystification to several newcomers, as few had eaten mutton before coming to Australia, but I do not recall any complaints from my parents, then or in later years. Of course some would have complained at the diet of frequent mutton but others just made do in gratitude for food on the table after the scarcities of the post-war years. I recall discussions between Bogdan and Valerie as to whether they would go to the mess or use some other tinned food they had in their room. The memories of Eastern European pickled vegetables, herrings, sprats, rye bread and potato salad would have been very distant by now and locked away in the halcyon days of childhood. However cravings are cravings and there were things that people searched for in Bonegilla or beyond in Albury. I remember my mother sometimes holding a large opened tin of herrings like a prize possession in our room and preparing it with tomatoes and onions with a gleam in her eye. We all ate this with fresh bread for dinner instead of the mess food some nights. East Europeans like herrings a lot – it is an incurable trait – and have untold ways of preparing them. In post-Soviet Eastern European supermarkets there are entire aisles devoted to varieties of herring and smoked fish as I discovered when I returned to visit Latvia and Poland in later years, walking by the barrels and vats of herrings in amazement. When I see herrings in oval tins with a red label which are still sold in supermarkets in Australia I cannot help but think with affection of those nights of quickly rustled up cuisine in Bonegilla.

My parents made friends with a young Estonian couple in the camp called the Malts, and I recall playing with their daughters Katri and Reti, both cheerful young girls around my age. The Malts went later to live in Melbourne and remained in contact for many years afterwards. They would no doubt have had long term jobs in the camp as had the Skladals, a Czech family, whom my parents befriended. I played with their daughter Annetta who was all of two years older than me and who like me had her hair in plaits with ribbons tied in. This fancy plaiting was standard for the young girls of Bonegilla. The

Bogdan, Valerie and Wanda in the camp

Valerie walking with young charges amidst the huts of the camp

Author at age 3 in Bonegilla

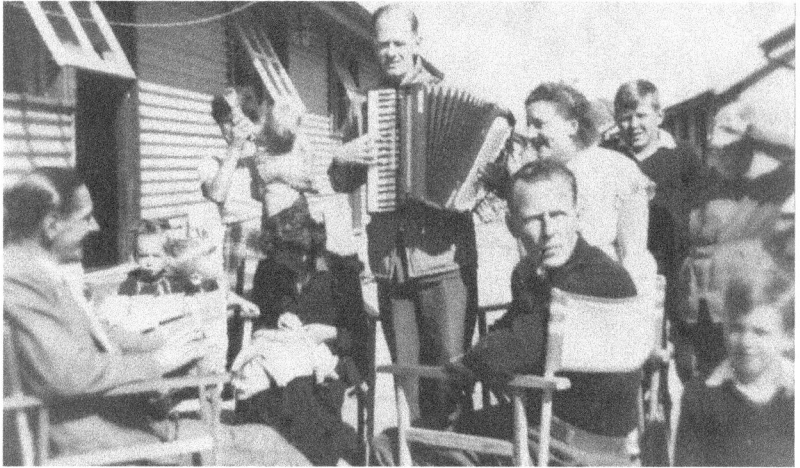

Improvised entertainment at the camp. 'Henry Bos is Playing the Accordion'
(From the Bonegilla Collection at Albury Library Museum)

Skladals later went to live in Canberra – before Bogdan and Valerie left – and this would have been a difficult parting. They left to live in the Canberra suburb of O'Connor and we all promised to meet each other again, which we did. The names of Katri, Reti and Annetta were a joyful refrain for me, like a windchime intoning delightful melodies of carefree periods of childhood in Bonegilla. Their names rang out so often from my lips during and after play, that long after we had left the camp. I kept saying their names to myself during childhood. And yes, I was very fortunate to have the chance to meet up with them again, once we had left the camp.

There was much discussion at nights and what to do and where good jobs might be among the longer term residents of the camp such as the Malts and Skladals. Groups of people used to visit someone's room at night where there was a small table set out with a few little treats, and perhaps glasses for tea, coffee or something stronger. I remember there were various groupings of the Skladals, the Malts, a 'Dr Rog' and a 'Dr Schnurr', and if I am not mistaken the latter two both went later to the United States and pursued their medical careers there, thinking it too difficult to redo their degrees in Australia. There were not so many barriers to professional recognition in America as there were here. Much of the discussion in the evenings was beyond my ability to understand as I was a young child but I do recall the tone of planning, at times conspiracy, a sense of urgency in the attempt to find a way to adapt and always forge ahead. Cigarette smoke often filled the air and plots were hatched as people exchanged views as to what they thought other places in Australia were like. I sat on the knees of various people and enjoyed exchanging a word here and there and apparently picked up conversational phrases of various languages in this way. I had no idea where Sydney, Adelaide or Melbourne were – as far as I was concerned the whole world was Bonegilla and little existed beyond its borders. The easy ambience between people from different places was as natural as the air one breathed. My father recalled that I would say hello to the Hungarians in Hungarian, to the Czechs in Czech, using some Estonian words to the Estonians and so on. I don't know how much else I knew at the time but apparently I rattled away in German too. Of course to our children's minds it was just a fact of life that people got on and communicated in this way and we were blissfully unaware of any complexities beneath the surface, though we were aware of 'something else' – the sense of there being a 'place' and 'time' where our parents had lived before – a strange realm we had not yet come to know.

The young in Bonegilla

The pervasive presence of children in Bonegilla would have been a constant distraction for the DPs. Birthday parties were held where crowds of children crammed into the small rooms with simple cakes set out on the tables, if one were fortunate enough to have a table. I have a photo of a group of Bonegilla children, myself among them, getting highly excited as Mr Helmut Malt, our Estonian friend, handed out balloons to his excited little crowd who were in awe of this tall man with a booming voice who could reach almost to the ceiling. Mr Malt and his great voice (of course he joined the Estonian choir) gave him a position akin to that of Moses on Mount Sinai and the children hovered eagerly around him to catch balloons.

An account of children's experiences in Bonegilla is given in a booklet entitled *The Young at Bonegilla* by Bruce Pennay He notes that 'Bonegilla was very much a young person's place. Very few of the adults were over 35 years of age, though there were a few exceptions. Sometimes as many as one in three of the migrants and refugees were under 16 years of age. Migration was generally a preserve of the

Simple methods of bathing for the young in Bonegilla. (Original in the Immigration Photographic Archive, 1946 – Today, held at the National Archives of Australia in Canberra)

Part of a very serious Bonegilla kindergarten class circa 1956/7

Mr Malt, of Estonian background, handing out balloons. He was a much admired entertainer at children's birthday parties in Bonegilla — the father of Katri and Reti Malt

More fun at a multilingual Bonegilla birthday party where 3 or 4 languages might be spoken by the children

young.'[140] Arthur Calwell also saw a strategic advantage in bringing the young in saying, 'When we bring alien children here, they can be more readily assimilated, will learn English and will absorb the Australian point of view more quickly than adults.'[141] Initially workers at the camp sent their children to school in Wodonga and Mitta Junction where enrolments rose rapidly. In 1952 a primary school opened in Bonegilla enrolling the children of resident staff. Then in 1953 English classes were started for children who were in transit in the camp until their parents obtained work placements. Pre-school kindergartens began for children over two-and-a half-years of age and a crèche was established for the children of hospitalised parents. These and some other simple recreational facilities helped the children adapt and develop socially in their new environment.

In 1953 the children at Bonegilla participated with some excitement in the Coronation of Queen Elizabeth II. There were celebrations with party food, games, balloons, films and floral displays. Pennay notes that in 1954 five buses carried Bonegilla children to Benalla for the Royal visit and that on the way the children, displaying ardent royalist sympathies, giving resounding renditions of 'God Save the Queen' about eight times.'[142]

Adapting to Antipodean life, remembering the past

The old world graciousness of pre-war Europe where men kissed ladies' hands created quite a stir in Australian settings beyond the gates of Bonegilla. I think when Bonegillians tried it as a polite gesture with some Australian ladies, the women were either awestruck or confused. My father and mother must have gone to dances in Wodonga as my father recalled the strange attitudes of the Australian men towards Bonegillian men who invited various women to dance. The women seemed pleased but there were mistrustful if not downright hostile glances from the men in the town who had not witnessed such goings on before.

Christmas must have been a poignant time for many ex-DPs in Bonegilla and other migrant camps around Australia, but again some attempt was made to 'get together' and make do with what one had. Another photo of the time shows me sitting on my father's lap one Christmas, near a Christmas tree in our allocated room, obviously decorated with care with whatever was available and a bottle of wine or schnapps on the table. My father smiles but deep wells of thought emanate from his face.

Bogdan had not seen his mother or sister since he was a teenager. He had learned at some stage that his mother, Wanda Maria, who had been arrested in Lublin early in the war, had been released from Ravensbrück concentration camp in which she had been incarcerated for four years. She was now back in Poland, realising she had to face the future under Soviet tyranny. After a long painstaking search, Wanda Maria managed to find her daughter in an orphanage after, in her emaciated state, she had walked back a good deal of the distance to Poland from Germany, catching such transport as she could along the way. She did this with her sister Janina and Janina's daughter Jadwiga, as transport was hard to find and many railway lines had been destroyed. In the acute accommodation shortages in Poland at the time Wanda Maria and her newly found daughter Alicia faced the daunting task of finding a place to live. The new Communist authorities allocated people to apartments and rooms, sometimes three and four families sharing a small space. Eventually Wanda met a friend, Zofia Tydda, who was at present living in a flat in Lublin. As mentioned in an earlier chapter, Zofia's husband Antoni Tydda, technical head of Lublin's Aircraft factory who had escaped south in 1939 with one of their sons, Jerzy, was not permitted to take anyone else in this hastily organised escape and always thought he could return. In fact, after having fought with the British Airforce and surviving extraordinary experiences he would have been a prime candidate for the gulags and hence could not return and lived alone in penury longing to see his family. And thus it was Zofia who invited Wanda Maria, also without a husband, as were many Polish women after the war who had lost spouses due to death, disappearance or enforced separation by the new regime, to share a small apartment in Lublin. Zofia had been allocated a 'place' in this apartment which she had to share with another couple. One was only ever allocated a 'place' which was often not more than a bed in a crowded apartment. Zofia organised it with the new Communist housing allocations group that Wanda and Alicia could move in and that is where they all lived. The other couple who also lived there eventually moved out. Thus the one bedroom apartment became a long term home for them all.

Zofia had a son Janusz who was making his way home to be with his mother after surviving several battles. Janusz had been forced at gunpoint to join in the Polish-Soviet army after it entered Poland in 1944, after he spent several years hiding in Włodawa in the east of the country. The reason he hid there was that the Germans were after him in Lublin, as they wished to 'transform' him into a German because of his Old Prussian surname 'Tydda' – a transformation he and his mother refused. His mother Zofia, persuaded a man from Włodawa who sold vegetables illegally in Nazi occupied Lublin to take her son to safety away from the pursuing Germans. So it happened that Janusz was taken from Lublin hidden under a mass of old vegetables on a horse-drawn cart to Włodawa, where some villagers hid him for several years. However, when the Polish-Soviet army marched in they ordered him to join them on pain of death. He was with this group from then on and almost reached Berlin as part of the Soviet advance.

In any case, after the war when Zofia's son Janusz came home to the little apartment in Lublin, and set eyes on the young Alicia, a romance blossomed and in the course of time they got married and continued to live in the small apartment with the two respective mothers. Not only that, but when the three children came along – Janusz, Andrzej and Wojtek – the two grandmothers, two parents, and three children all continued to live in the same one bedroom apartment in Narutowicza Street in Lublin. This was not at all an uncommon accommodation story in post-war Poland. At times Wanda Maria and Alicia used to sit at the table in this small apartment and read letters from Bogdan who lived in a far away strange place called Bonegilla and who sent the communications in a circuitous way so as not to arouse suspicion. They heard that he had married a Latvian called Valerie and looked at the photos he sent of his new home. They no doubt heard that he and Valerie called their daughter Wanda Alicia, after Wanda Maria who survived the concentration camp and Alicia his sister.

While in Bonegilla, Bogdan scrimped and saved to buy a box camera, which was a prize possession. Many of our Bonegilla photos were taken with it and made their way to Poland and later to Latvia, as I found out later when I visited the relations who had them. I cannot look at a box camera without thinking of Bonegilla and the efforts my father made to steady the box, while giving instructions as to where to stand, and line up for the photo, almost like the 19th century photos in which one had to remain still for a long time. In one Christmas photo the room in which it is taken shows a few possessions that made up our little world – the old guitar my mother had been given as a gift by Mrs Esch, which she could not play, but which she hung on the wall in our room at Bonegilla as an affectionate and memorable decoration. There was a cane chair and little table, some books on a shelf made by my father. There was another purchase which would have cost a great deal and crops up in another photo: a little cream coloured AWA radio, typical of the era, which stood on the shelf, and to which my father listened regularly. He was interested in current events and even in those early years reflected and philosophised about them from a now Antipodean distance.

Deciphering new political realities from far away Bonegilla

The political realities of Communist controlled Eastern Europe were discussed by Bonegillians in the context of the post-war, new world order. Although they were told they had to 'forget the past' by those in charge at Bonegilla, they clearly could not. Displacement and dispossession do not equate to elimination of memories which are inescapably vivid but which need some 'translation' and 'processing' in a new context. Many of the DPs had families who were victims of the Soviet regime, some of whom were either murdered or incarcerated in gulags while others lived in fear – and all of this would have weighed heavily on their minds. Nearly all of the newcomers had some family members behind the Iron Curtain and it was only natural that they wondered what had happened to them, living in such a radically different political system.

The years of mass DP arrivals occurred when Stalin was still in power and it was very difficult to get news in or out of any East European country, hence any letter from far away would be an event of great importance. As previously explained my mother had set up a connection with her friend Bronia in Latvia and through her could communicate with her parents which involved Bronia travelling 60 kms by train to deliver a coded letter to my mother's parents. In fact many in the new Latvia were strongly urged to join the Communist Party. However if one had relations in the West one had a 'bad biography' as occurred with my mother's sister Bronia who was relieved of the pressure to join for the reason that she had sisters in Australia. Her daughter Inga who was put into the Komsomol Youth League, marching with children forced to celebrate Communist 'feast' days and other events, was also told as she grew up she had a 'bad biography' because of her aunts Valerie and Zenia in Australia.

Through her roundabout letter-sending method, Valerie had learned in 1948, while still in Germany, that her father had died in a railway accident. He had been ordered by the new Soviet authorities to leave retirement and return to work for the now Soviet-run railways as he had a good pre-war knowledge of the railway system and bridges. In fact the Soviet authorities valued his judgement and desperately needed his knowledge of pre-war plans to restore transport. Near the town of Aglona, however, my grandfather Jazeps had apparently stepped off a carriage and then – as the story was told – was hit by a train. This episode was so strange, as my grandfather was unlikely to have made such a simple error as not to notice a train coming at him. My aunt Bronia thought in reality he might have been murdered, as he had a good position in the railways and in the new Soviet world, disposing of people was not unusual if they had something you wanted. An envious worker might have thought that this was an effective way to create a new vacancy. The suspicion of murder was strong but unspoken for many years by Bronia and grandmother Julija. Valerie simply heard that he had had 'an accident' as he had stepped off a train. There was no proof and no way of asking for evidence of the accident, no matter how strange it seemed. Bronia told me in later years that she and her mother had to suppress their suspicions, reduced to living in penury in the little rented room of a house the family had once owned.

While newer, grimmer, post-war Soviet realities had taken over, there was little time to mourn in Bonegilla, as the need to work and earn one's daily bread was pressing. Despite all, the little details of life went on in the camp and people discussed the political situation 'over there' when they could, searching the newspapers of the day for any information they could find. A Bonegillian, Dr Kalinovski, wrote:

Everything in your system is well thought over and tries to help us in our future in Australia … (except) this political side of the primary education of new settlers: Having here good food and accommodations [sic], studying English language, Australian customs, mood of life, etc, the newcomer has no newspapers which he can understand, no political information, lectures, etc … more than that you directly advise him not to be interested in the politics [sic] and think of the future life, sport. Etc.[143]

Despite being advised 'not to be interested' in politics, many at Bonegilla could not help but be interested. However, these victims of Soviet realities in Bonegilla were not 'connected' to the political parties, nor to those groups which had something to say about Communism, though in later years this changed. They were puzzled by westerners with pro-Soviet views held from a safe distance. No-one asked them what they thought of Communism but the Bonegillians were experiencing its effects. They would have been puzzled at the existence of a Communist party in Australia, given what they knew.

Bogdan related to me in later years that he, with others in Bonegilla, had discussed history and politics in pre-war and post-war Europe and speculated about Soviet intentions. He had certainly followed the progress of the Battle of Dien Bien Phu in Vietnam in 1954 when Communists overran the French town. With some friends Bogdan constructed a very high aerial at Bonegilla so they could all listen to ever more dramatic broadcasts coming from South-East Asia and thus have the first hand information they sought. He even recalled – I don't recall how this was done – the final transmissions of the French broadcaster at Dien Bien Phu and the sound of gunfire accompanying it. My father was deeply affected by it. He could never forget this episode of history, quoting verbatim the exact words of the final transmission. He heard it all sitting and listening in Bonegilla under the tranquil Southern Cross, gum trees and swinging possums with his friends from all nations and the tall home-made antenna. Perhaps it stirred memories of the Warsaw Uprising and the desperate pleas his confreres had made to the West for help against the Nazi and Soviet take-over. The ever-encroaching advance of Communism would have been discussed in the camp. It must have been quite a sight amidst the huts and the gum trees, to hear the snap and crackle of the transmission and the serious faces contemplating what was to happen next in the Vietnam War. Perhaps these young Bonegilla residents knew better what lay in store for the Vietnamese, than did a lot of other political analysts at the time.

Meanwhile, Valerie tried to communicate what life was like for her in Australia to her old university friend Ria (whom she had come to know at Bonn University in post-war Germany) through her letters to her. Ria lived in Gronau near Münster with her husband and child Christiane, and Valerie, writing from her wooden table, tried to describe Bonegilla as best she could to her eager German readers. As stated above, there was a gap in the barrack huts between the roof and the top of the ceiling and it was through this gap that occasional possums would try to get inside the rooms. Valerie told Ria of this and Ria must have read her letters with some alarm for Valerie tried to describe what she saw in the only way she knew how. Describing the antics of possums, Valerie could only say they were strange animals that came through the roof and obviously had no word for them in

German. So she described them as 'little monkeys'. The impression created for Ria living West Germany, was that Australia was infested with little monkeys – towns, cities and all – and you could never escape them, even in your bedroom. The fact that my mother lived in a town where they were ubiquitous would have just confirmed the impression that the whole of Australia was affected. One can only imagine the consternation felt on reading these letters on the other side of the world. Ria mentioned all this to her husband, child and wider family. So who knows where the story of Australia being filled with monkeys ended. Added to these misconceptions would be the fact that kangaroos and koalas, which were also mentioned in letters, would have made Australia seem a very strange place, one where furry marsupials roamed every street among helpless inhabitants who could not fight so populous an enemy.

After these letters, mother began to receive parcels filled with food and clothes from Ria, probably out of pity for Valerie's predicament and because of Ria's kind nature. Ria obviously thought my mother was undergoing considerable depredations as a pioneering explorer in quasi-exile and was in dire need. Even after we all moved to Sydney the parcels kept coming and no amount of explanation that things were better would prevent Ria from sending them. It seems that my mother's dramatic descriptions of the activities of possums in Bonegilla had deeply affected her German friend. In later years, as a young adult fresh out of university, when I visited Ria and her family in Münster, one of her first questions on my arrival was to ask me, with a deadly serious expression, how the monkey problem was in Australia. She looked straight at me with great compassion and I was taken aback, not quite understanding what she meant. It took me a while to work out that what she meant was 'possums' and not monkeys and then I had to reassure her several times that possums and kangaroos were not on the main streets of every Australian city and town. I think she finally believed me, though with a little reservation, perhaps thinking I was putting a brave face on it. What decades of misunderstanding had been caused by those early letters from Bonegilla! I then described Bonegilla to Ria's family and whatever I said to them, it still all sounded weird and wonderful as if it came straight from the movie *Zulu*. Ria always remained a very loyal and kind friend to my mother. Now that Ria and Valerie have passed away I correspond with Ria's daughter Christiane, a friendship inherited from our parents. The monkey problem was, at long last, sorted out for once and for all.

Health and survival

Although it is stretching it describe in detail a biography up to the age of five, there are several vivid memories I have of the early years spent at Bonegilla. Once, as a three-year-old I caused a lot of commotion when I swallowed a stone off the street, and was carted off to hospital by several shouting people and was made to drink a lot of milk till the situation resolved itself. I remember swallowing the stone with pleasure but the ensuing panic induced fear into me too. Health problems caused a great deal of worry as there was always an underlying fear of epidemics, with so many people living at close quarters. There was a major health scare in September 1949 during which 19 children died, 13 of whom were at Bonegilla. An inquiry found that children suffering gastro-enteritis had been on a limited diet for a long time. This led to improvements in the provision of foods such as eggs and milk and some basic amenities such as a fridge for each block, prompting immigration authorities to boast jubilantly in 1953 that child migrants had put on weight. Some, it was reported with pride, were too fat to take part in the fitness events at Bonegilla that year.[144]

On another occasion, when all the children were being immunised, I developed a severe allergic reaction to the triple antigen injection at age four, and it was thought, apparently, that I was going to die. I got uncontrollable diarrhoea as well as other symptoms and I remember being taken with urgency to an isolation ward, totally unaware of the distress of my parents and wondering what I was doing there. I recall a nurse changing me into clean pyjamas several times. There was a pained look in my parents' faces as they looked at me through a glass partition. They were then reluctantly led away – presumably to let me die in peace. The kind of reaction I had was usually fatal, but against the odds I survived. I emerged from hospital as a thin, rib-caged waif and could hardly stand where I had previously been so boisterous. But I quickly recovered and was back with playing with the Bonegilla girl-gang of Katri, Reti and Annetta.

My mother told me of some polio cases she had to attend to while she worked in the hospital at Bonegilla. There was a particular fear of such an epidemic spreading. She said it was necessary to get the symptoms early, but how can you do that with a one- or two-year-old child who cannot answer your questions? Valerie said that she developed the technique of giving a gentle type of push to the knees as children stood or tried to stand. Usually a child shows some resistance to this push and would be able to stand but the legs of children with suspected polio symptoms would always give way very easily. This was one of the theories of the time in any case. My mother recounted that on another occasion the Bonegilla hospital generator failed. She was caught in the situation where she with a few other hospital staff had to manually keep a primitive machine going for hours, their arms growing very tired in the process. A patient with a kidney problem was apparently totally dependent on this machine and the volunteers kept it going till the generator was repaired and thus saved the man's life. In the ebb and flow of hospital duties, it seems the doctors on duty allowed Valerie to take on some of their responsibilities and both she and they knew it. She administered medications and did medical check-ups. In one photo with her medical colleagues, she wears a white coat and is leaning on what looks like the Bonegilla ambulance.

Once when I was four I was being minded by one of the young women in the camp while my parents were at work. I don't think the babysitter had good childminding techniques as she locked me in a cupboard at one point as I must have been too active and annoyed her. By some means, I got away. I must have run a long way out of the room as I found myself surrounded by strange looking fields of brown – and, in what was a dramatic event in my life at that time, I did not realise I was walking into a muddy pond. I have no idea where this was in relation to Bonegilla but have seen a pond marked on a map of the area near the hospital since then. Apparently some sewerage was also thrown into the pond which would have made for pleasant aromatic experiences. For some reason I found my way to it and worse was to come. I remember being interested in these mysterious looking pieces of earth in front of me. Walking ahead I fell into the brown pond. In the way frightening events are frozen in time I remember struggling to get out but to this day do not know how I managed to do it but I did. Covered in malodorous sludge, I ran in the direction of the town and my father relates how horrified he was to see me running down a Bonegilla street near the post office wondering what had happened. I was delighted to see him and must have proceeded to cover him in mud as I hugged him. Simultaneously shocked and relieved that I had not drowned, he tried to piece together how it all happened. I cannot remember much of the aftermath of this incident but I think there must have been a big drama about it. That girl was not asked to baby-sit again. Like most things it all blew over. There cannot be many children who have memories of falling into a sizeable mud pond and living to tell the tale.

One of the centres of social life was the Bonegilla cinema and memories of a particular incident spring to mind. My father was always a great moviegoer and took Valerie and myself along from time to time. When I was four years old I embarrassed him by standing on his lap during an evening screening of a film on the life of Julius Caesar. Apparently I was yelling at the top of my voice as I was distressed by what I understood of the plot. I thought Caesar was a lady because of all of the Roman robes that flowed around him. So I called out, in loud, friendly Polish, an urgent request for all in the cinema to rally to the support of 'Auntie' Caesar, who was obviously being menaced by Brutus. I screamed out: "Auntie, auntie, run away run away, they're coming to kill you, they want to kill you", waving my arms around frantically which apparently brought the house down at this tense point of the plot. It took a while till my father could quieten me down. Another Bonegilla resident Laime Zole is recorded as going to the cinema with her grandmother 'and whispering the story line to her in Latvian through the show'. Then she would try to sing the songs she had heard all the way home.[145]

Also of note during these years were the visits to Bonegilla of my mother's relations who lived in New South Wales. At one point my mother's sister Zenia, the enterprising dentist, her husband Lazar and their son Michael came all the way from Sydney to visit us and that was a special event. There is a photo of my cousin Michael pushing the pedals of a toy car up the streets of the camp which seemed a very cool thing to do then for three and four year-olds. When I was four we also had a visit from my mother's aunt Anna, her husband Jed and their daughter Veronica, who had escaped from Latvia and been superb traders in the post-war DP camps After arrival in Australia, they had been sent to Greta, and then on to Dalby in Queensland, Veronica escaping from Greta to go to Dalby where her parents were working. Once in Dalby Veronica enrolled for nursing training at the local Hospital – nurses were in great demand in Australia at that time and training was done over two years in hospital. Veronica was very attractive and part of her duty involved taking care of a handsome Polish patient, Juzef Schmiehura, who hailed from Sieradz in southern Poland and who looked like Omar Sharif. It must have been quite a sight to have conducted a romance from a hospital bed. Juzef was also a DP and had survived years of forced labour in Germany. He obviously noticed and liked Veronica's caring ministrations. To cut a long story short, they ended up falling in love and getting married in Dalby and remained in the town for a few years.

The visit by Veronica and Juzef and Veronica's parents to Bonegilla is recorded by the box camera and shows a group of us standing at the Hume Weir, an ever-popular place for excursions outside the camp. Aunt Veronica was not one to do things by halves and in one photo she appears in a fur-trimmed coat looking very height of elegance. She exuded the style of Vienna and Paris on the streets of Bonegilla and looked very much a star next to austere concrete constructions of the Hume Weir and the dirt roads of the camp. She was known as a Latvian beauty in Dalby and had been paraded with some other immigrants on the back of a truck during town festivals to the applause of townspeople. Now in Bonegilla, she had much to say about sartorial elegance and my mother, also slim and attractive, soaked up her advice as they visited a material shop together in Albury. With Veronica's expert advice, Valerie asked a dressmaker in the camp to make her an outfit and posed with great sense of occasion when photos were taken of her in it.

Veronica Tjarve, Valerie's enterprising cousin from Latvia, who escaped from Greta Camp in NSW and made it alone at age 16 up to Dalby in Qld to rejoin her parents who had been sent to work there

At the Hume Weir, a favourite excursion spot near Bonegilla. Veronica (in front wearing the fur trimmed coat) is visiting Bonegilla with her husband Juzef (rear left), father Jed (rear right). Valerie is between them. Bogdan and Veronica's mother Anna are taking the photo with the cherished box camera

Author with a typical toy of the time, a pram with a slightly obscured view of Michael Kulic (son of Zenia the enterprising dentist) behind her in his toy car. This was on the occasion of the Kulic visit to Bonegilla camp. Valerie and Bogdan were shortly to leave Bonegilla for Sydney

Girlfriends at Bonegilla – from left Estonian Australian Katri Malt, Czech Australian Annetta Skladal, Estonian Australian Reti Malt and the Polish-Latvian Australian author nursing a sceptical air

Wondering about life beyond Bonegilla

Amidst the comings and goings in Bonegilla there was always much animated talk about future plans. Dmytro Chub from the Ukraine recalled in 1949:

> Mostly they talked about their jobs, who was being sent where to work … how much one had to work to buy a block of land and build a shack on it.[146]

My parents and her relations discussed, planned, considered options and wondered what to do. Veronica from Dalby had already taken steps to return to Sydney with her parents. In fact she did move there very soon, and her husband Juzef found employment in the General Motors Holden factory at Pagewood where he, along with many other immigrants, worked for many years. They had two children, Lucy and Anna, and three generations of the family lived for a long time under one roof not far from the GMH plant. In the years to come, Veronica was to put her nursing skills to good use and become a director of a nursing home called Hoban House in Maroubra. She was much appreciated by those she helped and was to receive a 'NSW Premier's award for Excellence' for her achievement.

Meanwhile, my aunt Zenia's husband, Lazar, had a job in the glass factory in Alexandria, mixing with the migrants of all nations and worked there all his life until his retirement as a senior supervisor. Lazar could not put his agricultural degree from Bonn University to any use in Australia but he was very genial and adapted to his circumstances. He was friendly and got on with his workmates and was always ready to have a discussion on any subject. He had an extraordinary bass baritone voice and I always thought he could have been an opera singer – he did in fact sing in the Serbian Orthodox choir for many years. Lazar and Zenia had made the first move to Sydney out of their migrant camp in Bathurst after Zenia's dental enterprises gave them the beginnings of a deposit on a house. Veronica and her family were soon to follow from Queensland. My parents, however, remained working in Bonegilla and were to make their move several years later. And so this group of people, who were frightened refugees fleeing Latvia and Poland over a decade before, were all moving out to their new lives, and in the case of my family heading for and congregating in Sydney. This gave my parents the impetus to consider a move to the big metropolis with its ever-expanding factories and offers of work, rather than to any other capital city, and so their gaze turned northwards, away from the world of Bonegilla.

10
Packing the bags for life beyond Bonegilla

After seven years of living in Bonegilla, it all came to an end for Bogdan and Valerie in late 1957. Plans were made in the tin huts under an electric light, huts that with time began to be part of the architecture of a vanishing post-war era. Words like 'Sydney', 'factory', 'pounds' and 'shillings' were exchanged with whispered hopes to find a permanent home. There must have been mixed feelings on leaving – but then perhaps not – after all, Bogdan and Valerie had been there a longer time than most and had seen their friends move on. The teachers, the nurses, the public service officials all eventually did move on to other places.

For those working in Bonegilla, there had been a kind of security in staying in the camp for such a long time – perhaps even a feeling they were needed there, for there was social contact with the more permanent and transient residents, even though the camp had radically changed since the late 1940s when the first groups of Eastern European DPs had arrived. Since that 'first wave', groups of assisted immigrants had arrived from Italy, Holland, Greece and Britain and a new phase at Bonegilla had taken hold. Some residents had moved to Wodonga and Albury and decided to stay there, near their point of 'first contact' in Australia. For example, Paul Peters who was born in Berlin, found himself in the Soviet sector with his family after the war and thus fled and became a refugee in his own country.

He came to Bonegilla with his family and moved out on finding work in Albury.[147] Peters was a master butcher by trade and after a stint of work in Albury, along with a partner, Irwin Grabbe, he opened a butchery and smallgoods-making business that, interestingly enough, began to supply Bonegilla camp kitchens. After small beginnings, this expanded in later years to four businesses and Paul Peters' son Lutz continued the business of Peter's and Son in the Albury suburb of Lavington. In fact, Bonegilla residents were to spread far and wide and to make significant contributions in all walks of life – health, education, business, the arts, academia and politics. Some well known former residents include Franca Arena, Arvi Parbo, and renowned chef, Stefano Manfredi.

The immediate problem for the DPs, on leaving the camp, was to make enough money to survive from week to week and this was the dynamic of the new life. After letters were written to relations in Sydney and inquiries made about work and accommodation, the bags were packed in Bonegilla and farewells said. My mother's old brown cardboard case from Germany was still in use and was packed with some Bonegilla possessions. My father's precious books were taken down from his home-made shelf and the AWA radio, the box camera and some clothes were packed into the suitcase. My mother carried the 'guitar from Mrs Esch' which was a reminder of post-war Germany. Their long journeys from Poland and Latvia had been interwoven with seven years of bush scenery, the presence of possums, magpie calls and the languid blue skies. With this store of Bonegilla memories, like pioneers on an ongoing journey, we all left the camp for Albury. I remember standing on the platform of Albury station – it may as well have been a NASA space centre for the awe I felt at the monstrous metal trains moving past me. I had never seen anything like it and was wide-eyed and terrified. Could such things exist? What was the meaning of it all? A vivid memory is that of holding on to my father and mother convinced that the platform was moving and not the train, thinking our lives were at stake. We finally boarded the train and so left Bonegilla heading for Central Station in Sydney and an unknown future.

The world outside Bonegilla

The reason we ended up in Sydney was that we could find a place to stay for a while with my enterprising and generous aunt and uncle, Zenia and Lazar Kulic. As previously stated, Zenia had used the earnings of her eagerly sought out dental skills in Bathurst Camp, along with the factory earnings of her husband Lazar in Sydney, to put a deposit on an old house in Randwick which was a much cheaper suburb in those days. Certainly the house was the oldest in the area – it had old unpolished floorboards through whose holes I remember seeing the earth beneath in places, an old gas stove, curled up lino on the kitchen floor and a bed in the kitchen. We all thought it was wonderful. Zenia and Lazar kindly offered us a room to stay in, till we found our feet in Sydney and we stayed nearly a year, until our move to Marrickville to a small semi-detached house. I met my cousin Michael again – now a more mature fellow aged six – in this house. I recall us staring at each other for quite a while, my hair in two long plaints tied with the perennial ribbons, looking every bit a young immigrant straight out of a camp and my cousin Michael looking very dapper in shorts and a shirt, now a dinky di Aussie keen on playing Cowboys and Indians. We both gazed at the strange object in our midst in the back yard of their house – the metal hills hoist – and thus were gradually drawn into the mysteries of Australian life, the mysteries of the backyards and streets, adapting to the Australian narratives of the 50s and 60s. I wished the hill hoist could be a large toy whose horizontal bars one could hold on to and swirl around on. I realised in later years this was the dream of just about every Australian child. Soon Michael and I were attending the local Catholic school together. I knew no English but like other DP children, I came face to face with suburban Australian schools, learning about pies, cream buns, peanut butter on toast, not to mention eating vegemite on Sao biscuits.

In Sydney we also met up with Veronica, Juzef, Anna and Jed who after their years of being chased by the Nazis and Soviet soldiers were now living in Pagewood, all working long hours, in factories, nursing homes and various businesses, bringing up their children, Lucy and Anna. We would all meet from time to time in between long shifts and sit around tables laden with food rejoicing in being together again after the separation of the various camps. Enterprising Anna Tjarve and Jed who survived both Nazi and Soviet attempts to kill him, took to raising chickens, pickling gherkins and making the occasional attempt at plum or other liqueur which all their relations and friends were welcome to savour.

My Polish grandmother Wanda Maria who had survived Ravensbrück had written to Bogdan in the late 1950s during the years of the post-Stalinist era (Stalin had died in 1953). She longed to see her son again and received rare permission to go to Australia. And so she sailed away from Poland in May 1958 to a great new adventure and an emotional re-union with the son she had last seen as a boy of 12 at the outset of World War II. I recall staring with curious apprehension at this new visitor from another world. She took from her suitcase a book written in Polish about a goat (*Koziołek Matołek*) to give to her little granddaughter as well as a collection of children's stories by the Polish writer Maria Konopnicka. She also pulled out a highly colourful 'krakowianka' Polish national dress from her trunk. I ended up being induced to wear this to the Kindergarten Ball in 1958 at the local Saint Brigid's school in Coogee. During this evening of sartorial elegance, while just about every other child at the ball wore cowboy suits, Annie Oakley outfits or Hawaiian skirts, this national dress was quite dazzling and induced the judges to award me first prize for an original costume. I remember being hoisted up onto the stage and being given a box of chocolates and not understanding why. In my puzzled state I thought I may as well eat them so I opened the box on the stage and pulled out a chocolate before I was handed back to my parents. My grandmother felt pride at having picked just the right costume for her granddaughter and spending her last zlotys on this in Poland had been well worth it for it had clearly advanced the cause of Polish Australian relations.

My grandmother or Babcia Wanda as she came to be known, had also come to stay at the house of Zenia and Lazar which already housed two families and now provided a bed for Babcia – in the kitchen – until Bogdan and Valerie found a place in which to live. Babcia Wanda actually was only permitted to come to Australia for two years but, to the shock of everyone, contracted stomach cancer at the end of her two year stay. In what was thought to be her 'final' phase of life she was given permanent residence by the Australian government as she could not travel back to Poland due to her illness. It was thought she would die but in fact she recovered entirely after an operation and lived out the remainder of her life in Australia from 1958 onwards. With her gentle smile, her broken English, this survivor of Ravensbrück was to become a tea lady for Tomasetti and Sons and then ironed clothes for other people, one in particular a Jewish holocaust survivor with whom she became good friends.

In order to survive financially, my father got a job in the Leyland car factory in Zetland and then after several years there, joined the water board, rising to be a senior technical officer. As previously stated, my mother went to do some of her studies again and worked briefly at Randwick Prince of Wales Hospital as a nurse, at Marrickville District Hospital after she qualified, and then as an assistant for a doctor in Paddington until ill health cut short a promising career.

The move out of Randwick to Marrickville for a few years involved enrolling at a new school. While in kindergarten, I was unable to speak English for some time. Now after a year, and in a new school, I could speak with a noticeable Aussie twang and sat in the class of 40 students at St Brigid's School in Marrickville, many of whom were Greek and Italian. We learned our prayers at this school and lined up on the street outside the Spanish mission style church to go to confession and Mass. When asked where I came from I said alternately 'Bonegilla', 'Poland' or 'Latvia' all of which seemed equally incomprehensible to those listening. Once when I had said 'Poland' a teacher thought I had said 'Holland' and called me 'the little Dutch girl'. I was too in awe of teachers to dare correct her. I even became tired of people not knowing where Latvia was so I tried to convince them my mother spoke Latin as this was a language everyone knew about at the time as it was the language of the Mass – but this ruse failed and only earned me suspicious stares from the teachers who insisted 'No that's not possible.'

Another memorable event along the way of initial post-Bonegilla adaptation to Australia involved salami sandwiches. At times I was given some of these to take to school. All those reffo children who ate salami sandwiches in the 50s and 60s will sympathise with this event. The very existence of salami often elicited long suspicious stares from some other children. My peers in second class berated me for having such 'urky purky' stuff in my bread and I was ostracised from the mainstream of Year 2 life. I convinced my grandmother to lend me a shilling so I could buy a pie and be cool like the other kids. I came with great anticipation and ordered a pie from the small canteen. I did not realise, however, it is not enough to buy a pie, one has to know how to eat a pie. Having received a pie in my hands for the first time in my life, I proudly took it out of the brown paper bag. My fingers gripped the top rim of the pie with the result that the bottom part filled with meat spilled out onto the front of my uniform making a terrible mess. A passing teacher exploded in anger and I was then berated for not even being able to eat a pie, which everyone who was a true Australian could do. I was relegated to an existence beyond the social pale for a while. But I was determined to practise this arcane art as much as I could and so I ordered more pies in the weeks to come. In time I learned to eat this iconic food without spilling it all over the place but this was still an event which the reffo kid from Bonegilla had to perfect with practice in between eating salami sandwiches.

Having an interest in school subjects helped to overcome the reffo aura and drew children like myself into the flow of Australian life and inevitably future dreams took shape. The memories of international life in the bush receded a little as the bold outlines of the city took over and I learned to say 'Circular Quay' not 'Kirkular Kway' and 'Gloucester Street' and not 'Glow – kaister Street'. The trams, the beaches, the Sydney buses, the town hall clock, the routines of school life and the languid summer afternoons eating watermelon became for me, as for other migrant children, some new constants that threaded the days. On a deeper level, however, the activities of this era mingled with thoughts of the 'other half of the family' over there 'somewhere', for as the children of DPs grew older, they were told something of where they came from, even if they could only grasp it in broad outline. As we became Aussies, that 'somewhere' also took hold.

There were secrets and past stories to be unravelled. For some families it involved details of deaths, murders, disappearances of family members, distant loved ones and fears of contact. Many migrant and reffo children wondered what those 'other people' in our families were doing under the rule of people like Stalin and Krushchev – they were part of the strange tapestry of our lives. Though shadowy figures in another world, the family we knew 'over there' were still our family – so how could we not care? I learned I had aunts, uncles and cousins in other countries and I yearned to know more about them. Children like myself watched our parents open letters with strange stamps from far away, looking at them like precious parchments, evidence of a lost world, never relinquished, always hoping for news, weaving new narratives with a constantly felt loss. The children of Bonegilla tried to understand the narratives but it would take years for their many threads to be put together, a process involving delicate integration of past and current narratives, not only paying tribute to the spiritual legacy of transmitted memories, but trying to decipher them.

In later life, having graduated from university and worked as a teacher and psychologist for several decades, I was to visit the places from which the letters had come. For it is clear throughout this book that while my parents came to Bonegilla, this very place was the beginning of my journeys through time to where they came from. By means of travel, reading and family meetings I tried to see beneath the surface details of what was remembered as the DPs' life in Bonegilla, the enigmas for which we children had no words in the camp. I was able then to set eyes on those places which had been the setting for the multiple journeys of my parents. Their journeys engendered my journeys across continents and in time I explored 'the other side' of Bonegilla through oral and written testimonies and gradually pieced together some of the stories. I walked the streets of Lublin, seeing where my father was born and Lublin Castle where my grandmother had been imprisoned. I walked along the streets of Mokotów in Warsaw where my father had fought as a boy and saw Vilno where my father and Alicia played and where my great-grandmother Helena is buried. I also visited Latvia seeing Rēzekne and Riga, gazing at the chestnut trees which my mother had climbed in her youth. I saw the school near Karsava which the Nazis had taken over, the station at Malta from which she caught trains, and I walked over the now silent land at Garkalne on which my grandparents' house had once stood before bombs destroyed it.

I met my father's sister Alicia and her husband and children – my Polish cousins Wojtek, Andrzej and Janusz – who had stood under snow-covered Christmas trees in photos sent to me at summery Christmas time in Sydney. While they had grown up in Communist Poland hearing about Marx and Lenin, I had heard about Saint Patrick and sang 'When Irish Eyes are Smiling' at St Brigid's School. When some years later, Janusz migrated to Australia with his wife Grazyna in the early 1980s, more threads of the hidden past permeated the new narrative, in ongoing conversations about ideas and ideologies lasting years. When I finally visited Latvia, after the end of the Soviet era, Bronia related first hand how life had been in the post-war years and how she had possessed only one dark coloured dress at that time. She wore that one dress on her wedding day. I heard first hand from people who suffered under Communist repression. Once, sitting in a train in Riga, a lady with whom I started a simple conversation about the weather ended up relating to me, a total stranger, how she had spent decades of her life in a Soviet gulag. Gradually I came to piece together the journeys before the journey to Australia and learned to make sense of the feelings which had permeated the all too old, 'young' faces of DPs walking the streets of Bonegilla.

Bonegilla's transmitted memories

There is much discussion of the transmission of memories through the generations especially the transmission of traumatic memories, and I am living witness to the fact that this happens. It was different for each person who was there but in time I found that memories of Bonegilla became associated with ongoing questions. For whatever I did in later life, Bonegilla remained as a reference point and every phase of my life had some connection to it. The 'riddle, wrapped in a mystery, inside an enigma' that was Bonegilla never let go. It was as if the riddle of the entire 20th century had gripped me there in an unending hold, requiring my response if I was ever to say who I was and what the camp itself was. Bonegilla seemed ephemeral yet it wasn't. It was a hastily adapted army base, yet became a home. It was a moment in time and yet it stayed forever in memory. It was a place of dust that was the source of solid hope. It had inhabitants aplenty and then one day they were all gone. It was a momentous town and then it disappeared into the silences of the bush. It was a temporary place and yet it acquired something of the fateful, the symbolic, the eternal.

Perhaps my experience has been qualitatively different from that of the non-refugees who also stayed in Bonegilla but many of them have said that something powerful was communicated there. For many first generation migrant children, and especially for those of the DPs, there was a wordless absorption of something from their parents' soulspace, the burdens which survivors of lost worlds carry on their journeys, what Rilke calls 'the long experience of sufferings, purely untellable things'. In this way Bonegilla, in addition to being a geographical launching pad for Australia's new economic and political plans, acquired a spiritual meaning. And that soulspace was inextricably post-war and mid-20th century, but also timeless, and this led me to ponder – as time went by – how the 'Dreaming' pervades

Some original suitcases the DPs brought to their new country
(Display from the permanent exhibition entitled 'Bonegilla Story' in the Albury City Library)

Photos and original utensils from the Bonegilla era
(On display at the Bonegilla Migrant Experience Museum in Bonegilla)

One of the original dormitories preserved as part of Block 29
in which up to 20 new arrivals slept

*One of the several preserved huts of Block 19 which constitute
the Bonegilla Migrant Experience Museum*

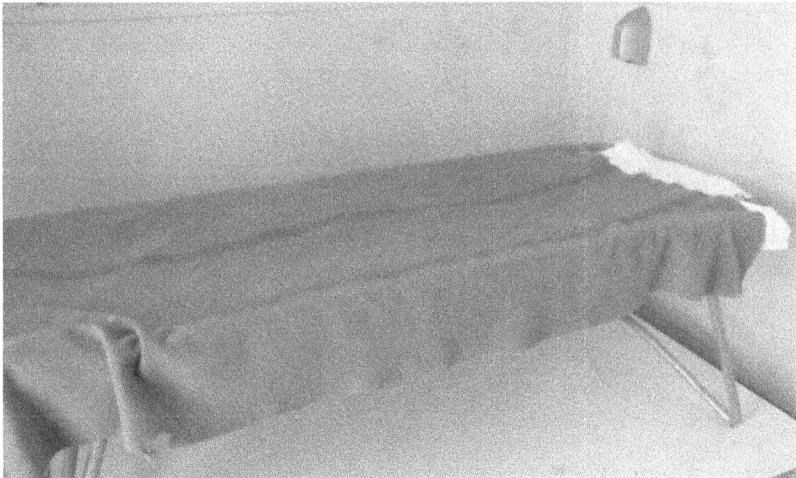

A typical camp bed of the era

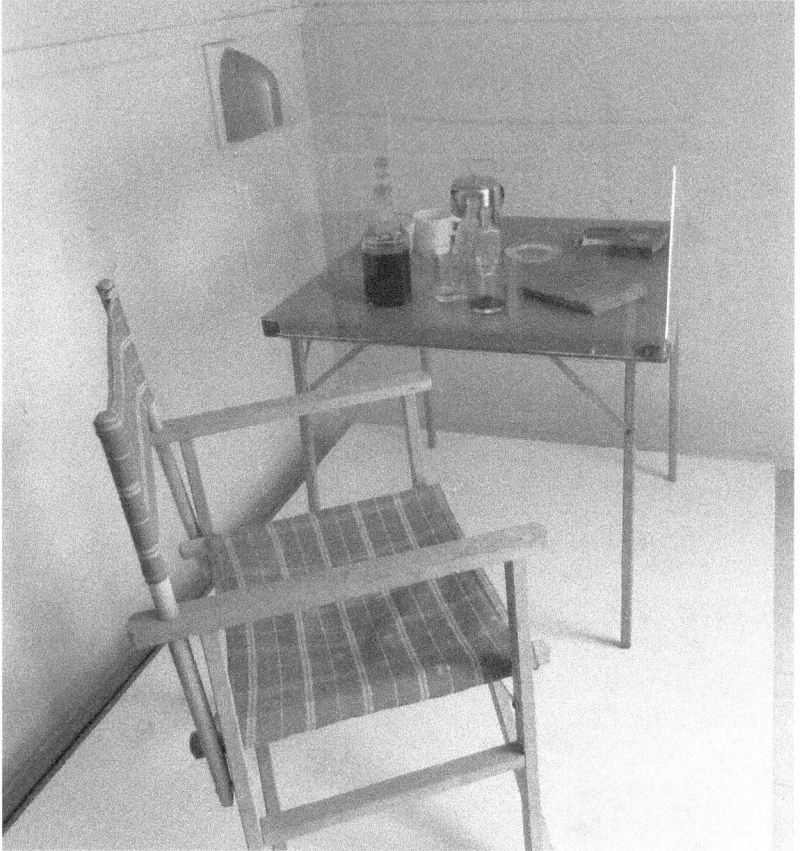

In one of the huts open to the public with makeshift furniture of the time

the lives of Australia's original inhabitants. And how each newcomer's intertwining of the past and present, carved through fragility and striving, suffering and hope, are the unique Australian inner soulscapes of all its inhabitants, each story framed by the endless horizons and evocative deserts of this Great South Land.

In later years, when I met people from Vietnam, Laos, Lebanon, Somalia and other places, people who had also experienced war and traumatic long journeys, I always felt there was a language of the soul that refugees and camp dwellers could understand. We could converse, even if words told only part of it. In the constant displacements of the 20th century, however, there are millions of such stories that will never be told, because the journey of displacement overwhelms the pilgrims, the depth of the experience cannot reach the form of words or – perhaps this is true for the majority – the pilgrims die with their stories along the way.

Going back

Some years ago I made a trip to Albury with the aim of seeing this now vanished world of my childhood. Bonegilla had long since closed. It was in the early 1980s and as I drove down and saw a road sign saying 'Bonegilla'. I stopped the car and was transfixed imagining the people, the tin buildings, the mess, the conversations, cigarette smoke, men kissing women's hands, the hospital, the shop, the Bonegilla cinema. I searched for familiar signs but I could not find any apart from silence and the sky. There was no-one around to ask. Had that world really vanished? From where I stood I could see nothing but gum trees lightly moving in the breeze and realised that nearly nothing of the old camp of my memories remained – its transience and that of all earthly things permeating my thoughts. Walking around a little more I did eventually come across a thin fibro building among the eucalypts with a sign saying 'cinema' on it. I realised this was probably the place where Bonegillians had watched movies of the 1950s and 60s with such intense interest and where I had called Julius Caesar 'auntie', urging him with loud screams to run away from Brutus. Weeds now grew around the edges of the fibro building which looked dilapidated and cracked in parts.

I was to learn that by 1971 the last Bonegillian had left. The DP era had ended, as had the subsequent phases of migrant placement there. In the unavoidable dynamic of progress, the army moved back with newer buildings, demolishing the older barracks, one by one. What had transpired there was now the realm of memories and history.

Before Bonegilla disappeared entirely

Not all the Bonegilla barracks disappeared. There are always some people, however, who want to retrieve something of past worlds and in this case it took the form of a Bonegilla Immigration Museum Committee which was formed in 1984. Its aim was to establish a national immigration museum and this culminated in the transfer of one section of the old camp, known as Block 19, by the Defence Department to the State of Victoria in 2002. Previously in 1986 the Defence Department had declared the remaining buildings at Block 19 surplus to its requirements and so these could form the basis of a museum, some physical evidence of the centre that once existed, as all the other 'blocks' had been destroyed. The Bonegilla Immigration Museum Committee fuelled the momentum to establish a national immigration museum and celebrate the role of migration, to understand in more nuanced detail the impact of various groups on Australian history. Block 19 was included in the National Heritage List on 7 December 2007 and thus, in this preserved section, the Bonegillians had become part of the living national memory of

Australia. The huts of Block 19 were transformed into a museum entitled the Bonegilla Migrant Experience with many authentic features remaining. The Australian Heritage website states:

> Block 19, Bonegilla, is a rare example of a post-war migration centre which retains considerable extant fabric. The existing buildings at Block 19 form a group of timber framed 'P' Series World War II army huts laid out symmetrically in a grid pattern, and used as migrant and staff housing, office accommodation, recreation and mess halls, kitchens and ablution blocks. The buildings illustrate the use of former wartime army camps as migrant reception and training centres. The rudimentary barracks buildings demonstrate the basic conditions typical of migrant reception places.[148]

I was able to visit Block 19 in February 2011 and, after a lifetime in Australia, saw the types of huts in which all former Bonegillians lived. Bogdan, Valerie and I had lived in a block near the hospital but Block 19, though it was in a different location, had typical features of most of the barracks. Of course I stared in some quiet amazement inside and outside the rooms and spent time imagining the former movement, bustle and multiple languages filling the air. It was a warm, still day and the only noises were the muted cries from the magpies. For a few hours I wandered around the empty buildings as the only visitor at that time, conversing with a volunteer in the shop attached to the museum which has displays of photos, suitcases and mementos of former Bonegilla residents evoking some details of the time.

In nearby Albury an exhibition of historical interest about Bonegilla has been set up in the city library. It is a work in progress and the library staff have collected memorabilia for over 25 years in order to establish a permanent collection for its exhibition. The

Albury City website notes:

> The exhibition relies on suitcases, packed with possessions ranging from a chamber pot to a piano accordion, to bring people's memories to life. One exhibit includes the smell of Bonegilla's notorious roast mutton dinners. Another features white elbow-length ladies dress gloves, along with a memory of Friday night dances. The suitcases serve as a reminder of one of the first challenges migrants' faced, as they had just one suitcase in which to pack all of the treasured and practical possessions they'd need to start their new life in Australia.[149]

The memorabilia are best symbolised by the huts and the suitcase – part of everyone's existence in the camp. Fragments are all that remain of that colourful, busy place. The bush beginnings could never disappear entirely for me as they had already established a place in my heart that the bigger cities I have lived in have never quite erased.

Bogdan and Valerie got to know the words of 'Waltzing Matilda', admired Holdens, understood what a Victa lawnmower was, gazed at the Blue Mountains, stood for the anthem in cinemas and rejoiced and mourned with their fellow Australians. Before them, however, lay long years of work, great joys and the immense tragedies that were to come. It is impossible to tell of the profound experiences awaiting them, many influenced by wartime life. As things turned out, Bogdan did not live long – he died aged 57 on 3 June 1985, no doubt weakened by the many diseases he had endured as a young resistance fighter in Poland. Valerie, after long years of ill health, died aged 70 on 6 September 1996 – far away from Latvia. When in Bonegilla they, along with other Bonegillians, were in a midpoint of a journey where some would go on to bigger and better things and some would

Author visiting Bonegilla in 2012

Brother and sister united. Bogdan and Alicia (who had tuberculosis in a Warsaw orphanage which was bombed by the Germans) met in 1978 and saw each other a few times before they passed away – Bogdan at 57, Alicia at 59

Sisters separated by war united in Australia. From left to right, Valerie, Bronia (who had lived in Soviet ruled Latvia all her life) and Zenia (the enterprising dentist of Bathurst camp). Valerie and Zenia brought Bronia out to Australia in 1990, the first meeting of the sisters in over 40 years

Wanda Maria, survivor of Ravensbrück (right) with some of her grandchildren, from left, Wanda, Janusz and Janusz's wife Grazyna in 1988. Wanda Maria migrated to Australia and died in the Marayong Polish nursing home in 1993 in Sydney

succumb to trauma, ill health and loss which overwhelmed their attempts to survive. But those are other stories that would take other much larger volumes to tell and this story is about that unique bridge of hope, that first contact with a new world which the DPs found in their unique bush town. As noted, the buildings of Bonegilla have nearly all gone, apart from the preserved section, and the wind blows over the sites of former huts. These empty spaces housed people with dreams, their dreams not of gold, but respite, perhaps some sanity and peace. The DPs grasped at new threads of happiness in Bonegilla and gave sound to the streets, their hands to new tasks and most importantly, their love to their new country.

I have come to understand in the end, as have many others, that Bonegilla is truly an iconic place in the land where the 'journey' takes on so much significance for the new Australians as well as the original ones. The journeys of Bogdan and Valerie, along with those of other DPs, and in fact all our journeys, had and continue to have unforeseen destinations, consequences and mysterious lines of fate. They were inheritors of an inescapable past which would always remain with them, an unavoidable present and unknown future. The farawayness of Australia from the scenes of their childhood imposed on them a sense of final separation and yet there remained continuities of the heart in their odyssey to another world. Their journeys, like those of the original inhabitants of the land, are caught in time and timelessness and their meanings are perpetually recast as new times and journeys of the spirit unfold, which indeed happens in the end for all of us, everywhere. The post-war Bonegillians and all migrants to this great south land, threaded their old lives with a new one, proof, as the original inhabitants well knew, that the meaning of all our journeys is never lost, just pondered over again and again, over time, for the journeying never ends.

Endnotes

CHAPTER 1

1, 2 This is the estimate of the Australian Heritage Database: http://www. environment.gov.au/heritage/ahc/national-assessments/bonegilla/pubs/ bonegilla.pdf (Accessed 19/3/2009).

3 James Jupp, *Arrivals and Departures*, (Melbourne: Landsdowne Press, 1966), 7. Numbers for the groups of Ukrainians, Yugoslav, Russian, Czechoslovak and others, expressed as percentages of the total number of Displaced Persons accepted by Australia, are given in: Bruce Pennay, *Receiving Europe's Displaced: Bonegilla Reception and Training Centre, 1947-53*. (Albury: Royal Australian Historical Society, 2010), 1. (Henceforth Pennay, *RED*).

4 Figures given as percentages of the total number of Displaced Personas are given in: Pennay, *RED*, 1; Lithuanian figures are given on the following site: http:// www.kirmus.ee/baltic_archives_abroad_2006/kogumik/eng/Budriuniene.htm (Accessed 7/4/2011). Estonian figures are given on the following site: http:// www.kirmus.ee/baltic_archives_abroad_2006/kogumik/eng/Barrow.htm (Accessed 7/4/2011).

5 Linas Saldukas, 'Culture in Adversity: the Lithuanian DP Experience', *Lithuanian Quarterly Journal of Arts and Sciences*, Volume 52, 3, Fall 2006. Also found on the following site: http://www.lituanus.org/2006/06_3_02%20Saldukas.htm (Accessed 7/4/2009).

6 A history of Latvian migration to Australia is given on the following website. http://museumvictoria.com.au/origins/history.aspx?id=36 (Accessed 5/3/2010).

7 The Australian Heritage Database can be found at: http://www.environment. gov.au/heritage/ahc/national-assessments/bonegilla/pubs/bonegilla.pdf (Accessed 9/4/2010).

8 James Jupp, "Immigration: Some Recent Perspectives", *Australian Historical Studies*, 95, October (1990), 286.

9 This is stated on the walls of the Bonegilla Migrant Experience Museum at Bonegilla itself.

10 Ann Tundern-Smith, *Bonegilla's Beginnings* (NSW, Triple D books: 2007).

11 The Australian Heritage Database can be found under the Publications and Resources section of: http://www.environment.gov.au/heritage/places/ national/bonegilla/index.html (Accessed on 9/4/2011).

12 Bruce Pennay, *The Army at Bonegilla 1940-1971* (Victoria Heritage Series, 2007). Most of the details of the army presence are taken from Bruce Pennay's account on p 2 ff.

13 Ann Tundern-Smith, *Bonegilla's Beginnings* (NSW: Triple D books, 2007), 25 ff.

14 More details can be found on the Australian Heritage Database. http://www.environment.gov.au/heritage/ahc/national-assessments/bonegilla/pubs/bonegilla.pdf

15 Viesturs P. Karnups, 'The Political Economy of the displaced Persons Immigration 1947-1954', *Lithuanian Quarterly Journal of Arts and Sciences,* 1984, 30, 4, The article can be found on the following website. http://www.lituanus.org/1984_4/84_4_05.htm (Accessed 3/9/2009)

16 Glenda Sluga 'Bonegilla Reception And Training Centre: 1947-1971.' Master's Thesis, University of Melbourne, August 1985. An online copy of this thesis in pdf format can be found at http://dtl.unimelb.edu.au/R/KN1KNARA54CSFC BJ15B8BJTBF7BQP8HJ4C95TEDGC7KTX617FV-01718?func=dbin-jump-full&object_id=66057&local_base=GEN01&pds_handle=GUEST (Accessed 4/7/2010).

17 http://www.lituanus.org/1984_4/84_4_05.htm (Accessed 8/4/2009).

18 http://www.migrationheritage.nsw.gov.au/exhibitions/somuchsky/(Accessed 13/4/2009).

19 The Australian Government website entitled 'Bonegilla Migrant Camp - Block 19 more information' expresses this view. http://www.environment.gov.au/heritage/places/national/bonegilla/information.html (Accessed 4/7/2010).

20 James Jupp, *Arrivals and Departures*, (Melbourne: Lansdowne press, 1966), 8.

21 Taken from the Albury City Bonegilla collection. See the following: http://www.bonegilla.com.au/collection/ (Accessed 2/12/2011).

22 Ann Tundern-Smith, *Bonegilla's Beginnings*, (NSW, Triple D books: 2007), 23.

23 This account is largely taken from the Australian Heritage Database. http://www.environment.gov.au/heritage/ahc/national-assessments/bonegilla/pubs/bonegilla.pdf (Accessed 10/4/2011).

24 http://www.environment.gov.au/heritage/places/national/bonegilla/information.html (Accessed 22/5/2010).

CHAPTER 2

25 http://www.poloniatoday.com/history-1-2.html (Accessed 2/11/2011). This gives a short history of Poland. Another similar history of Poland is that of Adam Zamoyski, *The Polish Way: A Thousand-Year History of the Poles and Their Culture.* (New York: Hippocrene Books, 1994).

26 http://en.poland.gov.pl/Kingdom,and,Grand,Duchy,,7279.html (Accessed 9/2/2009).

27 Lynne Olson and Stanley Cloud, *A Question of Honour: the Kosciuszko Squadron: Forgotten Heroes of World War II* (NY: Vintage, 2004), 17.

28 Zamoyski, *Warsaw 1920: Lenin's Failed Conquest of Europe* (Great Britain: Harper Collins, 2008), 7.

29 Olson and Cloud, *A Question of Honour,* 29 ff.

30 Ibid, 137.

31 Quoted in Norman Davies, *Rising 44* (New York: Penguin, 2004), 123.

32 Kenneth Koskodan, *No Greater Ally: The Untold Story of Poland's Forces in World War II.* (Great Britain: Osprey Publishing), 15.

33 Ibid, 16.

CHAPTER 3

34 Kenneth Koskodan, op. cit., 41.

35 Ibid, 41.

36 Taken from the site 'Kresy Siberia Virtual Museum' which details some of the stories of those killed in the 'Katyń Massacres', often pieced together by descendants. http://kresy-siberia.org/won/?page_id=19&lang=en&id=88809 (Accessed 2/3/2013).

37 Stefan has, with the assistance of others historically connected with these events, set up the KRESY-SIBERIA VIRTUAL MUSEUM which gives the stories of survivors of these Eastern deportations or accounts given by descendants of those who perished in them. This is and will be of immense importance to historians seeking first hand accounts of these times about which so little evidence exists compared with other facets of World War II. The English language version of the site can be found on: http://kresy-siberia.org/muzeum/?lang=en (Accessed 12/12/2012).

38 General Wladyslaw Anders, *An Army in Exile* (Tennessee: Battery Press, 2004,

originally printed in 1949), 69. Ander's own comment on this is given later in the chapter.

39 Jan Onoszko, *Syberia – moje Dziecinstwo* (Siberia – my Childhood) (Lublin: Institute Pamienci Narodowej, 2008).

40 Anders, *An Army in Exile*, (Tennessee: Battery Press, 2004), p 1.

41 The writings of Solzhenitsyn brought the word 'gulag' to prominence especially his work detailing life in the remote work camps in which millions died – The Gulag Archipelago written 1958 and 1968 but not published until 1973 in the west and not until 1989 in Russia. Gulag or Gulág is an acronym for the Russian term Glavnoye Upravleniye ispravitelno-trudovyh Lagerey (Главное Управление Исправительно-трудовых Лагерей), or "Chief Administration of Corrective Labour Camps". The shorter form of Gulag was commonly used.

42 Details of this period and many personal stories can be obtained from the English language site recently established: http://kresy-siberia.org/muzeum/?lang=en (Accessed 4/5/2012).

43 Dr Patryck Pleskot, researcher with the Polish Institute of National Remembrance gave an account of Russian understanding of the Katyń Massacres in the post-Soviet era in a public lecture at the Centre for Independent Studies on March 5, 2013 which the author attended.

44 Some details of this historic meeting in Iran can be found on the site entitled: ' We Meet the Brotherhood: An Unknown Episode. The history of an encounter of thousands of Polish Jewish soldiers with the Jews of Iraq and Iran in 1942-1943'. http://www.zchor.org/brotherhood/book.htm (Accessed 16/7/2011).

45 Anders, *An Army in Exile,* xiii.

46 Ibid, 69.

47 The published diary of the prison psychologist who interviewed many Nazi war criminals - Hans Frank among them recorded - Frank as saying 'A thousand years will pass and this guilt of Germany will not be erased' to the disgust of many of his Nazi peers. G.M. Gilbert *Nuremberg Diaries*, (USA: DA Capo Press, 1995, 1947), 276. Frank is said to have later recanted.

48 Chil Rajchman, *Treblinka: A Survivor's Memory* (UK: Maclehose Press, 2012, 2009).

49 Norman Davies, *Rising 44* (New York: Penguin, 2004), 76.

50 Jan Karski, *The Story of a Secret State: My Report to the World* (London: Penguin Books, 2011, 1944), 346-367.

51 A brief account of Karski and Ziegelboym can be found on: http://en.wikipedia.org/wiki/Szmul_Zygielbojm (Accessed 2/4/2012).

52 An account of the extermination of the Jews in Lublin is given on the following site: http://www.holocaustresearchproject.org/ghettos/lublin.html (Accessed 28/3/2010).

53 Davies, op. cit., 129.

54 Ibid., 26.

55 The experiment is described briefly in Polish by Jadwiga on the following website which details what occurred in Ravensbrück. Translation: Janusz Tydda. http://jtajchert.w.interia.pl/zyciorysykrolikow.htm (Accessed 1/3/2011).

56 http://jtajchert.w.interia.pl/zyciorysykrolikow.htm Accessed 1/3/2011).

57 Julian Eugeniusz Kulski, *Dying we Live: The Personal Chronicle of a Young Freedom Fighter in Warsaw, 1939-1945* (Holt, Rinehart and Winston, 1979).

58 Timothy Snyder, *Bloodlands: Europe Between Hitler and Stalin* (USA: Basic Books, 2010).

CHAPTER 4

59 Norman Davies, op. cit.; J.K. Zawodny, op. cit; Jan Ciechanowski, *The Warsaw Rising of 1944* (Cambridge University Press, 1974); George Bruce, *The Warsaw Uprising* (London: Rupert Hart-Davis, 1974); Julian Eugeniusz Kulski, *Dying we Live: The Personal Chronicle of a Young Freedom Fighter in Warsaw, 1939-1945* (Holt, Rinehart and Winston, 1979); Kenneth Koskodan, *No Greater Ally: The Untold Story of Poland's Forces in World War II.* (Great Britain: Osprey Publishing, 2009).

60 Czesław Miłosz, *The Captive Mind,* (New York: Vintage Books, 1990. First published in 1951), 184.

61 Jan Karski, *The Story of a Secret State: My Report to the World* (London: Penguin Books, 2011, 1944), 346-367. Reference was made to this in the previous chapter.

62 An account of the non-Jews killed by the German can be found in: Richard. D. Lukas, *Forgotten Holocaust: the Poles under German Occupation* (USA: University of Kentucky Press, 1986). Several paperback editions of this work have since appeared.

63 Timothy Snyder, *Bloodlands: Europe Between Hitler and Stalin* (USA: Basic Books, 2010), 297-8.

64 Norman Davies, *No Simple Victory* (New York: Penguin, 2008), 119.

65 J.K. Zawodny, op. cit., p 60.

66 http://www.warsawuprising.com/witness/nowak.htm

67 The fate of these Azerbaijanis who fought with the Nazis and who stayed on in Germany and the subsequent Islamic presence in Europe is described in Ian Johnson's *A Mosque in Munich: Nazis, the CIA, and the Rise of the Muslim Brotherhood in the West*, (USA: Houghton, Mifflin Harcourt Publishing, 2010).

68 Some information taken from a site dedicated to the Uprising: http://www.warsawuprising.com/timeline.htm

69 Julian Eugeniusz *Kulski Dying we Live: The personal chronicle of a young freedom fighter in Warsaw, 1939-1945* (Holt, Rinehart and Winston, 1979).

70 Norman Davies, *Rising 44* (New York: Penguin, 2004).

71 Almost all accounts of the Rising say that it lasted for sixty-three days. Historians conventionally count the period from the outbreak on 1 August to the final shot on 2 October'. Davies Rising 44, 425. The numbers of fighters, wounded and other dead are taken from Davies' account.

72 Norman Davies, op. cit. Article quoted in full in Appendix, 671- 3 This quotation taken from p. 672.

73 J.K. Zawodny op. cit., 47.

74 Norman Davies *Rising 44* (New York: Penguin, 2004), p172.

75 John Paul II, *Jan Pawel II Autobiografia* (Poland: Wydawnictwo Literackie), 23. Year of publication not given.

76 As the museum in the Catholic University of Lublin relates – Father Idzi Radziszewski founded the university in 1918. Lenin strangely allowed the priest to take the library and equipment of Saint Petersburg Roman Catholic Seminary back to Poland to launch the university just as Poland regained its independence. No doubt he was pleased to get rid of these signs of 'religion' in Russia and considered its removal to Poland a temporary measure until the Soviet Union would take over Poland. There were 39 students in 1918–1919 and this grew to 1440 in 1937–1938. After being closed at the outbreak of the Second World War and many of its students and professors being killed, the University carried on its teaching activities in secret. After the invasion of Lublin in July 1944 by the Red Army, the university reopened on 21 August 1944 and was closely observed by the Communist regime. It currently has 19,000 students.

77 Various recordings of the song are available on youtube, as on the following site: http://www.youtube.com/watch?v=qXT7DwpsG8Q&feature=related

Accessed 2/4/2011). The words of the song are as follows:

Rozszumiały się wierzby płaczące,/ Rozpłakała się dziewczyna w głos,
Od łez oczy podniosła błyszczące,/ Na żołnierski, na twardy życia los.

Nie szumcie, wierzby, nam,/ Żalu, co serce rwie,
Nie płacz, dziewczyno ma,/ Bo w partyzantce nie jest źle.

Do tańca grają nam/ Granaty, stenów szczęk,
Śmierć kosi niby łan,/ Lecz my nie wiemy, co to lęk.

Czy to deszcz czy słoneczna spiekota,/ Wszędzie słychać miarowy, równy krok,
To na bój idzie leśna piechota,/ Na ustach śpiew, spokojna twarz, wesoły wzrok./
Nie szumcie, wierzby....

English translation

The weeping willows were trembling/ A girl started crying and
She raised her tearful eyes to look/ At the soldiers life's, his harsh fate

Willows, don't tremble for us/ In sorrow over our fate
Don't cry my dear girl/ For the partisan's life is not all bad

An orchestra plays for us/ With grenade blasts and the rattle of a Sten
Death mows us down like a field/ But we don't know the meaning of fear

No matter if it's rain or hellish heat/ Steady, marching steps can be heard
It's the forest army on the move to battle/ A song on their lips, calm faces and cheerful eyes.
Willows, don't tremble...

78 Kenneth Koskodan, op. cit., 197.

79 Ibid, 193.

80 J.K. Zawodny op. cit., quoted on p.163,

81 Norman Davies, op. cit., 48.

82 Ibid, 175.

83 Ibid, 179 ff.

84 Davies makes a similar point: On the evening of 2 August Churchill addressed the House of Commons on the political problem within the Alliance by stressing both Poland's courage and 'Russia's need for friendly neighbours'. (He pointedly made no reference to Poland's need for friendly neighbours.) He then ordered the RAF to fly supply missions to Warsaw from their bases in southern Italy, thereby initiating the long saga of the Warsaw Airlift.

The Foreign Office, in contrast, displayed an extraordinary degree of lethargy, which can be partly explained by divided counsels and partly by the existence of Soviet moles in its ranks. (Christopher Hill, the historian, who was later shown to have been a secret member of the Communist Party, was in charge of the Foreign Office's Soviet Desk). Taken from: http://www.warsawuprising.com/paper/davies1.htm (Accessed 1/11/2011).

85 Ibid, 154.

86 http://www.warsawuprising.com/doc/dispatches2.htm

87 Original radios and technical equipment from this time are on display at the Uprising Museum in Warsaw which was opened in 2004 and is one of Poland's best museums. It has interactive displays, photographs, video footage and miscellaneous exhibits. It is located on the site of a former tram power station and details the chronological story of the Uprising.

88 J.K. Zawodny op. cit., 63-4

89 An account of this incident and the evaluation of the chances of the AK in an Uprising is given in Timothy Snyder, *Bloodlands: Europe Between Hitler and Stalin* (USA: Basic Books, 2010), 297 ff.

90 This excerpt taken from: http://www.warsawuprising.com/witness/kulski2.htm (Accessed 3/8/2010).

91 Ibid.

92 Ibid.

93 J.K. Zawodny, op. cit., 58.

94 Another person to escape from Auschwitz is Witold Pilecki, who actually volunteered to be captured and sent to this concentration camp to attempt to set up some 'resistance' within it. The entire story is recounted in *The Auschwitz Volunteer: Beyond Bravery. Catpain Witold Pilecki Auschwitz Prisoner No. 4859.* Translation of the original 1945 Pilecki report by Jarek Garlinski (USA: Aquila Polinica, 2012).

95 Quoted on the following website: http://www.warsawuprising.com/witness/kulski2.htm

96 Norman Davies, op. cit., 346

97 Ibid, 631.

98 Norman Davies 'Britain and the Warsaw Uprising'. http://www.warsaw uprising.com/paper/davies1.htm (Accessed 9/4/2010).

99 Ibid. (Accessed 1/12/2011).

CHAPTER 5

100 http://www.ft.com/cms/s/0/0d441dfa-ecf1-11d9-9d20-00000e2511c8. html? nclick_check=1 (Accessed 2/11/2010)/

101 Lynne Olson and Stanley Cloud, *A Question of Honour: the Kosciuszko Squadron: Forgotten Heroes of World War II* (NY: Vintage, 2004), 158 ff, 372 ff.

102 Davies, *Rising 44*, 510.

103 Ibid, 496.

104 http://www.bu.edu/jeremymb/papers/paper-y1.htm (Accessed 3/5/2010).

105 Primo Levi, *If This is a Man*, translated by Stuart Woolf (United Kingdom: The Orion Press, 1960), 32-3. First published in Italy as *Se questo è un uomo*. (Giulio Einaudi editore S.p.A, 1958).

106 Viktor Frankl, *The Search for Meaning* (United Kingdom: Avon, 1971). First published in 1946 as *Ein Psychologe erlebt das Konzentrationslager*.

107 Davies, op. cit., 541

108 An account of this can be found in Davies, *Rising 44*, 541-544.

109 All Australian post-war shipping records, indicating which boats the DPs and the later 'assisted' immigrants to Bonegilla came on, are accessible to the public.

CHAPTER 6

110 This description has been adapted from the Latvian Institute website: http:// www.li.lv/index.php?option=com_content&task=view&id=69&Itemid=441 (Accessed 4/5/2009)

111 *The Chronicle of Henry of Livonia: Henricus Lettus*, Records of Western Civilisation Series, translated by James A. Brudage (USA: University of Wisconsin Press, 1961). An updated edition was published in 2003 by University of Columbia Press with a new introduction and notes.

112 Much of the information in this section is taken from the following detailed site http://www.nationmaster.com/encyclopedia/Livonian-Order (Accessed 3/7/2009).

113 On November 18, 1918, the Republic of Latvia is proclaimed. However this did not last long for on December 1, 1918, The Red Army invaded Latvia and formed the Latvian Socialist Soviet Republic. After fierce fighting on February 1, 1920, ceasefire between Russia and Latvia came into effect and on August 11, 1920, the Latvian-Soviet Peace Treaty was signed.

114 This is well described in Timothy Snyders' extraordinary and well referenced account of the period, *Bloodlands: Europe Between Hitler and Stalin* (USA: 2010, Basic Books), Chapters 1-3.

115 http://www.eunet.lv/VT/south-east/tour1.html (Accessed 3/7/2009).

116 http://www.li.lv/index.php?option=com_content&task=view&id=100&Itemid=469 (Accessed 4/8/2010).

117 The following website compiled by descendants of a Jewish family which had once lived in Rēzekne and left prior to World War I, contains old photos of the town and interesting historical details.

http://horwitzfam.org/boris_rezekne.htm (Accessed 4/3/2010).

118 http://www.li.lv/en/?id=21 (Accessed 4/3/2010).

119   http://en.wikipedia.org/wiki/History_of_the_Jews_in_Latvia#War_crimes_ trials (Accessed 6/3/2010).

CHAPTER 7

120 These figures were taken from the following site but can be found in several historical accounts of the era. http://www.communistcrimes.org/en/Database/Latvia/Historical-Overview/1941-1953. This site states: 'Many Latvians were actively involved in a resistance movement against persecutions of the German occupation regime. Civic circles in Latvia were also dissatisfied with the German occupation regime and secretly plotted to reinstate a democracy. In order to carry out the independence scheme an underground organisation was established, the Latvian Central Council, which published the outlawed publication *Briva Latvija* (*Free Latvia*). The periodical was notably democratically inclined and propagated the idea of renewing democracy in Latvia after the war.'

121 Ilmars Salts, *A Stolen Childhood: Five Winters in Siberia*. Translation from the original Latvian by Gunna Dickson. (USA: SIA Liktenstasti, 2008).

122 Aigars Dabolins and Juris Kanels, *Latvia A Guide Book*. (Puse Plus Ltd), 17.

CHAPTER 8

123 Yalta was the second of three wartime conferences among the Big Three leaders (Churchill, Roosevelt and Stalin). It had been preceded by the Tehran Conference in 1943, and it was followed by the Potsdam Conference in July 1945, which was attended by Harry S. Truman in place of the late Roosevelt, Stalin, and Churchill, with Churchill replaced mid-point by the newly elected Prime Minister Clement Attlee. These conferences were places at which the

fates of countries were bargained and traded without the knowledge of those affected by the decisions. The decisions taken affected the future of most of the DPs, the geopolitical future of Europe and the world.

124 Personal communication with the author via email dated 29/8/2008.

125 Ibid.

CHAPTER 9

126 Glenda Sluga 'Bonegilla Reception And Training Centre: 1947-1971'. Master's Thesis, University of Melbourne, August 1985, 52. Henceforth Sluga *BRTC*.

127 It was not until decades later, in 2008, that this record intake was surpassed. *The Sydney Morning Herald* of 25 September 2008, states: 'Immigration added a record 199,064 people to Australia over the year to March – the biggest annual rise in history, figures released yesterday by the Bureau of Statistics show. This surpasses the boom after World War II, which peaked at about 149,000 people in 1950.

128 This description largely from the following site set up in remembrance of Lithuanian DPs in Australia. http://salithohistory.blogspot.com/2008_08_01_archive.html (Accessed 4/3/2010).

129 http://www.naa.gov.au/collection/explore/migration/alien-registration.aspx (Accessed 4/6/2010).

130 Sluga *BRTC*, 68, footnote 11.

131 A letter quoted in Sluga, *BRTC*, 45. Taken from: Desmond O'Grady, 'Migrant Camp Blues', *The Bulletin*, 11 November, 1961, 13-14.

132 Sluga *BRTC*, 57.

133 Taken from a Migration Heritage website entitled 'Belongings': http://www.migrationheritage.nsw.gov.au/exhibition/belongings/mergl/ (Accessed 3/6/2012).

134 http://www.migrationheritage.nsw.gov.au/exhibition/belongings/potocnik/ (Accessed 3/6/2012).

135 Bruce Pennay, *The Young at Bonegilla: Receiving Young Immigrants at Bonegilla Reception and Training Centre, 1947-1971* (Wodonga: Parklands Albury Wodonga, 2010), 12.

136 James Jupp, *Arrivals and Departures*, (Melbourne: Lansdowne press, 1966), 10.

137 Among some works focusing on this problem *before* the diagnosis came into existence in 1980 were: H. Krystal, *Massive Psychic Trauma*. (New York: International University Press, 1968); J.T. Shuval, "Some persistent effects

of trauma: Five years after the Nazi concentration camps," in *Social Problems* (1957), 5, 230-243; J. Bastiaans, "The KZ-syndrome: A thirty year study of the effects on victims of Nazi concentration camps," in *Revue Medico-Chirurgicale de Jassy*, (1974), 78, 573-578; A. Kardiner, *The Traumatic Neuroses of War*. (NY: Paul Hoeber, 1941).

138 This was referred to in the recollections by HBM Murphy in: Sluga *BRTC*, 68. The original article from which this was quoted is referenced in footnotes as follows: H.B.M. Murphy, 'The Assimilation of Refugee Immigrants in Australia', *Population Studies*, 5:3, March, 1952, p 182

139 Egon Kunz, *The Intruders* (Canberra: Australian National University Press, 1975). This book is difficult to get and would now be only available in some libraries.

140 Bruce Pennay, *The Young at Bonegilla: Receiving Young Immigrants at Bonegilla Reception and Training Centre, 1947-1971* (Wodonga: Parklands Albury Wodonga, 2010). (Henceforth Pennay *YB*) Comment on inside cover.

141 Ibid, 2. There reference is given as Arthur Calwell, *Commonwealth Parliament Debates (CPD)* May 1945.

142 Pennay, *YB*, 8.

143 Sluga, *BRTC*, 85.

144 Pennay, *YB*,3.

145 Pennay, *YB*,15.

146 http://www.migrationheritage.nsw.gov.au/exhibitions/somuchsky/whatjob.shtml (Accessed 7/7/2011).

CHAPTER 10

147 Lee Mylne, 'Return to Bonegilla', *The Australian*, 20 October 2008.

148 http://www.environment.gov.au/heritage/ahc/national-assessments/bonegilla/pubs/bonegilla.pdf (Accessed 6/2/2012).

149 http://www.bonegilla.com.au/news/2009111923694.htm (Accessed 4 May 2011).